D0147143

The Moderns
Time, Space, and Subjectivity in Contemporary Spanish Culture

Paul Julian Smith

OXFORD
UNIVERSITY PRESS

OXFORD
UNIVERSITY PRESS

Great Clarendon Street, Oxford, OX2 6DP
Oxford University Press is a department of the University of Oxford.
It furthers the University's objective of excellence in research, scholarship,
and education by publishing worldwide in

Oxford New York

Athens Auckland Bangkok Bogotá Buenos Aires Calcutta
Cape Town Chennai Dar es Salaam Delhi Florence Hong Kong Istanbul
Karachi Kuala Lumpur Madrid Melbourne Mexico City Mumbai
Nairobi Paris São Paulo Singapore Taipei Tokyo Toronto Warsaw

and associated companies in Berlin Ibadan

Oxford is a registered trade mark of Oxford University Press
in the UK and certain other countries

Published in the United States
by Oxford University Press Inc., New York

British Library Cataloguing in Publication Data

Data available

Library of Congress Cataloging in Publication Data

Data available

ISBN-0-19-816000-3
ISBN-0-19-816001-1 (Pbk.)

1 3 5 7 9 10 8 6 4 2

Typeset in Imprint by Regent Typesetting, London
Printed in Great Britain
on acid-free paper by
Biddles Ltd,
Guildford and King's Lynn

For my mother MARGARET;

and in memory of my father BERT

Preface

I would like to thank the University of Cambridge for sabbatical leave in 1996–7 during which most of the research for this book was carried out in Madrid, Barcelona, and San Sebastián. Sophie Goldsworthy, my editor at OUP, supported the project throughout. Mrs Coral Neale, the departmental secretary, provided invaluable support for me in my role as head of department. The sense of a common project with other scholars working on Spanish cultural studies in the UK (most particularly Jo Labanyi and Chris Perriam) has also been invaluable, as has continuing contact with friends and colleagues in the USA and the Spanish state. Emma Widdis first suggested I look at Lefebvre and urban space.

Material from this book was read as lectures and papers in the Institute of Romance Studies (London), at the universities of Oxford, Rutgers (New Brunswick), Tulane (New Orleans), Brown (Providence), and at the annual meetings of the Modern Language Association of America in Washington (1996) and San Francisco (1998). Earlier versions were published as: 'Back to Front: Alberto Cardín's Queer Habitus', *Bulletin of Hispanic Studies* (Liverpool), 74 (1997), 473–81; 'Social Space and Symbolic Power: Fernando Savater's Intellectual Field', *Modern Language Review*, 93 (1998), 94–104; 'Modern Times: Francisco Umbral's Chronicle of Distinction', *Modern Language Notes*, 113 (1998), 324–38; and 'Between Heaven and Earth: Grounding Medem's *Tierra*', *Bulletin of Hispanic Studies* (Glasgow), 76 (1999), 11–26.

P.J.S.

Contents

Part III. Subjectivity

List of Plates

between pp. 116–117.

1, 2. Víctor Erice, *El espíritu de la colmena* ('The Spirit of the Beehive', 1973)
Photo: BFI Stills, Posters and Designs; Elías Querejeta PC

3. Cristina García Rodero, 'Jugando a la Pasión, Riogordo 1983' ('Playing at the Passion, Riogordo 1983')
Photo: Agence VU

4. Rafael Moneo, Airport, Seville (1987–91)
Photo: Studio of Rafael Moneo

5. Rafael Moneo, National Museum of Roman Art, Mérida (1980–6)
Photo: Dida Biggi

6. La Cubana, *Cegada de amor* ('Blinded By Love', 1994)
Photo: La Cubana

7, 8. Bigas Luna, *La teta i la lluna* ('The Tit and the Moon', 1994)
Photo: Tartan Video

9. Antonio López García, 'Madrid visto desde Capitán Haya' ('Madrid seen from Capitán Haya', 1987)
Photo: Museo Nacional Centro de Arte Reina Sofía

10. Santiago Calatrava, Bach de Roda Bridge, Barcelona (1985–7)
Photo: Royal Institute of British Architects

11, 12. Julio Medem, *Tierra* (1995)
Photo: Tartan Video

13. Carlos Saura, *Carmen* (1983)
Photo: BFI Stills, Posters and Designs; Emiliano Piedra PC

14. Chus Gutiérrez, *Alma gitana* ('Gypsy Soul', 1996)
Photo: BFI Stills, Posters and Designs; Samarkanda Cine & Vídeo

List of Plates

While every effort has been made to contact copyright holders, the author welcomes corrections and additions.

Introduction: Time, Space, Subjectivity

Contemporary Spanish culture is a uniquely rich and varied field. Yet Spanish cultural studies is still in its infancy.[1] Academic scholars have rarely ventured beyond literature and, more recently, cinema;[2] and popular commentators are unversed in critical theory.[3] The aim of this book is thus twofold: to change the object of contemporary Hispanism, by incorporating new media, such as photography, town planning, and popular music; and to analyse that new object by engaging for the first time with (mainly French) cultural theory on such themes as (post)modernity, urbanization, and everyday life.

Clearly it is impossible to address the entirety of a nation's cultural production in any period; and the range of texts examined here is neither exhaustive nor representative of post-Franco Spain. This study thus concentrates on three nodes or themes treated in three successive sections: time, space, and subjectivity. These sections are themselves divided into three chapters, each addressing in turn an intellectual, a film-maker, and a topic (the replaying of history, the city, and the gypsy) that is refracted or 'cross-cut' over a variety of media. I have chosen to focus on the

---

[1] Helen Graham and Jo Labanyi's *Spanish Cultural Studies: An Introduction. The Struggle for Modernity* (Oxford: Oxford University Press, 1995) is the basis for any project in the field.

[2] But see Teresa Vilarós's *El mono del desencanto: una crítica cultural de la transición española (1973–1993)* (Madrid: Siglo XXI, 1998), a pioneering attempt to theorize contemporary Spanish culture from a broadly psychoanalytic perspective. Vilarós concentrates, unlike myself, on the 1970s; and she treats none of the cultural products I discuss in this book. See also Eduardo Subirats, 'Postmoderna modernidad: la España de los felices ochenta', *Quimera*, 145 (Mar. 1996), 11–18. Marsha Kinder's *Refiguring Spain: Cinema/ Media/Representation* (Durham, NC: Duke University Press, 1997) contains two essays on television and one on regional museums.

[3] Rafael Conte's *Una cultura portátil: cultura y sociedad en la España de hoy* (Madrid: Temas de Hoy, 1990) is a typically uneven survey with contributions on theatre, film, television, fiction, poetry, thought, classical and popular music, and art. Agustín Sánchez Vidal's *Sol y sombra* (Barcelona: Planeta, 1990) is a light-hearted and anecdotal description of cultural fashions of the 1960s.

journalistic and philosophical essay or *ensayo* not only because the genre remains almost unstudied, compared to fiction, but because it is a privileged medium for a rapidly changing nation to represent itself to its citizens and to others.[4] Likewise cinema is selected not so much for its formal properties (although these are indeed analysed in some detail) as for its national and institutional implications as a communal medium par excellence.[5] Finally, the topical 'cross-cuts' address social and intellectual issues beyond the limits of literary Hispanism, while continuing to raise aesthetic questions proper to the various media examined.

Some of the figures I treat are more familiar than others. Francisco Umbral (Chapter 1) has spent some twenty-five years producing a newspaper chronicle of cultural life in Madrid that is as meticulous as it is ironic. Famously prolific, he focuses in his essays on minute details charged with emblematic significance: a typical essay published in the year before the death of Franco contrasts the 'little moustache' ('bigotillo') of the Falangist 1940s with the smooth-shaven technocrats of the 1960s, and the unkempt rebels of the youthful 1970s.[6] Fernando Savater (Chapter 4) has also engaged in journalistic cultural commentary over two decades, but this time from the professional position of an academic philosopher based, until very recently, in the troubled Basque Country. A self-styled solipsist and anarchist, Savater also employs irony as a double-edged sword in his critique of democratic Spain, writing in 1977 that the 'anti-Francoists' were amongst the most 'repugnant products of the Dictatorship'; and in 1990 that the best that can be hoped for from democracy is an 'Enlightened pessimism'.[7] Alberto Cardín (Chapter 7), on the other hand, is almost unknown in Spain and died young in 1991 without having access to the prestigious publishers enjoyed by Umbral and Savater. However, as a self-declared gay intellectual and chronicler of the AIDS epidemic in Spain, he is unique in his bitter and mordant testimony to social change and despair at the margins (sexual, discursive, medical) of the Spanish state. If, then, Umbral chronicles modern times and Savater traces symbolic spaces, Cardín testifies to the emergence of new subjects, even as they are excluded from the dominant discursive consensus.

The three film-makers are chosen, rather, for their engagement with

[4] For the particularity of the modern *ensayo* see Jordi Gracia's introduction to *El ensayo español*, v: *Los contemporáneos* (Barcelona: Crítica, 1996), 9–67.

[5] The best general history of contemporary Spanish cinema remains John Hopewell's *El cine español después de Franco* (Madrid: El Arquero, 1989); for a detailed survey of Catalan cinema until 1990, see Miquel Porter i Moix, *Història del cinema a Catalunya* (Barcelona: Generalitat, 1992). Alberto López Echevarrieta's *Cine vasco: ¿realidad o ficción?* (Bilbao: Mensajero, n.d.) covers only the period to 1931.

[6] Reprinted in Gracia's *El ensayo español*, 272–5.

[7] Reprinted ibid. 310–30.

contemporary nationalisms. Víctor Erice's trilogy focuses explicitly on time: from the confrontation of children with the aftermath of the Civil War to the concentration of an artist (Antonio López) on a nature that is in constant flux. In Chapter 2 I examine his early masterpiece *El espíritu de la colmena* ('The Spirit of the Beehive'), focusing not on the late Francoist period in which it was produced, but on its reception in the decades that followed. My aim is to show how Spanish readings of the film became progressively abstracted and dehistoricized as the dictatorship receded, neglecting that trace of time, which (I argue) is implicitly encoded in the film's cinematography, performance style, and scriptwriting. The national narrative of the Spanish state, embodied and contested in Erice's bleak Castilian landscapes, is replaced in Chapter 5 by Bigas Luna's lushly sensual Iberia, celebrated in his trilogy of that name. More particularly, Bigas's *La teta i la lluna* ('The Tit and the Moon') reveals an oblique response to a Catalan nationalism that is itself, I argue, caught between the spatial or territorial model of land and the dematerialized model of language. Overtly international, with its polyglot dialogue and stereotypical characters, Bigas's film also testifies to a new kind of local history: the interaction of human habitation and geographical location. Finally, Julio Medem's cinematic trilogy addresses, to varying degrees, the richest and most problematic of nationalisms, that of the Basque Country or Euskadi. While Medem's three films suggest the emergence of new, unanchored subjects (women who are no longer defined by men, Basques who need no longer aggressively assert their position), *Tierra* goes furthest in contesting the historically violent relation between identity, land, and language. Rhapsodic and oneiric, Medem's filmic practice is also implicitly political in its grounding of Basque metaphysics, an artistic endeavour analogous to that of the brave theorists of recent Basque 'postnationalism'. If the progressive abstraction of Erice's cinema colludes to some extent with the dehistoricizing of his films by post-Franco critics, then Bigas's localized carnality and Medem's more problematic terrestrial subjects echo the emphases of demythologizing thinkers in the historic nations of Catalunya and Euskadi. By rehistoricizing (locating, grounding) these films, I also attempt to take up the intellectual and social challenge of positionality.

The three cross-cut chapters, more extensive and extended than those on *ensayo* and cinema, continue the exploration of time, space, and subjectivity. Chapter 3 examines the widespread phenomenon of the 'replaying' of recent history in post-Franco culture. I argue that the ethnographic photography of Cristina García Rodero and the modestly monumental architecture of Rafael Moneo conserve a faith in modernization, even as they cite the past. Inversely, the kitsch multimedia performances of La

Cubana and novels of Álvaro Pombo retain a sense of the trace of time at odds with their apparent superficiality. Chapter 6 treats the city in Spanish narrative, painting, architecture, and urban theory. Here I argue that Juan Goytisolo's novels and Antonio López's graphic works employ the vocabularies of high art to stage the desolation or evacuation of urban space. Santiago Calatrava's bridges and Manuel Castells's theory of the informational 'flow' of the technopolis, on the other hand, attempt to heal the urban wound and resurrect the dead city. Finally, Chapter 9 addresses the figure of the gypsy, as a subject newly refigured in Spanish popular culture. Thus while Carlos Saura's *Carmen* and Chus Gutiérrez's *Alma gitana* ('Gypsy Soul') refuse modernity, nomadism, and hybridism, the flamenco fusion music of Ketama and dance of Joaquín Cortés embrace or incorporate these same contemporary characteristics. Refusing to be confined by what was previously prescribed as their proper place, practitioners of gypsy culture have thus fully participated with other Spaniards in the newly globalized order of the cultural market place.

It is clear, then, that in spite of the particularities of the Spanish state (most especially the continuing conflict between a modernized economy and a premodern sociality), Spanish culture is not immune to the pressures of international change. Hybridization and deterritorialization, more fully examined in the context of Latin American cultural studies,[8] are undoubtedly of the essence. But turning away from the sometimes apocalyptic theories of postcolonialism and globalization, I appeal in this study to the less familiar accounts, broadly sociological, offered by French theorists since the 1960s. The most important proponent of a philosophically informed sociology is Pierre Bourdieu, whose work I address in the three chapters on intellectuals. Neither empiricist nor idealist (in spite of his affection for both numerical data and aesthetic regulation), Bourdieu is my source for three concepts: distinction, the field, and the habitus. Distinction is the process by which the aesthetic is separated off from the social by a magic circle of nominators and nominees. In the case of Umbral I examine how the intellectual *mondain* at once confers distinction on others and attracts distinction to himself in a finely balanced exercise of the 'judgement of taste'. Paradoxically, the latter is employed more typically in the sphere of everyday life (from cooking to clothing) than it is in high art. If distinction is subject to time (even as it presents its judgements as eternal), then the field is defined by social and symbolic space.

[8] See William Rowe and Vivian Schelling, *Memory and Modernity: Popular Culture in Latin America* (London: Verso, 1991), 231. 'Hybridization' is defined as 'the ways in which forms become separated from existing practices and recombine with new forms in new practices'; 'deterritorialization' as 'the release of cultural signs from fixed locations in space and time'.

The realm of interaction between intellectuals, texts, and institutions, the field serves as a stage on which Savater plays multiple and apparently irreconcilable roles: professorial journalist, Basque postnationalist, ethical egotist. At times of crisis, warns Bourdieu, the cultural field will fragment, revealing the hidden social forces which subtend it. Distinction and the field can thus be read as the temporal and spatial equivalents of my third term: the habitus, the mechanism which aligns objective conditions with subjective dispositions. Underwriting the discursive status quo, the habitus overrules cultural and intellectual interventions such as those by Cardín: a Castilian speaker in Catalunya, an effeminate homosexual versed in Marxism, and an articulate person with AIDS in a society which provided no proper place from which such a discourse of disease could be enunciated. While Bourdieu provides an account of the historical origin of the judgement of taste and the rules of art only for France, his version of a logic of practice can in its broad outline be adopted and adapted for the very different case of Spain, whose multiple nationalisms I document in the chapters on film.

The three cross-cuts feature different theorists chosen for their relevance to each chapter's respective theme. For 'Replay' (Chapter 3) I appeal to Gianni Vattimo and Jean-François Lyotard. While this pair clearly have little in common with the sociologists I cite elsewhere (and Bourdieu is scathing of 'licensed heretics' such as Lyotard), as the most influential foreign theorists of postmodernism in Spain they serve as a touchstone against which to test the character of a period of culture in which use of the epithet 'postmodern' was as ubiquitous as it was indiscriminate. Focusing on time, I argue that in Vattimo and Lyotard the 'crisis of the future' and of metaphysics implies a temporal dislocation that raises the prospect of social and cultural dissolution. In Spain, however, anachronism and dislocation are combined unstably with a persistent faith in the possibility of historical change and cultural intervention. 'City' (Chapter 6) invokes the major theorist of urban space, Henri Lefebvre. Connecting the architectonic to the social and the mental to the physical, Lefebvre offers both a diachronic and a synchronic account of the city. For example 'spatial practice' refers to how space is perceived, 'representations of space' to how it is conceived, and 'representational spaces' to how it is lived. More particularly, Lefebvre distinguishes between the city as 'work' and as 'product'. While the first is the unique creation of the artist's mark, the second is the reproducible result of mechanical gestures. At once work and product (unique and reproduced) the urban space of Spanish writers, artists, architects, and theorists is peculiarly rich and complex. Finally Chapter 9 rereads the 'Gypsy' as one of Michel de Certeau's 'practices of everyday life'. Reclaiming the lost continent of 'ordinary culture' and arguing that

5

belief can be expressed only indirectly through 'subjects supposed to believe', Certeau also distinguishes between tactics and strategies. While the former are temporal, unstable, and indefinite, the latter are spatial, proprietorial, and delimited. Hybrid and rhythmic, the tactic is for Certeau 'the art of the weak', and characteristic of activities such as dance and (I argue) nomadic subjects such as gypsies.

It is Pedro Almodóvar (the figure still most representative of contemporary Spain to foreigners) who reminds us that those said to embody the *movida* at the time of the Transition did not use that word themselves; rather they identified themselves as 'the moderns'.[9] The name can be taken in several senses. First it suggests a parallel between a period of exceptional cultural effervescence in Spain and some antecedents abroad: from Paris in the 1920s to London in the 1960s.[10] Secondly it suggests that cult of the new that remains so characteristic of Spain, even as traditional dispositions undermine contemporary conditions. Finally, and more profoundly, it suggests that the promise of political modernity and technological modernization is not to be denied too soon.[11] For even as it claims to have 'leapfrogged' its European neighbours, Spain remains by many social indicators culturally underdeveloped.[12] If postmodern theory disputes the possibility of any simple break with the past, then Spanish practice reminds us that radical political and historical change has indeed been effected in recent decades; and that however disappointing that change may have come to seem, the cultural practices examined in this book could never have existed without it. Franco may have died in his bed and *desencanto* may have been born with democracy, but the temporal, spatial, and subjective dislocations of contemporary Spain have produced a culture whose 'ambiguous modernity'[13] is richly particular.

[9] José Luis Gallero, *Sólo se vive una vez: esplendor y ruina de la movida madrileña* (Madrid: Ardora, 1991).

[10] See Alan Rudolph's feature film *The Moderns* (1988) and Christopher Booker's impressionistic chronicle *Neophiliacs: The Revolution in English Life in the Fifties and Sixties* (London: Pimlico, 1992).

[11] Graham and Labanyi, *Spanish Cultural Studies*, 18.

[12] Carlos Alonso Zaldívar and Manuel Castells cite statistics showing that Spaniards spend the least on culture and reading and the most on restaurants and hotels of any nationality in the European Union. Paradoxically, the percentage of Spaniards engaged in full-time education is exceeded only by France and Belgium; *España, fin de siglo* (Madrid: Alianza, 1992), 57–8.

[13] I take the phrase from Eduardo Subirats, *Después de la lluvia: sobre la ambigua modernidad española* (Madrid: Temas de Hoy, 1993). Subirats's own reading is itself ambiguous in that he both identifies the hidden persistence of the *ancien régime* under the spectacular signs of postmodernity and seeks out, beyond the mere 'simulacrum of democracy', civil participation in society and the restoration of civic identity in architecture, education, and the intellectual field (p. 14).

PART I

Time

1 | Modern Times: Francisco Umbral's Chronicle of Distinction

If, in Vattimo's apparent tautology, 'modernity' is that time in which 'the modern' is the highest or only value,[1] then the Spain of the 1980s is surely the most modern of societies. And the journalist and novelist Francisco Umbral is its arbiter of elegance: both a commentator on and a contributor to social and aesthetic manners. The author of over one hundred books, Umbral is perhaps best known for his daily newspaper column, once in the Socialist-supporting *El País*, now in the maverick upstart *El Mundo*. An idiosyncratic chronicle of the *Zeitgeist* and the *genius loci*, Umbral's column (which has been run under titles which include the Baudelairian 'Spleen of Madrid' and the Proustian 'Pleasures and Days') charts the specific intersections of time and space in a thousand book launches, film premières, and press conferences. But in its knowing combination of politics and poetics, as in its fleeting references to such fashionable concepts as Vattimo's 'weak thought' or Lacan's 'discourse of the other', Umbral's column has ambitions far beyond those of gossip writers in other countries or his rivals in Spain itself. For his aims are at once total and partial: to give a general account of the glittering social life of a 'Dior-issimo' Madrid and a specific social critique of that same elite's decadence and arrogance as the ironically named 'Red Decade' advances. As dandy and moralist, Umbral presents himself as a 'Proustian Marxist',[2] an apparently trivial *mondain* whose devotion to the daily discipline of writing transmutes the ephemera he chronicles into the resonant symbols of profound social malaise. The 'portable culture'[3] of the period is thus

---

[1] Gianni Vattimo, *La sociedad transparente* (Barcelona: Paidós, 1990), 73.
[2] *La década roja* (Barcelona: Planeta, 1993), 56.
[3] Rafael Conte (ed.), *Una cultura portátil: cultura y sociedad en la España de hoy* (Madrid: Temas de Hoy, 1990).

subjected to an increasingly explicit critique of the Left which Umbral mounts (or claims to mount) from within the Left itself.[4]

Umbral's column thus serves as a chronicle of distinction in a double sense: it both marks out those figures worthy of the reader's attention (a painter, a politician, a supermodel); and confers value on itself through the writer's intimacy with those same figures: in Pierre Bourdieu's terms, each secures social and symbolic profits 'by exhibiting signs of recognition' to the other.[5] In this chapter I shall argue that Umbral's writing practice, unique in Spain, is exemplary of Bourdieu's concept of 'distinction' or 'the judgement of taste'. For Bourdieu the sense of distinction is always subject to 'the mark of time' (p. 295): 'art and cultural consumption are predisposed . . . to fulfil a social function of legitimating social differences' (p. 7). But if distinction is culturally constructed, it is not determined or exhausted by social class: even what Proust called the 'abominable, voluptuous act called "reading the paper"' (the consumption of grotesquely varied events over coffee and croissants) is a complex, mediated experience (p. 21); and where culture is concerned, 'class condition' is not identical with 'social conditioning' (p. 101). Thus the most crucial aesthetic education (the most socially significant and the most difficult to acquire) is not that of the legitimate arts such as painting or music, which can be formally taught, but rather that of 'illegitimate' tastes, such as clothing or cookery, widely and erroneously held to be the result of innate 'sensibility' (p. 13). Or again, the middle-brow contempt for popular culture (Bourdieu's example is a sugary photograph of a First Communion) is not shared by the 'aristocracy' of cultural capital. Ironically coinciding with the most impoverished in education, the 'nobles' manifest the acquired disinterestedness of their taste by declaring that 'any object can be perceived aesthetically', however vulgar or banal (p. 39).

As we shall see, both of these points hold for Umbral who prefers to demonstrate his mastery of the finest distinctions of taste in the vulgar fields of fashion and food, rather than in the high arts such as classical music, to which he professes indifference; and whose titles of cultural nobility rest as much on his aestheticization of everyday life as on his sensitivity to the works of the artistic and political elite. Like the Almodóvar he has so consistently supported, Umbral attempts the 'conquest of the present' (*La década*, 125) or the memorialization of the every-

---

[4] *Los cuerpos gloriosos: memorias y semblanzas* (Barcelona: Planeta, 1996), 281. Umbral here likens his political position to that of Fernando Savater and distinguishes it from that of philosopher Aranguren.

[5] *Distinction: A Social Critique of the Judgment of Taste* (London: Routledge, 1996), 485. All quotations from Bourdieu are taken from this source.

day: that which is too self-evident properly to be distinguished. If, as Bourdieu argues (against Kant), the aesthetic is created as a category through 'the denial of the social' (*Distinction*, 11), then for the dandy Umbral the social is recreated as an aesthetic category, one which retains, nonetheless, weakened traces of its political past: it is no accident that Umbral should choose to interview a former Communist leader in a fine restaurant and to comment indulgently on his gastronomic savoir faire (*La década*, 131). Where Bourdieu found even in the France of the 1960s evidence of a 'fun ethic' which was a 'systematic reversal of the ascetic morality of the bourgeoisie' (*Distinction*, 370), in Umbral's hedonistic Spain of the 1980s the aesthetic has been exploded, wholly dissolved into everyday life. Truly, in Marsha Kinder's words, 'pleasure is the new Spanish morality'.[6]

How does Umbral respond to this in-difference or non-differentiation? At first sight he merely mimics it, the successive 'flashes' of the column a kaleidoscopic collage of drag queens and philosophers, starlets and professors. As the decade progresses, however, Umbral confronts the skewed chronology of the period: the history of the Socialists' achievement and consolidation of political power is also the history of the definitive collapse of the ideology which sustained them through the long years of underground resistance and the shorter period of democratic opposition. The postmodern clichés of 'the society of the spectacle' or 'the simulacrum' are thus to be read in the specifically Spanish context of a divorce between institutional triumph and ideological disaster.[7] What I argue in this chapter, then, is that in his typically fragmentary and ironic way Umbral moves from an aesthetic treatment of the political passions of 1982 to a political treatment of the aestheticized indifference of 1992. His recent self-styled 'anachronistic' return to a rhetoric of moral denunciation is, however, undermined by the practice of aesthetic distancing which Umbral had not only chronicled and celebrated in such artists as Almodóvar, but had also pioneered day after day in elegant essays which wilfully and wittily confused politics and poetics, news and fiction. If 'distinction' is derived etymologically from the Latin verb meaning 'to mark off, separate, or divide',[8] then in a typically ironic twist, Umbral's chronicle acquires its unique status by refusing to discriminate between aesthetic and banal objects, engulfed as they both are in a journalistic

[6] 'Pleasure and the New Spanish Morality: A Conversation with Pedro Almodóvar', *Film Quarterly* (Fall 1987), 33–4.

[7] See Eduardo Subirats's denunciation of the authoritarianism and incomplete modernization of Socialist Spain, *Después de la lluvia: sobre la ambigua modernidad española* (Madrid: Temas de Hoy, 1993).

[8] William Smith and John Lockwood, *Latin–English Dictionary* (Edinburgh: Chambers, John Murray, 1976), s.v. 'distinguo'.

roman fleuve or (Umbral's term) 'novelized memoir'[9] indistinguishable (or so it appears) from life itself.

Distinction is thus both active and passive: it is the process of differentiating between objects and the quality thus conferred on those same objects. Just so is writing to Umbral: the daily duty of the column, aided by coffee and whisky, is the labour of either a hero or a martyr, a 'perpetual writing' which is at once the affirmation of a self and the renunciation of a life.[10] Writing is thus coextensive with (even identical to) the subject or the body: Umbral's minute chronicle of his own hypochondria (of his chills and hair loss, myopia and rheumatism) is inextricable from his account of the grand personages and events of the day. Moreover his reflections on 'the column' are incorporated into that column, or the periodically published collections of the same. Thus he gives a succinct assessment of his own style: as the 'sonnet' of journalism, the column must sacrifice both the prosaic detail of 'news' and the false lyricism of 'costumbrismo'.[11] The column is not the description of an event, but rather the trace ('rastro') of topicality, resolved in a metaphor like one of Rimbaud's *Illuminations* (p. 11). The trick is to isolate a fragment and submit it to unwonted even excessive attention; and never to confront great issues directly, but rather to enter through the 'bloody wound' of a tiny detail. In pictorial terms, the column will focus on the 'still life' of a meal in the corner of a picture rather than on the 'central (and remote) scene', which claims to be the main subject of the painting (p. 12).

Brevity, fragmentation, indirection: Spanish imitators of Umbral have reproduced such techniques. Mario Mactas's book of interviews (or 'perversions')[12] with Umbral begins with an ironic introduction narrating the extended and bizarre negotiations required by a subject who is obsessed with protecting his own image when the journalistic tables are turned on him. And that image is sketched by Mactas with ironic details worthy of his master: 'so many years of *foulards* and polemics, of insolence and posing, of sitting down to write morning after morning' (p. 12). Umbral has also given a pen portrait of himself, focusing on his trademarks: thick black spectacles ('he is falsely shortsighted, like Borges was falsely blind') and extravagant waistcoats (*Los cuerpos gloriosos*, 285–6). But amongst

---

[9] See Umbral's typically hybrid narrative, *Y Tierno Galván ascendió a los cielos: memorias noveladas de la transición* (Barcelona: Seix Barral, 1990). The narrator here claims that there is no ideology 'unstained' by autobiography, citing Felipe González's rural origins as an example (pp. 129–30).

[10] See Umbral's meditation on César González Ruano, another inveterate columnist (who, Umbral claims, wrote his last piece on the day of his death), *La escritura perpetua* (n.p.: Mapfre-Vida, 1989), 9, 11.

[11] *Spleen de Madrid 2* (Barcelona: Destino, 1982), 9.

[12] *Las perversiones de Francisco Umbral* (Madrid: Anjana, 1984).

such apparent self-indulgence, Umbral has championed what his fellow columnist and political ironist Eduardo Haro Tecglen has called 'the defence of writing'[13] in the face of the ubiquitous incursions of the audio-visual. And if we look at three significant moments in Spanish history of the period we find that style and substance (poetics and politics) are inseparable.

The first is the Socialist victory in the general elections of 1982. Umbral stresses the euphoria and utopianism of the moment, which he expresses with characteristic marginality in the image of the emergence of 'queers' ('maricones') in the streets 'who in these historical moments become the flowers of liberty' (*La década*, 18). Having greeted the masses from the balcony of the Palace Hotel, Felipe González descends for a lavish dinner with his journalist supporters at *El País*. They are celebrating 'the coming of social justice' (p. 20); but Umbral's attention to Felipe's wardrobe (long hair, boots, no tie, and 'Fidel's cigar') suggests already that socialism is just another style and the new leader's 'modernity' nothing more than his photogenic qualities when reproduced on a political poster (p. 32). The second moment comes four years later with the bitterly fought referendum on Spanish membership of NATO, a *cause célèbre* to the anti-American Left. Claiming to take part in fly posting at midnight and massive demonstrations in the streets of Madrid with famous actresses and philosophers (whose names he does not fail to mention), Umbral focuses nonetheless on a small detail: the ambiguities of the campaign slogan, which can be read as either 'no' or 'not yet' to the referendum (p. 121). This, then, is the epitome of double think and the symbol of a Socialist Spain which, with the imminent visit of President Reagan, will be 'mortgaged' to the triumphalist USA as surely as the Francoist dictatorship was (p. 124). The final moment is 1992 with its 'Pharaonic'[14] Happenings: the Barcelona Olympics, Seville Expo, and Madrid's nomination as Capital of European Culture. Here the Socialist project is 'finished up or finished off' ('consumada y consumida') (p. 281). Empty and gratuitous, the Happening 'stops time, abstracts history, places us in an absolute and fictitious present' (p. 294). It is the end of Felipe's 'discourse of corduroy' (p. 320): the now distant appeal to a conspicuously modern informality of clothing, which had appeared to herald the democratization of the public sphere.

In these three epochal moments, then, aesthetics and ethics are made to rhyme, both metaphorically and (in a too frequent stylistic tick) literally.

---

[13] 'Umbral: defensa de la escritura', *Cuadernos Hispanoamericanos* 450 (Dec. 1987), 39–47.

[14] Beyond simple monumentalism, the word has a special resonance in Spanish, since it recalls *La corte de faraón*, a zarzuela widely held to be a satire on the home life of Franco.

But if the dandy and the political polemicist are made to walk hand in hand down the Castellana (just as Umbral composes a guest list of 'countesses and communists'),[15] the 'empty' Happening of state display is contrasted with the marginal and ephemeral events which mark definitive changes in the life of a person and a nation. There is thus amongst the sheer volume of Umbral's writings an occasional 'flash' of the event not as empty Happening, but as moment of pure difference. The anecdote cited by Umbral is typically self-serving but no less accurate: Amerindians, it is claimed, say the fruit is either on the tree or on the ground—nobody sees it fall. Umbral's achievement is to have narrated that fall: the imperceptible, yet definitive, Transition to democracy.[16] There is thus a productive structural conflict in Umbral's chronicle between a grand narrative of circularity or stasis (in which Felipe comes to be the same as Franco) and a little story of the body (of the multiple and fleeting memory traces of which a subject or a nation's life is composed). The theoretical question for the analyst of distinction (of vision and division of culture in time) is to articulate these two temporal and spatial paradigms. It is a double bind which Umbral himself resolves, intermittently at least, by appealing to women, whose exclusion from the vicissitudes of political life makes them exemplary witnesses to the flow of personal time; and gay men, whose lack of sustained social presence makes them pure expressions of the moment, elegant but ephemeral 'flowers of freedom'.

The twin stories of the nation and the body are centred, anachronistically, perhaps, during the birth of the *estado de autonomías*, on the old imperial capital. Credited with the 'invention of Madrid',[17] Umbral transforms what he himself describes as the 'grotesquely swollen Manchegan village [*poblachón*] interspersed with Francoist Manhattan skyscrapers' (*Spleen*, 35) into a fashionable metropolis favoured by the figures he denotes in iconic and laconically abbreviated Anglicisms as the 'jet [set]' and the 'beautiful [people]'. Playing at once the pedant and the *mondain* (combining, in Bourdieu's words, 'understanding without pleasure' and 'pleasure without understanding'; *Distinction*, 11), Umbral at once dissects and celebrates the social scene of the early 1980s, immediately before the first Socialist victory. At a time of impending definitive change and transparent historical gravity (the first democratic handover of power from one party to another), Umbral seems at first to be uncharacteristically and uncompromisingly serious. At the première of the flamenco

---

[15] *La década*, 205.

[16] *Spleen*, 196. The anecdote is attributed to respected politician Francisco Fernández Ordóñez (under Umbral's pet name 'Pacordóñez').

[17] Pedro Rocamora, 'Francisco Umbral o la "invención" de Madrid', *Arbor*, 118.462 (1984), 53–7.

version of *Bodas de sangre* he contrasts the old pessimism of Lorca, Gades, and Saura with the new optimism of democracy, shared by Umbral's fellow columnist, Basque philosopher Fernando Savater (*Spleen*, 55–7); a review of contemporary journalism finds Umbral urging his colleagues to 'assume their responsibilities': democracy is not, he insists, a 'perpetual orgy' (p. 142); even the pop stars of the moment, the boy band Pecos ('Freckles'), plucked from the slums of southern Madrid to enjoy brief celebrity, become a *memento mori* of the deadly fate of the rest of their class: while record companies sell the myth of 'individual salvation through music', the 'lumpen' are condemned to mass unemployment (p. 300).

But at such epochal moments in political and cultural life (when the present seems infused by both the persistence of the past and a premonition of the future), there is a curious sense of stasis and aestheticism in the air. At the première of Almodóvar's first feature of 1981, *Pepi, Luci, Bom*, Umbral finds in the post-punk subculture of the 'pegamoide'[18] 'one of the multiple flights from History and from the present which youth is currently trying out' (p. 250). Where others were to see the essence of modernity and *joie de vivre*, Umbral diagnoses a 'desperate extension of childhood', 'a fear of life disguised as aggression against life'. Or again the tragicomic attempted *coup d'état* of Tejero which took place on the 23 February 1981 is deflected onto the frozen and aestheticized image of the early plum blossom with which it coincided, now rendered 'sacred' because democracy is in danger (p. 151). The typical technique of the emblematic and indirect detail serves here (in the rhetorical sense of the Latin *distinguere*) to 'mark the pauses' or 'punctuate' the flow of text and time, to register a 'stop' (*distinctio*), in which image and moment are set apart from the indistinct flux of existence.

This distinctive sense of stasis is thus both in the world (in, say, the escapism of Spanish youth) and in Umbral (in his aestheticization of the political). And it is reconfirmed by one of Umbral's most consistent techniques: the refusal to give dates to his fragments and the principled rejection of objective chronology in favour of subjectivized memoirs. Topicality is thus deflected into the past or into an aesthetic distancing whose irony is not always precisely directed. Thus when Umbral mocks an ETA terrorist atrocity by calling it 'kitsch' ('folklórico'), his aim is true: to kill for a flag is obscene when there are shanty towns in Bilbao and Madrid (p. 25). But the indifference of the Basque separatists to the real conditions of the working people they claim to defend is reproduced by Umbral when he makes horror merge, imperceptibly, with literature. The nightclub at

---

[18] The name is derived from the pop group of the period fronted by Alaska, star of Almodóvar's *Pepi, Luci, Bom* and later a celebrated DJ.

which forty-three young people meet their death in a fire becomes, with the assistance of Madrid's 'literary' mayor, the 'professor' Tierno Galván, 'a fleeting, romantic cemetery' (p. 15); the manifesto against the normalization of Catalan signed by Castilian-speaking intellectuals is linked with the anniversary of the first Spanish grammar (by Nebrija) and thus to 'five centuries of the Renaissance' (p. 17); after a dinner party Umbral is asked by his hostess whether he would prefer to see a video of Tejero's coup or (the hitherto censored) *Last Tango in Paris* (p. 23): political and artistic transgressions are homogenized, indistinct. And if the première of *Bodas de sangre* suggested a definitive break with the legacy of the past, both political and cultural, then the first night of a theatrical production of *Doña Rosita* has the opposite effect: it takes the form of a stately 'minuet' in which 'the Spain divided for ever by the death of Lorca performed its steps and played its part to perfection' (p. 224).

Such performances are to be found at the highest level: the King (who had recently and bravely supported democracy during the 'Tejerazo') is now sketched by Umbral in the 'infantile' spotted kerchief he is using temporarily as a sling for an injured arm. At once a metaphor for deeper wounds (the mutilation of Juan Carlos and of Spain under the dictatorship) and an icon of the new informality of democracy, the kerchief poses the question of how far monarchy can be 'dissolved' into democracy without losing its charismatic aura (p. 66). Here Umbral carries out a minor example of Bourdieu's 'sociology of taste' (revealing the social meaning of an aesthetic detail); but he also, in characteristic fashion, privileges that detail through his unwonted attention, fetishizing a minute distinction of dress (the inappropriate pattern of a fabric) in a way which reinforces that primacy of form over function which is for Bourdieu the very definition of the aesthetic sense's denial of the social.

Umbral himself rejects the charge of aestheticism at this time, posing as a 'moral dandy', a 'Stoic' who sets himself against the 'vulgarity' ('horterismo') of the current political times (p. 301). And he claims that while 'aesthetic dandyism' is reactionary (leading to the provincial conservativism known as 'señoritismo'), moral dandyism is 'permanent revolution' (p. 302). However it is unclear what political purchase such a position can obtain, with its defiant subjectivism and wayward literary references: the dispute over fishing rights with the French is reduced to Umbral's briefly observed diet (lightly boiled hake) (p. 71); the proposal to legalize divorce leads Umbral to suggest 'separation by gunshot', as was the case for that most 'transgressive' of couples, Rimbaud and Verlaine (p. 47); the epidemic of heroin addiction in Spain (like that of AIDS which will follow it) turns junkies into 'martyrs or stylists of the cult of nothing, of the religion of the passing of time' (p. 215). And if Umbral cites Lacan on the discourse of the other and on the 'narrow margin of subjectivity' which remains to the self ('el yo residual'), then he draws a very un-psychoanalytic moral from this abjection: it is to serve as the 'ashes or seed of a latent romanticism opposed to the massifications of both Right and Left' (p. 295).

Hence, even before the Socialists' victory (and the disillusion which followed hard on its heels), Umbral was hinting that political programmes are indistinguishable from one another. While initially this bears out his belief in Europe (and at one point Eurocommunism) as a 'third way' between Reagan's America and Brezhnev's Russia, it soon finds him arguing, obscurely, 'neither for nor against NATO' (claiming the decision to join is dependent on the specific and changing circumstances of the moment) (*Spleen*, 28). It is in this confused context that Umbral, a constant chronicler of his supposed amatory successes, turns to women. When history proves perplexing, women remain reassuringly the same: distinct from both men and the compromises of the public sphere men inhabit. The child actress Ana Torrent overwhelms Umbral: his forty years cannot withstand her pubescent thirteen, cannot bear to bear witness to the maturity which he had anticipated when first he saw her on screen (p. 210). Umbral eulogizes the bare, freckled shoulder of stage actress and director Nuria Espert: where once, when fighting for democracy, it seemed reactionary to compliment a woman on her beauty, now with democracy more or less achieved, Spain is experiencing 'the resurrection of the flesh' (pp. 231–2). Finally Umbral hymns actress and singer Ana Belén, another icon of the female *progre* (political progressive): 'you are what has remained of the hopes of 1977 . . . You are the immediate past, that which is most painful, the absolute present which is suddenly perfumed like the past. History is swiftly growing old' (pp. 305–6).

Where men are actors in history (albeit condemned to the empty posturing of the political and cultural 'event') women are merely mediums for history: the mirror in which Umbral sees, in would-be romantic fashion, his own ageing, his own fleeting desires, his own dis-course of the other. While he claims of Pilar Miró, film director and future minister, that 'by looking at men in another way, she taught us to look at women in another way' (p. 244), he in fact sees women in time-honoured style as purely passive, the 'electric conductor' of time. Indeed, as we have seen, the coming of the morality of pleasure (what Bourdieu would call the 'selective democracy' of consumerist choice) (*Distinction*, 399) is used as an alibi for the erotic objectification of women, a process which must be defended against the supposed puritanism of feminism and political correctness. Studiedly indifferent to commercial or social change (to fishing rights and divorce reform), Umbral also contrives to miss the revolution in the status of women which is perhaps the most profound transformation of Spanish society in the period,[19] even as he celebrates the perfume, the breasts, and the vaginas of the women he so publicly desires.

Umbral has always claimed that impartiality and impersonality are not synonymous. And if we flash forward ten years to 1992, and the long twilight of the Red Decade, we find him claiming that Spanish society has finally caught up with him: just as his journalism has always been personalized, so Spaniards, grown indifferent to politics, are now fascinated by politicians and the 'soap opera' of their daily lives (*La década*, 61). Proud that he has never stooped to reporting 'news', Umbral mounts a defence of gossip and rumour, which, he claims, always bear within them a kernel of narrative truth (p. 53). Now Umbral's hero is realist painter Antonio López, who was seen by Umbral, as he returned from a tumultuous demonstration, quietly painting the deserted Gran Vía, taking advantage of a momentary effect of the light. Against vain 'historical acceleration' López values what is fleeting but lasting: 'the persistence of simple things, the growth of a plum tree' (p. 72).

This quietism is, however, also that of Spanish youth, once living the 'intensity of immediacy, the smell of the street' (p. 126), now bored but uncomplaining lodgers in the parental home (p. 230); and of an ageing leadership which has not simply decelerated but 'arrested' history: Felipe is at one with the bonsai trees he collects: stunted and frozen in time (p. 108). The extraordinary sight of a Red Flag flown over Franco's old palace of El Pardo, on the occasion of Gorbachev's visit to Madrid, is the symbol not of a revolution in Spanish life but rather of the 'end of the great experiment of the twentieth century' (p. 246) and the new indifference of ideologies. Likewise the ravages of the AIDS epidemic, far graver in Spain than in northern Europe, are not the sign of a specifically Spanish crisis in health care, but a metaphor for a generalized defencelessness: now the fears formally provoked by religion and politics are gone, AIDS is for Umbral a 'punishment for the crime of believing ourselves to be free' (pp. 299–301). Even homosexuality, once exploited and celebrated by Umbral in his column and novels as a defining instance of modernity,[20] is now faded: flowers for a day in the 'grotesque fiesta of liberty', today's gay men have become 'ordinary people', living their lives like 'strange but acceptable' businessmen (pp. 155–6).

In his successive celebrity profiles, Umbral colludes with this arresting

[19] See, amongst many others, Carlos Alonso Zaldívar and Manuel Castells, 'La revolución silenciosa: las nuevas españolas', in *España, fin de siglo* (Madrid: Alianza, 1992), 53–6.

[20] To take two examples from the novels: *El giocondo* (Barcelona: Planeta, 1970) begins in the fashionably mixed gay piano bar Oliver; *Un carnívoro cuchillo* (Barcelona: Planeta, 1988) in the public toilets where respectable politicians meet up with muscular ragazzi di vita.

of time in which, in Bourdieu's words, the aesthetic distancing of the 'art of living' merges indistinctly with the moral agnosticism of social indifference (*Distinction*, 47). Thus on meeting Camilo José Cela ('one hundred kilos of literary history'), the newly 'Nobelized' novelist's thoughts on the Spanish contempt for intellectuals, as contrasted with the respect he claims is characteristic of the French and Latin Americans, are met by Umbral's mock solemn advice on personal grooming and the proper choice of cufflinks (*La década*, 189–91). In his parade of intimacy with the great and the good (who reciprocate his favoured term of endearment: 'amor'), Umbral thus asserts that circularity of legitimization by which signs of distinction are recognized and, in Bourdieu's words, 'classifying subjects [are] classified' (*Distinction*, 482). Just as the history of the aesthetic object is (for Bourdieu) the experience of its increasing relation not to the world but to previous art objects, so Umbral's chronicle of the cultural scene (of the 'theory of Madrid')[21] begins to refer only to itself, and to a cumulative effect of minute distinctions and relations of value it itself has set into play. The primacy of form over function is thus reconfirmed both by the nature of the profile (in which Umbral gleefully confesses to 'fictionalizing' lives lacking in intrinsic interest) and by its contrast with the 'event' of an earlier time, when the subjective stories of celebrities were set in a collective context. Where once Umbral glimpsed 'heavenly bodies'[22] in street demonstrations, now he loiters with them in fine restaurants. One typically ironic and well-chosen detail embodies the weakening or evacuation of political gestures: attending a birthday celebration for the 'historical' Communist Dolores Ibárruri ('Pasionaria') Umbral finds himself raising his fist in the time-honoured sign of struggle, but doing so 'as if [he] were trying to get on to a bus' (*La década*, 144).

But if Umbral, like the women he desires, is a medium (an 'electric conductor') of this historical inertia and weightlessness, he also finds time to submit that phenomenon to analysis. For Felipe, he says, has pioneered an 'aesthetics of disappearance' in which his absence from parliamentary debate is magnified by the frequency of his television appearances, which serve (paradoxically) to 'distance' him from the bedazzled electorate (p. 69). And while the opposition on the Right has been left without a discourse which the Left has appropriated for itself (p. 105), the Socialist government has embraced European integration as an alibi: the refusal to make a choice between the policies of Left and Right (p. 208). Felipe is thus a 'political transvestite' (p. 162), adopting or adapting Francoist

---

[21] *Teoría de Madrid* (Madrid: Espasa-Calpe, 1981) is a book of minutely detailed line drawings by Alfredo González accompanied by impressionistic texts by Umbral.

[22] *Los cuerpos gloriosos* is composed entirely of celebrity profiles.

triumphalism (p. 295). And the fashion designer of the decade is Adolfo Domínguez (inventor of the slogan 'the wrinkle is beautiful'), who has 'consecrated' a pseudo-casual socialism sold back to its own creators as a luxuriously distressed commodity (p. 119). In Bourdieu's telling phrase, consumers are sold 'the choice of the necessary' (*Distinction*, 372), the commodity consecrated by the dominant taste in both politics and fashion.

But if power is detached from the political (with an impotent and image-obsessed government mired in corruption and scandal), then the political becomes progressively detached from power (with new oppositional movements making their presence felt in unexpected ways). While Umbral embraces once more the 'anachronism' of the denunciation of the abuse of power (*La década*, 245), there is an uncanny persistence, in this the age of 'weak thought' (p. 207), of class conflict, alienation, and economic exploitation, beyond the collapse of that Marxist analysis which attempted to explain such phenomena. Umbral thus mourns the death of Tierno Galván, the mayor of a 'dialectical' Madrid, who had himself decried the city's lack of respect for its ruins and 'erasure of history' and had 'given back the people to the street and the street to the people' (pp. 147–53); he explicitly invokes posterity as a witness to a shameful moment (a 'flash') in which a Socialist government proposed the abolition of socialized medicine (p. 181); and with the rebirth of trade union militancy, he rejects the 'personalizing' interpretation of political struggle (the claim that it is merely 'a challenge to Felipe') as the denial of the true nature of social conflict (p. 186).

But if Umbral agrees with Fernando Savater that he 'would never vote for the Right, even if all [the Socialists] are sent to jail' for corruption (*Los cuerpos gloriosos*, 281), then his political and artistic judgements become increasingly reactionary. While the government champions 'Europe' as a universal panacea for Spain's ills, Umbral ironically proposes a greater loyalty to dull, provincial Extremadura than to Eurocratic Brussels (*La década*, 121); and if he here adopts a strategic, Spanish-speaking localism, he mocks the renewed energies of regionalism in the person of 'the Valencianist Valencian' who, as he addresses parliament, brandishes 'an orange in the face of Europe' (*La década*, 103), an orange which he leaves pointedly on Felipe's empty desk. And the one-time champion of modernity slips into an aesthetic *señoritismo* (provincialism and traditionalism). Where once he was an early champion of an Almodóvar dismissed as a prankster by much of the press, now he neglects challenging new directors such as Julio Medem (not to mention difficult older auteurs such as Víctor Erice). In art he prefers the realist López to the younger conceptualists who represent Spain abroad; in theatre his tastes are for the farceurs and ingénues of Madrid boulevard comedy, not the experimental physical theatre of Catalunya, which draws the critics' plaudits. Finally in fiction, he repeatedly hymns Camilo José Cela, a self-styled 'heretic' now definitively institutionalized by his many prizes, and mocks with him the 'decaffeinated', Anglophile, and internationalist style of younger novelists such as Javier Marías (*La década*, 195).

Once more we find here the double gesture of distinction: a setting apart of one group (one work) from another and an internal legitimization of that group which has granted itself titles of cultural nobility. Umbral thus speaks at the launches of books by famous authors, who kindly return the favour; and he serves on prize juries whose many awards are invariably directed to those who are already part of the aristocracy of culture, including himself. If the artistic boundary between high and low has been abolished (if Umbral consecrates and is consecrated by his mastery of everyday life), then the magic circle of distinction (in which, Bourdieu says, 'social subjects comprehend the social world which comprehends them' (*Distinction*, 482)) remains uncannily intact. In just the same way the Socialists' politics of the image and cult of personality are repeated and reversed in Umbral's own appeal to iconic details and his ironic, but always flattering, devotion to celebrity. The final irony, then, is that if Umbral comes to attack Socialist Spain for the uneven modernization of the Red Decade (for Felipe's drift into archaic authoritarianism or 'nacionalfelipismo'), then Umbral himself is 'anachronistic' not only in his new-found return to a politics of leftist denunciation (of a critique of the Left from within the Left), but also in the reactionary cultural, social, and sexual attitudes he takes such wilfully scandalous pleasure in exhibiting.

Bourdieu says of 'the habitus and the space of life styles':

The popular realism which inclines working people to reduce [cultural] practices to their function, to do what they do and be what they are . . . is the near perfect antithesis of the aesthetic disavowal which . . . masks the interest in function by the primacy given to form, so that what people do they do as if they were not doing it. (*Distinction*, 200)

There could be no better definition of a Socialist Spain in which, in culture as in politics, function is masked by form and action disavowed by words. For the sense of distinction serves to set apart image and object, rulers and ruled. But if there can be no return to the politics of substance (and, in the Spain of mass unemployment and pay-per-view television, precious few 'working people' to serve as the touchstone for authentic action and identity), then perhaps Umbral is saved by his love of language. The disengagement of representation from the real and of aesthetic form from its social implications is contradicted by Umbral's minute attention to what Bourdieu calls 'the expressiveness of popular language' (p. 34). Revelling in slang (from the *pasotas* of the 1970s to the gays and junkies of the 1980s and the pallid and insipid youth of the 1990s), Umbral reveals (and implicitly respects) the language that is an inextricable part of social being, a truly democratic practice of infinite distinction (of discrimination and embellishment) in time. As oral historian, Umbral practises anamnesis: the re-membering of an improbable past, obliterated daily by the consumer's reiterated quest for novelty and the politician's willed amnesia to the promises he has repeatedly broken. And like the anamnesis which is the patient's history of his own condition, Umbral's chronicle is at once psychic and somatic, internal and external. His column thus stands, in its very contradictions and confusions, as a great novel of Madrid in the Socialist era, worthy of the Parisian precedents Umbral invokes so frequently, in its dogged devotion to the necessity and the impossibility of modern times.

2 | Between Metaphysics and Scientism: Rehistoricizing Víctor Erice

1. Transcending Time

There seems little doubt that Víctor Erice is the consummate Spanish art director. A recent reading of his first feature, *El espíritu de la colmena* ('The Spirit of the Beehive', 1973), by Santos Zunzunegui begins by stating that there is a 'fundamental agreement' amongst critics that Erice's work constitutes not only the high point of Spanish cinema of all time, but also one of the most notable examples of contemporary Spanish art in general.[1] It is characteristic of Erice's reception abroad that in Britain *El espíritu de la colmena* is distributed in a video collection which bears the name 'Art House'. The most cursory examination of Spanish press coverage of Erice's career reveals the preconceptions implicit in such a term: his films are favourably contrasted with more commercially successful Spanish cinema; praised for their austerity, purity, and poetic lyricism; and held to be destined for an elite, minority audience.[2] Moreover, central to this question of art cinema is a questioning of the very possibility of cinema itself: Vicente Molina Foix cites Erice's second feature *El sur* ('The South', 1983) as an example of an 'unrealized', utopian cinema, hampered by financial limitations;[3] Erice himself claims with reference to his third

I would like to acknowledge the help of the staff of the Filmoteca Nacional and Biblioteca Nacional (Madrid) and the British Film Institute (London); and to thank Andrés F. Rubio, for kindly sending me material from the archives of *El País*, Madrid.

[1] 'Entre la historia y el sueño: eficacia simbólica y estructura mítica en *El espíritu de la colmena*', in *Paisajes de la forma: ejercicios de análisis de la imagen* (Madrid: Cátedra, 1994), 42–70 (p. 42).

[2] See, for example, Elsa Fernández Santos, 'Los buscadores de luz', *El País* (3 May 1992); Ángel Fernández Santos, '"El sol del membrillo", de Víctor Erice y Antonio López, provoca una fuerte división de opiniones', *El País* (12 May 1992).

[3] 'El año en que triunfamos peligrosamente', *El País* (25 June 1983); see also Ángel Fernández Santos, 'Una hermosa elegía inacabada', *El País* (25 May 1985).

feature *El sol del membrillo* ('The Quince Tree Sun', 1992) that, compared to that of painting, the language of cinema is 'wholly decadent', even 'dangerous'.[4]

In this chapter I hope to examine the role of the unrealized or unrepresentable in *El espíritu de la colmena*, most particularly in relation to cinematic techniques, such as off-screen space and sound; but I also hope to historicize the question of art cinema, auteurism, and their relation to cinematic language by examining the emergence of a press persona for Erice in representative writings by and interviews of the director over twenty years and the complex Spanish responses to this very self-conscious project over the same period. Here I attempt a revised version of Erice's own critique of the supposed opposition between history and poetry. Finally I look at three specific contributions to the production of *El espíritu de la colmena* which both supplement and qualify the myth of the auteur as unique and solitary artistic creator: cinematography (Luis Cuadrado); performance (Ana Torrent); and scriptwriting (Ángel Fernández Santos). My aim is not to minimize Erice's achievement but rather to historicize its reception and to call attention to the contributions of others without whom *El espíritu de la colmena* would not exist. The original synopsis of the film states that 'El viejo caserón donde viven las niñas se va llenando de la presencia de algo impalpable que sólo Ana parece fundamentalmente decidida a descubrir.' ('The big old house where the girls live is gradually filled with the presence of something impalpable which ultimately only Ana seems resolved to uncover.')[5] If *El espíritu de la colmena* is reliant on the positing of an unrepresentable (or untouchable) which is to be uncovered or drawn into visibility, then Erice's career has also benefited from just such a resonant absence, an unexamined appeal to the category of 'art' which can now be submitted to analysis.

A sense of wilful isolation or abstraction is stressed by Erice in a very early interview with José María Palá in *Film Ideal* on the release in 1969 of *Los desafíos* ('The Challenges'), the portmanteau movie in which Erice had directed one of the three segments.[6] Erice calls attention to the particular circumstances of the shoot. Filmed far from Madrid in a remote country location (a village abandoned by its inhabitants when a new reservoir was created), the film required a sense of 'convivencia' (of cooperation or communality) amongst cast and crew. Indeed, on returning from the

---

[4] Ángeles García, 'Víctor Erice dice que "El sol del membrillo" es para minorías que "están en todas partes"', *El País* (20 Jan. 1993).

[5] Unpub. typescript in the Filmoteca Nacional, Madrid.

[6] José María Palá, 'Conversación con Víctor Erice y Julia Peña', *Film Ideal* (1969), 217–22.

location to their hotel Erice claims that some of his colleagues chose to swim across the reservoir, rather than take the boat (p. 218), a detail which he says is important in that it helped to create an 'atmosphere' of 'mystery' around the film, a mystery to which even he as director did not fully have access (p. 219). Unaware of his characters' motivations, Erice trusts to the actors who add a contribution which they have learned themselves during the collective enterprise of film-making. Such privileged knowledge, claims Erice, is not learned in film school. Attacking not just Francoist censorship but also 'anachronistic' Spanish production practices, Erice states that he is interested only in auteurist cinema and that at the moment of self-expression one cannot give up 'what one is' (p. 220).

Erice's artistic isolation and presence-to-self are here qualified in a somewhat unexpected manner by his sense of cinema as 'convivencia', a paradox I will explore later. But on the opening of *El espíritu de la colmena* some four years later Erice insisted once more in interviews on the purity of his artistic vision.[7] Condemned to publicity work in the long interval between his first projects because of an inability to procure funding for features, Erice claims modestly that he must remain faithful to himself, as his 'limitations' make him unable to take on any project in which he does not believe. The only concern of an auteur is to maintain a rigorously moral posture, an absolute commitment to oneself, and a complete fidelity to one's beliefs (p. 35). Inversely, however, Erice stresses that 'cinema is an industrial entity' and claims that the poor reception of some films comes not from their auteur's lack of vision but rather from a mundane, commercial limitation: the distributors' frequent ignorance of the films for which they are responsible means that Spanish publicity campaigns are often inappropriate for the films they are promoting and fail to match product and audience (p. 36).

For Erice, then, the auteur is defined both by his artistic integrity and by his antagonistic relation to the commercial norms of the industry. And this is true not only of Spain, but also of Hollywood. It is no accident, then, that Erice should edit with Jos Oliver a collection of critical essays on the apparently unlikely figure of Nicholas Ray.[8] In their introduction to the volume the editors stress the existential isolation of Ray, who experienced the 'decisive' alienation of modernity (p. 13); his work constitutes not so much a break ('ruptura') with cinematic norms but rather an act of 'dissidence' within them, establishing a problematic link between the past and the future of film, without giving up on aesthetic innovation. Ray thus experienced exile as an 'internal condition', one which he lived in his native land (p. 14), condemned to solitude (p. 15) as the product of

[7] Juan Comas, 'Víctor Erice nos dice; entrevista', *Imagen y Sonido* (Jan. 1974), 35–6.
[8] *Nicholas Ray y su tiempo* (Madrid: Filmoteca Española, 1986).

'classical humanist training'. In his own, brief essay on Ray (pp. 17–21), Erice claims that the latter's life and work are inseparable: his films are not discursive, do not communicate a truth: rather they are 'pure exteriority . . . unfurled to the infinite' (p. 19). But this sense of an impossible, unrealized cinema, itself based on a primary alienation (Erice cites the 'most beautiful and revealing' title *We Can't Go Home Again*), is coupled with a tragic destiny at the hands of the industry: Erice and Oliver state that some of Ray's films were 'mutilated' by his producers (p. 13).

As geniuses frustrated not by artistic but by commercial constraints, the identification between Erice and Ray is clear. And when *El espíritu de la colmena* was revived on the tenth anniversary of its release the Spanish press agreed with this assessment. For example, a positive piece in the rightist *Ya* (written to coincide with a round table on the film at the prestigious Ateneo in Madrid) was in no doubt that Erice's first two features were amongst the best Spanish films of all time.[9] However, although the writer stresses the universality of Erice, whose films are addressed to 'any human being capable of thought and feeling', he also claims that Spanish spectators are the only ones able to understand their 'complex network of references and feelings' and to intuit that the central theme of Erice is the 'continuity of tradition and life' in Spain. *El espíritu de la colmena* is thus inserted into a narrative of national identity which becomes increasingly problematic: rejecting the claim frequently voiced in an earlier era that the 'Spanish genius' was less suited for film than it was for other media such as painting, the journalist goes on to state that Francoist censorship was never an obstacle to great film-makers: proof of this (he claims) is that both *El espíritu de la colmena* and *El sur* could have been shown under the dictatorship without any problem. Although freedom of expression is, of course, necessary and welcome, it must always be adapted ('adecuarse') to the customs of each people ('pueblo').

It is clear, then, that Erice's poetic abstraction and metaphysical absorption were easily coopted by the Right even under the Socialist government of the 1980s and even as consensus as to the nature of Erice's achievement became ubiquitous. But what was the response of the national press and the specialist film journals to the release of *El espíritu de la colmena* in the last days of the dictatorship? Was there the same degree of unanimity?

Although *El espíritu de la colmena* won the main prize (Concha de Oro) at the San Sebastián film festival of 1973, its reception was mixed. The interview already cited above claims that the cheers from critics in the stalls of the main screening theatre were matched by the jeers and stamps of the public in the balcony. The journalist also proposes another significant division: while the Madrid press was positive towards the film,

[9] Manuel Fernández, 'Diez años de "El espíritu de la colmena"', *Ya* (23 Nov. 1983).

the Barcelona papers were hostile. Examination of press clippings held at the Filmoteca Nacional (many of which lack full attributions) reveals that even the established and mainly Madrid-based critics of late Francoism had mixed feelings about the film. One supporter of Erice states that one of the film's great merits is its 'universality', a universality which does not, however, prevent it from being purely auteurist: personal and subjective.[10] Another supporter claims that for once Spanish cinema, normally 'impoverished, shaky, and colourless', has produced a 'miracle' worthy of French masters such as Godard or Truffaut or of the 'essential form' of silent pioneer D. W. Griffith.[11] Even those who doubt the value of the film as a whole praise it for transcending the particularities of the time and place in which it is set: Erice has 'raised himself' ('se ha elevado') up to the level of the internal world of child psychology; here he finds poetic inspiration, classical simplicity of narration, and purity of expression.[12] When one critic, uniquely, praises Erice's 'social commitment' it is only in the context of celebrating the emergence of a 'sensitive, profound, and lyrical auteur'.[13] More typical is the reviewer who cites Erice's lack of concern for the social conditions of the time in which *El espíritu de la colmena* is set (1940): scorning the temptation to call attention to this 'dramatic date in our history', Erice, we are told, 'gains universality' and shows his 'independence of any kind of ideology'.[14]

Universality is thus an alibi for the refusal to consider any social or political considerations to which the film might give rise. It is thus inevitable that the most right-wing critics of the film (those who show most hostility towards it) are also those who distinguish most sharply between the 'success' of the scenes centring on the children and the 'failure' of those concerning the adults. Thus *El Alcázar* wrote that the world of the girls was 'a true creation', while that of the adults exhibits 'vacuous meandering'.[15] *El Pueblo* praises the intelligence of bees, who, unlike Erice's characters, work together towards a clear aim: in *El espíritu de la colmena*, on the contrary, all is 'Baroquism' and 'confusion', with the married couple lacking 'human vitality'.[16]

The enigmas and ellipses of Erice's plot are thus both celebrated by some critics for their poetic lyricism and decried by others for their dangerous obscurity: *El Pueblo* claims the film is a 'crossword puzzle without answers'. In the face of such wilfully fragmented narration, the

[10] A. B., '*El espíritu de la colmena*', no source given.
[11] Miguel Rubio, '*El espíritu de la colmena*', *Nuevo Diario* (14 Oct. 1973).
[12] Pascual Cebollada, *Ya* (10 Oct. 1974).
[13] Pedro Crespo, '"El espíritu de la colmena" de Víctor Erice', *Arriba* (10 Oct. 1973).
[14] '*El espíritu de la colmena*' (9 Oct. 1973).
[15] Félix Martialay, *El Alcázar* (12 Oct. 1973).
[16] Anon., *El Pueblo* (17 Oct. 1973).

critic's breast cannot swell with the 'patriotic pride' that would normally be felt at a Spanish film's international recognition. The debates on universality and obscurity are thus inseparable from competing discourses of nationalism: opponents (such as *El Alcázar*) attack Erice's genuflection to 'modern' (read: 'foreign') experimentalism and supporters (such as *Nuevo Diario*) qualify their comparisons with French or US masters by claiming that *El espíritu de la colmena* is Spanish 'through and through'.

The short review in trade journal *Cineinforme*[17] coincides with the rightist view in attacking the 'weakness' of *El espíritu de la colmena*'s plot and the 'falseness' of the roles of the parents, while celebrating the 'lyricism' and 'humanity' of the psychological study of childhood. Such timeless qualities, however, are somewhat qualified by the context of the review, which is fortuitously placed according to alphabetical order between two features more characteristic of films released commercially in the Spanish market that month: a French *policier* and an execrable Italian *peplum* (classical epic).[18] And if we turn from the daily national press to the specialist monthly film journals we find, perhaps unexpectedly, a much greater attention to the historical specificity of Erice's film, in relation to both the period in which *El espíritu de la colmena* is set and the moment in which it was released and was battling for an audience with more commercial productions, often from foreign sources.

Dirigido Por named *El espíritu de la colmena* 'film of the month'. Jaume Genover's sensitive review[19] begins by stressing once more the 'puzzle'-like structure of Erice's plot, which requires an active participation from the audience which some spectators will be unwilling to give. Citing the isolation of each character from the others (as previous critics had also done) Genover moves beyond the stylistic vindication of Erice's poetic dislocation of narrative to draw a crucial connection between film form and history: the separation of each member of the family, confined to their own 'cell' of the eponymous hive, directs the spectator to the 'historical moment in which the action is situated' and to its unvoiced correlatives: the presence of the 'intellectual' father in an impoverished and uncultured village and his 'unusual' profession of beekeeping are transparent signs of his political unorthodoxy; the mother's letters to an unknown recipient reveal 'all the anguish of the War'. Moreover, the necessary failure of the young girls' fantastic aspirations is a transparent 'symbol' of the unavoidable repressions of the period. The film is thus not confined to the time

[17] A. F., *Cineinforme*, 186 (Nov. 1973), 23–4.

[18] *Il était une fois un flic* (Georges Lautner, 1971); *Maciste, il gladiatore più forte del mondo* (Michele Lupo, 1970).

[19] *Dirigido Por*, 9 (Jan. 1974), 25.

and place in which it is set; but those circumstances and that location are 'specific' and 'concrete'.[20]

Alvaro Feito's argument in *Cinestudio* is rather similar. Feito argues that *El espíritu de la colmena* is the first Spanish film of its time to be wholly 'modern' (controversial, open to differing interpretations, requiring the active participation of an adult spectator); and that the characters are by no means as 'symbolic or universally abstract' as 'triumphalist' (i.e. Francoist) critics would have us believe (p. 47). On the contrary, the spirit of the beehive is, quite simply, 'the spirit of Spanish society in 1940': hierarchical, functional, and wholly closed in on itself. The repressions and fears of the children are thus as much socio-political as psychological, the 'creation of a historical period . . . which does not eliminate, but rather amalgamates the diverse influences to which any human life is subject, situated as it is in a specific historical context' (p. 48).

Writing in the broadly Marxist tradition of progressive opponents of the regime, Genover and Feito are thus impatient with what they see as the idealizing abstractions of the daily press, and take for granted a necessary relation between artistic form and historical moment, but one which is inevitably complex and mediated. One of those mediations is the contemporary Spanish film industry. Thus Genover stresses the role of producer Elías Querejeta (unmentioned in the national press), who brought to the project his customary 'team' of technicians including cinematographer Luis Cuadrado; and Feito mentions the class component in Erice's reception: *El espíritu de la colmena* has received extravagant praise from the progressive bourgeoisie ('progres') and perhaps coincides too cosily with the expectations of a certain intellectually elite metropolitan audience, amongst whom are to be found members of the national press and of festival juries (p. 48). The institutionalization of Erice's art cinema by an ascendant liberal establishment is thus already clear even to those critics who vindicate *El espíritu de la colmena*'s political and social challenge to the Francoism which still clung to power on its release.

Ironically, as democracy became definitively established in the Spanish state so readings of the film became increasingly abstracted, thus justifying the warnings of leftist intellectual critics on *El espíritu de la colmena*'s release. A crucial moment in this process is Vicente Molina Foix's typically subtle essay of 1985 in a special number of the prestigious *Revista de Occidente* on war, Francoism, and film.[21] Reading the film as 'the war behind the window' (that is, the domestic replaying of a national scenario) Molina claims that *El espíritu de la colmena*'s theme is the 'obligation to absent themselves from reality produced in the characters by the Civil War

[20] *Cinestudio*, 127 (Dec. 1973), 47–8.
[21] 'La guerra detrás de la ventana', *Revista de Occidente* (Oct. 1985), 112–18.

and its political effects' (p. 113). For Molina, all of the characters (not just the children) are defined by their relation to fiction: the mother by her letters and the father by his diary, both of which are directed to an unknown addressee (p. 113). The film, then, is not (as previous art critics had suggested) a 'symbolic film on the War', since it lacks both a contrast between 'the two Spains' and a dialectic between the worlds of winning and losing parties (p. 115). All possible elements of historicity are thus 'erased' from *El espíritu de la colmena*, rendering it not so much a metaphorical reflection on the War as a study of the simulations of the real enacted by fiction on the world (p. 116). Transcending the barrier between *énonciation* and *énoncé* (Spanish *decir* and *lo dicho*) Erice expands the boundaries of filmic verisimilitude, lending his images the quality of phenomenological reality itself (p. 118).

With his customary subtlety, then, Molina suggests that the resonant absences and silences of the film (its appeal to the unrepresentable) are themselves an imaging of the effects of history, of a political repression which rendered its victims speechless and diverted their energies from the public, social arena into the private realm of fantasy. But in his contention that *El espíritu de la colmena* represses the dialectic of power, neglects metaphor in favour of simulation, and thus blurs the binary between fact and fiction, Molina not only problematizes previous Marxian readings made on the film's release, a time of more urgent political commitment; he also prepares the way for later, increasingly abstract readings which will expand his own reference to the structuralist poetics of, say, Christian Metz and wholly neglect any socio-political implications of the film, just as the Francoist critics of *El Alcázar* and *El Pueblo* had done before them.

The most developed and theorized of such readings is Santos Zunzunegui's essay, which, the author tells us, won a prize as best unpublished essay at a conference on Cinema and History held in Orihuela in 1992 ('Entre la historia y el sueño', 42). Zunzunegui claims to base his study on Erice's own challenge to the Aristotelian binary of history and poetry: Erice has shown that there is 'no real division' between the two (p. 43). Zunzunegui argues convincingly that Erice's critical writings must be taken in conjunction with his filmic works as part of a single project; but his chronological narration of that project (which seeks quite properly to avoid any facile linearity) remains wholly intracinematic: it is a succession of encounters with the work of filmic masters on the screen (Visconti, Pasolini, Mizoguchi) (pp. 44–8). Tellingly, Zunzunegui cites with approval what Erice claims to have learned from von Sternberg's Dietrich films: a 'path towards abstraction' (p. 48).

For Zunzunegui, then, *El espíritu de la colmena* follows a road of abstraction or 'dereferentialization', which lends the 'signifying practice' a 'particular density' (p. 49). Abandoning anecdotal elements in the narrative, Erice also lends objects a resonant (yet non-specific) opacity by shooting them straight on: a frontal angle which lends locations such as the abandoned building in which the fugitive hides an anthropomorphic quality (p. 53). With its multiple openings (credit sequence; unestablished first shots; 'primal scene' of the *Frankenstein* screening) the film is devoted to an 'internal referentialization' which renders 'external referentials' (reality effects) wholly secondary (p. 55). In a rather similar way, the narrative as a whole can be abstracted into 'mythemes' (paradigmatic 'coagulations' of syntagmatic strands) (p. 56) and a structural logic in which temporality is negated, giving way to a circular 'figurativization' which always refers back to itself (p. 59) and a 'mythic operator' in which all movement is eliminated (p. 65). Here Zunzunegui calls attention to one of Erice's (or perhaps more properly Luis Cuadrado's) most significant formal techniques: the lack of establishing shots, which means that 'all shots function as close ups', that is, are 'abstracted from their space-time coordinates' (p. 66). Surpassing 'banal referentialism', *El espíritu de la colmena* thus points to an impossible space beyond the image which Zunzunegui calls 'essentiality' or 'firstness' (p. 69).

Zunzunegui is to be praised for his close attention to film form. But although he does not deny that Erice's 'disconnections' gesture towards a concrete referent (the 'double physical and moral void' of the post-War (p. 69)), it is clear that the 'path towards abstraction' Zunzunegui discerns in Erice is also his own.[22] This is not the place to ask why the structuralist and semiotic poetics of Greimas, Lévi-Strauss, and the early Barthes (all cited reverently by Zunzunegui) should still be so influential in Spanish literary and cultural studies some twenty years after it fell out of favour in other countries. Zunzunegui himself offers a fragmentary genealogy of film studies in Spain when he refers to a piece on *El espíritu de la colmena* by Javier Maqua and Marta Hernández which, he claims, introduced the use of narratological terms to film study in Spain, thus clearing the way for a criticism which would no longer be reliant on gossip and impressionism: Zunzunegui cites film journals such as *La Mirada* and *Contracampo* in the period 1978–87 as exemplary here (p. 48 n. 20). I would suggest, however, that specialist film journals of the Transition were often more politically engaged and less enamoured of abstraction than Zunzunegui suggests;[23]

[22] In recent publications the prolific Zunzunegui has both developed his interest in the formal analysis of film and attacked US studies of Spanish cinema for their ignorance of or indifference to local cultural and historical context; see *La mirada cercana: microanálisis fílmico* (Barcelona: Paidós, 1996); and *El extraño viaje: el celuloide atrapado por la cola, o la crítica norteamericana ante el cine español* (Valencia: Episteme, 1999).

[23] See the references to *Contracampo* critics of the late 1970s and early 1980s in my *Laws of*

and, ironically, Zunzunegui's universalism merely echoes that of the 'impressionistic' press he so despises. In spite of his title, then, Zunzunegui's 'logical model' neglects not only history, but also dream: the scientist rigour and technical lexicon of structuralist poetics is notably inappropriate for the study of a film such as *El espíritu de la colmena* in which desire and fantasy are so prominent: Zunzunegui can only point, beyond his graphs and diagrams, to an unrepresentable 'essentiality' which goes wholly unexamined. The cult of the text (of its circularity, self-reference, immanence) is thus complicit with the cult of the auteur who also aspires to self-sufficiency and transcendental abstraction, who claims that history and poetry are one.

Yet we have seen that Erice himself acknowledges, intermittently at least, that cinema is an 'industrial entity' and the product of a community of co-workers. Having considered both popular and academic approaches to *El espíritu de la colmena*, we can now look more closely at how auteurism is qualified by collaboration in the film with reference to the three areas of cinematography, performance, and scriptwriting. My aim is both to historicize the act of film-making and to materialize elements often held to be transparent, innocent, or invisible: light, childhood, and off-screen space and sound. Rather than succumbing, then, to Erice's path towards abstraction, I follow a different route, one which attempts to acknowledge both technical virtuosity and psychic virtuality.

2. Cinematography, Performance, Scriptwriting

Luis Cuadrado's cinematography is invariably cited by critics as being an essential contribution to the success of *El espíritu de la colmena*. More difficult, however, is to assess the exact nature of that contribution. In his volume on the history of Spanish cinematography Francisco Llinás reproduces an extended interview with Cuadrado by Jaime Barroso which sheds light on both his working practices and his conceptualization of the relation between film and the real.[24] Cuadrado begins modestly by stating that the cinematographer's role is simply to reproduce in the form of images the director's ideas (p. 229). However, it is not quite as simple as it sounds: for the question of creating, or, more properly, recreating, cannot be limited to 'capturing' or 'photocopying' the world. As film is incapable of reproducing the natural look of objects, the 'naturalness' sought by the director must be 'invented' by the cinematographer. Moreover, although

Desire: Questions of Homosexuality in Spanish Writing and Film 1960–90 (Oxford: Oxford University Press, 1992), 134–6, 142–3, 153, 158, 160, 163.

[24] 'Entrevista con Luis Cuadrado', in Francisco Llinás, *Directores de fotografía del cine español* (Madrid: Filmoteca Española, 1989), 228–47.

'creative discussion' with the director is important, no director has been able to advise Cuadrado on the technical means he uses to produce the final effects of the film; indeed, only Carlos Saura has any specialist knowledge of cinematography at all (pp. 230, 231). Scouting for locations before the shoot is also a collaborative process, but one in which Cuadrado's contribution is definitive: while it is important, once more, that the director should explain how he intends to shoot each scene, exteriors are determined by the cinematographer's priorities: the direction of light and position of the sun at each point in the working day; the adaption of his own preferred lighting design to the kind of lighting required by the film. Cuadrado's preference in interiors is for indirect lighting, reflected off a sometimes complex combination of white cards, sheets, or translucent papers. This is particularly appropriate for a frequent and tricky shot (prominent in *El espíritu de la colmena*): filming an actor by a window (p. 246).

It is clear, then, that according to Cuadrado's account of his working practice, the 'magical' or 'mysterious' effects praised by critics and often attributed to Erice are the result of strictly technical means. But, moreover, that technique (to which the director has no access) is inextricable from a certain theory of representation elaborated by the cinematographer from his practice: Cuadrado claims to favour 'realist photography'; but by this he means an 'expressionism' which reproduces the 'sensation' of the real, the emotion it provokes in the spectator, not its exact appearance ('realidad minuciosa', p. 233). That relation between history and poetry (between the particular and the general), that tension between referentiality and abstraction that we have seen in both the writings of Erice and the responses of critics to *El espíritu de la colmena* (generally considered to be 'Erice's film'), are thus also present in the theory and practice of *El espíritu de la colmena*'s cinematographer, who also and uniquely controls the technical means without which there would be no film.

One of those means is colour. Jesús González Requena has given an original account of the 'consciousness of colour' in Spanish cinematography which pays particular attention to Cuadrado and *El espíritu de la colmena*.[25] Like Zunzunegui, González Requena's theoretical touchstone is semiotic or formalist: citing Shklovski he claims that the role of art is to transform the object, defamiliarizing the everyday, and substituting revelation for mere recognition (p. 121). But González Requena also offers a historical account of colour. Thus, in general, the second half of the twentieth century has seen three major changes: the massive expan-

[25] 'La conciencia del color en la fotografía cinematográfica española', in Llinás, *Directores de fotografía*, 118–65.

sion of audiovisual technologies, which have 'invaded' perceptive experience with intense, even 'violent' colours; the inversion of the historical relation between matter and colour, whereby the latter is no longer dependent on the former, and indeed often flaunts its status as an arbitrary choice, independent of the object to which it is attached; finally, the rise of plastic, which has 'sacralized' this arbitrary relation, creating ever more pure and dense colours, and sacrificing texture to wholly homogeneous surfaces (pp. 119–20). More particularly in Spain, these developments had quite specific effects on cinematography: the expansionist 1960s were a time of increasing consumerism in which the middle class saw itself reflected in the vivid colours of advertising and the garish Kodak tones of the dominant genre of the period: the bourgeois, urban comedy. 'Flat and brilliant urban colours, reminiscent of plastic, of postcards, and of sunsets, irrepressibly modern and commercial . . . these were the colours that dominated the Spanish cinematographic landscape of the 1960s' (p. 122). González Requena traces next the 'clean break of the 1970s': rejecting both the 'granitic greys' of Francoism and the Kodak colourized consumerism a new tendency emerges, which replaces plastic colours and TV kitsch with local landscapes in their diversity of texture and colour, with subtle, shaded, and warm tones, and with intimate, atmospheric, and metaphorical photography (p. 123).

El espíritu de la colmena clearly belongs to this reactive tendency. For González Requena the novelty of its look was, paradoxically, its direct link to the 'perceptive memory' of Spaniards who could see beyond the 1960s: for them, its setting was at once recognizable and dense with associations. The browns, creams, and greys of the exteriors, the warm yellows and oranges of the interiors, both palettes suggest to González Requena 'dense, subtle . . . atmospheres' (p. 123). This chromatic density is confirmed by contradictory forces in the composition. On the one hand, we find the static symmetricality of the composition of exteriors (the two windows of the abandoned building; the horizontal long shots of a road or railway in a deserted landscape). But on the other we find the unsettling liminal nature of interiors and the 'vertical affirmation of the subject' (the mother writing by a window; the child standing against the landscape). Most importantly, González Requena stresses texture: the human face is presented as 'a rough surface which . . . reveals that it shares its matter with other surfaces' (p. 123). Thus the face of the woman announcing the film show in the opening sequence is similar in texture to the rough walls of the buildings which surround her; the facial wounds of the villagers are extended into the highly textured features of the village itself (p. 124) (Plate 1).

Compared to the mythic immobilism of, say, Zunzunegui, González

Requena suggests a textured temporality: Cuadrado's cinematography is not abstract, but reveals rather the trace left by time in bodies and buildings. Moreover, in place of Zunzunegui's 'essentiality', González Requena cites the Lacanian 'real': that impossible place outside representation, which is not, however, wholly separate from the trace of textual and psychic movement.[26] And if we look now at the question of performance we shall see that just as the magic of light may be historicized, drawn itself into visibility, so the supposed innocence and abstraction of childhood can also be read for its insistent historicity and inevitable temporality.

It is notoriously difficult to read performance in film, so specific are codes of facial and bodily movement to cultural context. The problem is multiplied when the actor is a child and the performance offers itself as purely 'natural'. Erice has suggested that the sequence in which Ana (the character) sees *Frankenstein* for the first time was the first time that Ana (the actor) had herself seen the film.[27] This 'firstness' or priority of the unrepeatable event, captured by Erice uniquely on a hand-held camera, points towards the 'magical' moment of 'primeridad' cited by Zunzunegui in *El espíritu de la colmena*. In an interview in the women's magazine *Dunia*, run under the emblematic title 'The power of the look',[28] the adult Ana Torrent has confirmed this identification of presentation and representation in a unique moment of innocence: she was not aware of giving a performance but was simply 'playing' before the camera.

Torrent also acknowledges, however, that Spanish audiences have internalized their memory of her as a child (p. 136). And if we look back to press cuttings of the 1970s a more complex story emerges. Posed against a varied range of backgrounds (an aquarium, a DC9 aeroplane, a cinema in which *El espíritu de la colmena* is playing) the child Ana is shown always with the same impassive face she presents in the film: the dark, blank stare which embodies 'the power of the look' (Plate 2). Journalists invariably comment on the 'special attraction' of her 'large, wide' eyes, the 'most expressive look of our cinema'.[29] But while in the late 1980s *Dunia* read the meaning of those eyes as being that 'there was still a place [in late Francoist Spain] for a forbidden ideal of freedom', earlier interpretations are quite different. An extended interview in *Ya* praises not only the 'naturalness of her performance' but also the 'simplicity of her Hispanic face', claiming

---

[26] González Requena does not however give a reference in Lacan's text for this term; nor does he acknowledge that its meaning is problematic and much debated. For one version of the real see Slavoj Zizek, 'Pornography, Nostalgia, Montage', in *Looking Awry: An Introduction to Jacques Lacan through Popular Culture* (Cambridge, Mass.: MIT, 1992).

[27] Elsa Fernández Santos, 'Los buscadores de luz', *El País* (3 May 1992).

[28] Juan Pando, 'Ana Torrent: el poder de la mirada', *Dunia*, 18 (1989), 136–7 (p. 137).

[29] Antonio García Rayo, 'Ana María Torrent: con nueve años, dos películas', *Ya* (23 Nov. 1975).

that there are 'many Anas' in Spain, many young girls of her generation, facing so many difficulties with such a great capacity for endurance. The 'magical face' invoked in *Telva* magazine (15 March 1976) is also quite specifically Spanish, held to embody both the spirit of the nation (there are frequent references to the dark eyes of Goya portraits) and the history of that nation at a particular moment.

The most sensitive and revealing interview is by novelist and contemporary chronicler Francisco Umbral on the release of Saura's *Cría cuervos* two years after *El espíritu de la colmena*.[30] Umbral also cites Torrent's 'dark tragic eyes, worthy of a sad child in a Goya portrait'; but he seems equally taken by her tiny hand covered in elastoplasts and her 'catastrophic' teeth. On the one hand Umbral claims that she is 'a little girl and nothing more' and that the impression she makes on film comes from a simple, even mechanical technique: she is forbidden to smile on camera, and her gaze thus takes on a 'veil' of adult seriousness. But on the other hand Umbral compliments Torrent on her beauty, asks her where babies come from, and compares the pleasure she takes in snacks and sweets to an 'ordered orgy'. He ends with an exclamation: 'Oh, those eyes, dear God, those terrible eyes.'

These hints of infantile sexuality (which could hardly be voiced by a women's magazine such as *Dunia*) are confirmed in a later piece in *El País*, in which Umbral, five years later, looks back on the earlier encounter and compares himself to the 'dirty, old man' ('hombre del saco'), seducing children with poisoned sweets as evening falls in the park.[31] But if the journalist plays the part of the paedophile (even 'vampire') then the child herself is cast as 'Lolita', her innocence 'stolen' by the adult whose heart is swollen with 'blood and embarrassed love': in the figure of the child, in the doll-like, Goya eyes, Umbral saw the body of the adolescent she was to become coming towards him: 'nicely grown up [*crecidita*], reader. Nicely grown up.'

Just as the 'universality' of *El espíritu de la colmena* served critics as a screen protecting them from the film's political implications, so the 'naturalness' of Torrent's performance, the 'darkness' of her look, work as a veil, masking both the nationalist dimensions of her image (the mirror of Spanish womanhood) and the disturbingly sexual resonances of the plot (in which a child gives herself to a monstrous man in the dark). Playfully ironic and archly seductive, Umbral not only discloses the repressed eroticism of the spectator's response to child actors; he also reveals a less sublimated yet more complex process: the way in which audiences trace the chronology of their own lives in the shifting appear-

[30] 'Ídolos sin pedestal: Ana Torrent', unidentified press clipping [1975].

[31] 'Spleen de Madrid: Ana Torrent', *El País* (5 Sept. 1980).

ance of performers on screen. By anticipating the erotic evolution of Ana (the actor, and perhaps the character) Umbral illuminates the historicity of our own libidinal response to cinema, a historicity which at once responds to and recoils from the 'magical' suspension or abstraction of bodies imaged and unchanging on the screen. He points, then, to an off-screen space in which Torrent scratches her hand, eats sweets, grows up, but in which she and her audience will carry with us the material trace of the power of her look, a power that is at once poetic and historical, experienced in isolation and as part of a community of spectators, of citizens.

We have seen, then, that both cinematography and performance made specific contributions to that process of 'convivencia' described by Erice in the shoot for *Los desafíos*, contributions which are perhaps more self-conscious than has previously been supposed. Even the adult Torrent, who claims she had simply 'played' before the camera, is contradicted by the child actor Ana, who reveals differences in working practices: with Erice, unlike with Saura, she learned her lines before shooting began.[32] The question of the contribution of co-scriptwriter Ángel Fernández Santos is more complex as it raises the problem of artistic priority. For while the two share the credit for the screenplay, in the typewritten script held in the Biblioteca Nacional[33] Fernández Santos's name comes first; while in the film itself it comes second. In a lengthy piece in *El País*, published to celebrate the tenth anniversary of *El espíritu de la colmena*,[34] Fernández Santos (a faithful supporter of Erice's subsequent films, in which he himself played no part) gives his account of the origins of the script. According to Fernández Santos this was such an intimate process of collaboration that the childhood memories of each man alternated in the narrative: thus Erice provided the mushroom picking and monster games of the children; Fernández Santos the well, the fugitive, and the school anatomy lesson. Fernández Santos attributes to Erice a decisive stroke: the 'amputation' of the original frame narrative set in the present in which the adult Ana returns to the village in which she grew up to visit her dying father. This cut led to an internalization of the narrative: deprived of an on-screen story-teller, spectators are obliged to recreate the story inside their own consciousness, using the 'secret look, indebted to a secret identity and poetic time, which exists behind the eyes of every human being'.

Fernández Santos thus takes the internalization of the narrative to be also a universalization of it: the two men's private memories become, immediately, those of the audience. What he reveals, however, is that that

---

[32] Fernández Santos, 'Los buscadores de luz'.

[33] 'El espíritu de la colmena' (Madrid: Elías Querejeta, 1973).

[34] 'Mirar desde detrás de los ojos', *El País*, no date [1983].

abstraction is the effect of a specific and conscious decision on the writers' part and one which arose from a familiar problem in scriptwriting, the attempt to retain a unified point of view. And if we go on to contrast the Biblioteca Nacional script with the final film version we note a continuing erasure of the historical frame of the narrative which extends into analogous changes in shooting style and the relation between sound and image. To start at the very beginning: the opening shots of the film (after the title pictures drawn by the child actors) are long shots of the truck carrying the movie apparatus and of the building in which the film will be shown, followed by medium shots of the projectionist unloading his equipment surrounded by boisterous children and the town crier announcing the show. The script opens on a black screen in silence on which the title appears, fading out on to a shot of a 'hermetically closed' beehive, without a single bee in sight. A dissolve links this to the following montage, also shown in silence:

Vista general de un pueblo. La mayoría de las casas se reúnen en el fondo de una hondonada, junto a un pequeño río.
En el interior, pero especialmente en la afueras de ese pueblo, vemos algunas casas derruídas, y otras vacías, sin habitar.
Muros derruídos.
Muros ennegrecidos.
Ventanas de cristales rotos.
Una casa, en las afueras, en medio de la llanura, de labranza, abandonada. Junto a ella, el brocal de un pozo de agua.
Una pieza de artillería, enmohecida, destrozada por un impacto, convertida en chatarra.
Una trinchera abandonada.
Un par de botas de soldado, en el fondo de una zanja, las suelas reventadas.
Una fosa común. Una cruz. Junto a la tumba, muchas flores silvestres. (fo. 1)[35]

Master shot of a village. Most of the houses are grouped together around a hollow, by a small river.
Inside the village, but mainly on the outskirts, we can see ruined houses, and others that are empty and uninhabited.
Ruined walls.
Blackened walls.
Windows with their panes broken.
A house on the outskirts, in the middle of the plain, a farm labourer's house, abandoned. Next to it, a well.
An artillery gun, overgrown with moss, destroyed by a blast, turned into scrap iron.
An abandoned trench.

[35] Zunzunegui ('Entre la historia y el sueño', 52) also cites this passage from the published version of the script: *El espíritu de la colmena* (Madrid: Elías Querejeta, 1976).

A pair of soldier's boots, in the bottom of a ditch, their soles in tatters.
A common grave. A cross. By the tomb, a lot of wild flowers.

Here there is a very explicit reference to the trace of history in the landscape (guns, boots, and graves), not to mention an emphatic parallel between the emptiness of the hive and the mortal decrepitude of the village. The next shot in the script (of a bee feeding at a flower) hints, like the blossoms by the grave, at the possibility of a rebirth also absent from the opening of the film as it finally appeared. If the loss of this historical frame renders the opening sequence of *El espíritu de la colmena* abstracted, non-specific, what remains nonetheless is the texturality of the images cited by González Requena: the traces of time in the faces and buildings we are shown.

Elsewhere Erice (or Cuadrado) eliminates spectacular camera effects or movements specified in the script. Thus the sequence in which the children watch *Frankenstein* begins in the script (but not the film) with a 'blinding white light directed straight to the camera lens' (fo. 8), a reverse angle from the screen's point of view. Or again, the sequence in which Ana looks down the well on her second visit to the abandoned building ends in the script with the camera, hitherto held motionless in extreme long shot, 'violently penetrating the interior of the well, focusing on the opening from the darkness surrounded by walls on all sides: this opening against which we see [Ana's] head leaning over, standing out against the sky' (fo. 43). In the film, we simply cut to closer shots of Ana and the well, followed by a shot from her point of view looking down into the well. Once more the showy subjective shot from the point of view of the 'thing' (screen or well) is cut.

Eliminating both historical reference and virtuoso camera movement, the film also intensifies the use of off-screen space and sound already hinted at in the script by rendering what we see and hear more abstracted and less grounded within the frame. For example, the script is divided throughout into two columns on each folio, with visual instructions on the left and sound and dialogue on the right. Sound effects off screen are precisely orchestrated as they are in the film itself: Teresa (known as 'the woman' in much of the script) thus pauses as she writes her letter and looks to the window as the distant whistle of a train is heard (fo. 10); or again, the script specifies that in the scene in which Fernando joins his estranged wife in bed and she pretends to sleep, he does not appear in frame as we hear him approach and remove his clothes and shoes (fo. 33). Indeed he is wholly impersonalized in the direction which reads: 'Someone opens the door off screen.' The script also refuses to specify the motivation or sometimes, indeed, the actions of the characters: when the two girls first visit the abandoned building we are told that Ana 'seems' to follow her sister faithfully, 'as if' obeying an agreement they had previously made (fo. 41). In the same sequence we are told that Ana 'may' be cold and that it is 'impossible' to know if the two girls speak to one another (fo. 42).

Historical abstraction, technical discretion, and undecidable motivation thus seem to go hand in hand. What is important to note, however, is that the consistent use of sound bridges (the staggering of sound and vision from one sequence to another) is always in the form of sound off, not sound over: that is, unlike the voice-over of, say, *El sur*, in which the main character offers an authoritative commentary on the action from a disembodied position outside it, the effects or dialogue which play over a sequence in *El espíritu de la colmena* always derive from another location within the diegetic space: thus we know, for example, that the ominous clumping noises heard as the girls discuss *Frankenstein* late at night derive not from the monster but from the father we have seen pacing in his studio in a previous shot. Strictly speaking, then, *El espíritu de la colmena* is a film not so much of the unrepresentable but of the unrepresented. The dislocation of image- and soundtracks points not to an 'essentiality' to which actors and spectators have no access, but rather to an atomization of filmic space in which no subject accedes to an intersubjective realm beyond their immediate, sensual experience. This atomization and dislocation can be read (as Molina Foix does) not as metaphysical, but rather as historical in origin.

In the last sequence of *El espíritu de la colmena* Ana invokes the monster, addressing the night sky with the words 'Soy Ana' ('It's me, Ana'). A female voice is heard, singing eerily and wordlessly on the soundtrack. This is another example of the path towards abstraction followed by Erice (by Cuadrado, Torrent, and Fernández Santos): in the script she sings a song on a woman waiting at night for her lover, taken from a sixteenth century *Cancionero* (fo. 128). But the sequence also reveals the role of the Other in the constitution of a sense of self: it is by giving herself to the monster (to the unknowable lover whom she awaits) that Ana finds her own (sexual?) identity. There is no denying the magical, mysterious effect of this scene on many audiences, like its predecessor in which, eyes closed once more, the child offers herself to the monster by the river. What I have suggested in this piece, however, is that such effects are the result of quite specific technical means (of cinematography, performance, and script-writing); and that those means are themselves subject to the commercial constraints of the film industry and the discursive limitations of those critics, whether journalistic or academic, who are paid to comment on its products. Like Ana, then, the director has no unique and solitary identity, no sense of self without the Other (crew, industry, audience) with whom and to whom he offers his vision.

But if we, like the Nicholas Ray whom Erice admires so much, 'cannot go home again' to the old myth of auteurism or, still less, the unquestioning reverence of the 'Art House', nor should we take refuge in metaphysics or scientism, which remain the dominant critical approaches to *El espíritu de la colmena* in Spain.[36] For, as we have seen, the first is complicit with a rightist politics of nationalism (of the 'Spanish genius' or 'spirit of the nation'); while the second can address neither the historical nor the psychic dimensions of film (neither the 'war behind the window' nor the 'look behind the eyes'). The connection between film form and social practice will always be complex; and any study of reception risks impressionism and triviality. The challenge, then, is not to suspend too soon the conflict between history and poetry, between reference and abstraction; to elaborate a reading of *El espíritu de la colmena* which does justice to its extraordinary resonance and complexity without either reducing it to empirical evidence or abandoning it to the ecstasy of abstraction.

---

[36] I have attempted to offer just such a reading (both historical and theoretical) for another contemporary Spanish film-maker in *Desire Unlimited: The Cinema of Pedro Almodóvar* (London: Verso, 1994).

3 | Cross-Cut: Replay

1. The Resurrection of History

One curious characteristic of post-Franco culture is the persistence with which artists in many media replay the past. Under the Socialists, cinema, freed at last from censorship, tended to specialize not in contemporary political dramas but rather in period pictures. An important genre of the 1980s was the cinematic adaptation of progressive literary texts from before and after the Civil War such as *Bernarda Alba*, *Réquiem por un campesino español*, and *Tiempo de silencio*. The culmination of this process of screening the past was *Belle Époque*, Fernando Trueba's original screenplay of 1992, winner of the Oscar for best foreign film. Nostalgic and narcissistic, this narrative replayed pre-War Spain as a utopian moment in which sexual and political options are unlimited: a youthful army deserter (ingénu Jorge Sainz) sleeps his way through the four daughters of an indulgent anarchist father, played by veteran Fernando Fernán Gómez.

Belle Époque is exemplary of a phenomenon that Baudrillard calls 'History: A Retro Scenario'.[1] Writing in the early 1980s, and prompted by such meticulous and lifeless recreations as Kubrick's *Barry Lyndon*, Baudrillard claims that 'today history . . . invades the cinema' (p. 43). 'Exorcised by a slowly or brutally congealing society,' continues Baudrillard, 'history celebrates its resurrection in force on the screen.' Rehearsing postmodern motifs he himself originated, Baudrillard writes that 'the great event of this period [is] the death pangs of the real and of the rational that open onto an age of simulation . . . history has retreated, leaving behind it an indifferent nebula, traversed by currents, but emptied of references. It is into this void that the phantasms of a past history recede' (pp. 43–4). People no longer believe in the ideologies of the past, but they need to 'resurrect the period when at least there was history, at least there was violence (albeit fascist), when at least life and death were at stake' (p. 44).

Baudrillard's hypothesis of a 'void' or 'leukemia of history and politics'

---

[1] *Simulacra and Simulation* (Ann Arbor: University of Michigan Press, 1994), 43–8.

or of a 'haemorrhage of values' (p. 44) that precipitates this uncanny 'resurrection' of history would seem more appropriate to France after the disillusion of 1968 than to Spain, even given the so-called *desencanto* of the period. For the 1970s and 1980s had seen in Spain a swift sequence of irrevocable historical events. The death of Franco in 1975 was succeeded by the first democratic general elections for forty years (1977), the Constitution establishing the *estado de las autonomías* (1979), the Socialist landslide and disintegration of the rightist UCD (1982), and the incorporation of Spain into the EEC and NATO (1986). It seems difficult to qualify such a decade as 'the retreat of history'; and there is little evidence for Baudrillard's nostalgia for violence, Fascist or not, in a Spain racked by terrorism even as it experimented with democracy. The cult of novelty was such that the artists who stamped their imprint on the period, such as Almodóvar, identified themselves simply as 'the moderns' before they were pigeon-holed by the press as the 'movida'. Or again, the erosion of public space, another leitmotif of the postmodern condition, is hardly applicable to Spain. To the contrary, the newly elected governments, both central and peripheral, became the largest public sponsors of architecture in the nation's history, commissioning regional assemblies, airports, and museums at a prodigious rate.

Writing in the United States (and publishing in Mexico) in 1988 Eduardo Subirats also rehearses the postmodern leitmotifs of the period: the death of art and the anti-aesthetic, the simulacrum and the end of progress, the twilight of the idols and the performativity of experience.[2] But even here Subirats's analysis of the 'lost object' (compare Baudrillard's loss of the referent) gives way finally to a relative optimism in the proposal of a 'discrete principle of hope' (p. 203) and a 'poetic experience of the world' that can 'recover the lost time of history, transcend the dialectic of domination . . . and grasp the promise of happiness' (p. 225). Subirats makes only fleeting references to Baudrillard and even to the Guy Debord whose theory of the 'spectacle' gives him the title of his book; and he is not here concerned with Spain. But within Spain itself commentators on postmodernism also rarely engage with the foreign philosophers who were most influential in theorizing the term and characteristically hold out for the continuing promise of modernity in their own country. This holds true across a wide range of different disciplines. In 1986 a collection on 'leisure, art, and postmodernity' edited by the Spanish Association of Art Critics[3] featured only one essay out of seven that mentioned

[2] *La cultura como espectáculo* (Mexico: Fondo de Cultura Económica, 1988), 29, 35, 49, 84, 122.
[3] Asociación Española de Críticos de Arte, *Ocio, arte, y postmodernidad* (Madrid: Fundación Actilibre, 1986).

Baudrillard and Lyotard; and in the same year a conference on 'utopia and postmodernity' held at Salamanca's Pontifical University[4] saw academics from Madrid's Complutense arguing, with Marx, that it was not enough to interpret the world in order to change it (p. 39); that the 'myth of postmodernity is nothing more than an anti-utopia that power opposes to a culture of emancipation' (p. 44); and that, finally, we must continue that 'age old wager on reason and freedom . . . the transcendental legacy of the historical cycle that is now coming to an end' (p. 66).

Ten years later the debate had hardly moved on. A journalistic survey of 'postmodernity and the end of the millennium'[5] in 1994 briefly cites Lyotard and Baudrillard in an impressionistic 'eulogy of postmodernity' and 'sweet nihilism' (pp. 83, 93); but it also attacks the supposed 'despotism of minorities' and 'political correctness' (pp. 44–5). One moral philosopher in the same year[6] attacks the 'hegemonic system' that promotes as the 'only form of postmodernity French poststructuralism [sic] and the significantly named *pensiero debole* [of Gianni Vattimo] [theories] that are nothing but decadence, the abandonment of rationality, of communication, and even of the very idea of man' (p. 13). Confronted by the 'evidence of the failure of the idea of progress as historical necessity' we must 'resist injustice', promote 'ecumenical solidarity' against 'individualist indifference', and 'continue to believe in reason, progress [sic], and democracy'. A second moral philosopher in 1996[7] also proposes ethics in the face of postmodern scepticism. Setting up a range of targets (Foucault, Derrida, Rorty) he claims they merely 'react to the unilaterality of the programme of modernity (universality, identity, rationality, necessity) with another unilaterality: nothing exists but the variable, particular, different, irrational, and contingent' (p. 92). Needless to say, there is no detailed engagement with the texts of the supposed irrationalist postmodernists whose thesis is once more contrasted with an 'ethical paradigm: justice, solidarity, and sovereignty [*autonomía*]' (p. 111).

Surprisingly, perhaps, a more thoughtful engagement with the foreign theorists of postmodernity comes from two relatively early and unlikely sources: the proceedings of a Marxist conference on 'modernity and postmodernity' held in 1987 and a collection of essays published by the editor

[4] María Teresa Aubach (ed.), *Utopía y postmodernidad* (Salamanca: Universidad Pontificia, 1986).

[5] José Javier Esparza, *Ejercicios de vértigo: ensayos sobre la posmodernidad y el fin del milenio* (Valencia: Barbarroja, 1994).

[6] Jesús Ballesteros, *Postmodernidad: decadencia o resistencia* (Madrid: Tecnos, 1994).

[7] José Rubio Carracedo, *Educación moral, postmodernidad y democracia: más allá del liberalismo y del comunitarismo* (Madrid: Trotta, 1996).

of *El País* in the same year. The Marxists[8] note that postmodernism is not or not merely antimodernism (i.e. the neo-conservative attack on the Enlightenment values of equality, freedom, and progress), but rather the investigation of 'the aporias in the modern project' that is as yet 'incomplete': 'rather than breaking with Modernity, [postmodernism] would establish a certain continuity with it . . . proposing a certain right to difference' (p. 13). The 'dissolution' or 'dispersal' of the social and political subject leads, then, not to atomistic hedonism (as most Spanish commentators believe) but rather to a new kind of solidarity (p. 14); or again while 'global projects' are impossible 'Postmodernity does not renounce political struggle or the project, although it is conscious of the difficulty of relating different perspectives together without diluting or eliminating them.' The authors thus propose a 'struggle for a Postmodernity that buries along with capitalism the (modern) prehistory of humanity and finally opens the way to a history that would now be a posthistory' (p. 14). One concrete example of this theoretical posture is town planning (p. 15), combining as it does of necessity the general project and the local intervention, the material evidence of the past and the posthistorical possibility of the future.

Such theoretical repositioning of Marxism could be read, cynically, as a tactical response to the precipitous decline of the electoral fortunes of the Spanish Communist Party in the 1980s. But Juan Luis Cebrián, the Socialist-supporting editor of *El País*,[9] also combines a sympathetic engagement with the foreign theorists with a relatively optimistic approach to the possibilities of the postmodern, inseparable as it is in Spain from the modern project that remains unfinished. Writing in the mid-1980s at a time when the 'insufficiencies of politics and the wretchedness of intellectual and cultural life' (p. 10) were already visible, Cebrián gives an accurate account of the development of the postmodern debate as theory (the rejection of progress, dialectics, and the Enlightenment) and as practice (the 'ludic' North American architecture of the façade) (pp. 32, 33). This debate presupposes a break ('ruptura') with the previous 'mental universe' in Spain, that of 'palaeo-Marxists' and 'palaeo-Christians' alike (p. 34). The resulting 'absence of a reliable framework of values' is, however, salutary for Spain, putting as it does the nation state into crisis (p. 35). With the end of the 'confrontation between Left and

[8] Pedro Castrortega et al., *Encuentros sobre modernidad y postmodernidad* (Madrid: Fundación de Investigaciones Marxistas, 1989).

[9] *El tamaño del elefante* (Madrid: Alianza, 1987). The 'elephant' of the title is the great and diverse Spain that has been released from captivity and is now 'in the middle of the street'. Cebrián writes that this state of affairs is 'risky for scientific progress [but] a triumph for democracy and an invitation [to Spaniards] to leave behind [them] the world of darkness' (p. 11).

Right' (p. 38), it may be possible 'to modernize Spain . . . finally to have a French Revolution' (p. 37) and to produce a 'civil society' independent of the violent appropriations of the nation state (p. 38).

However, Cebrián is not always so sanguine. In this 'world without values' youth have no 'historical memory' (p. 40) and the 'ideal of solidarity' has disappeared (p. 41). Political demonstrations have become fiestas (p. 42) and, in a country with 'more visitors than inhabitants', tourism is not so much an industry as a 'culture' (p. 44). Postmodernism has destroyed 'the concept of rightness and error', thus leading Spaniards to 'accept idiots' (p. 46), such as the proponents of the *movida*: 'a cultural phenomenon so concerned with the façade that it forgot to build the house' (p. 47). If Cebrián echoes here the moral philosophers' critique of hedonistic individualism, it is not, however, because he rejects out of hand the postmodern project: the Spanish 'idiots' with their 'fireworks' are compared unfavourably to the Italian Vattimo and the French Lyotard, seriously engaged in the 'task of thought' (p. 46). With the Marxists, then, Cebrián acknowledges that postmodernism is implicit in modernity (a modernity he identifies unambiguously with 'democratization and development' (p. 67)); and in an experience of time and history that is not simply haemorrhaged away as it is in Baudrillard's 'retro scenario'.

In this chapter I return to the texts of Vattimo and Lyotard (which remain more invoked than read) in order to explore four Spanish cultural products that replay history in ways that illustrate this problematic and fluid cohabitation of the modern and postmodern. The first is the photography of Cristina García Rodero, whose famous documentary collection of traditional Spanish festivals was first published in 1989 as *España oculta* ('Hidden Spain'). The second is the architecture of Rafael Moneo, the best-known builder of public projects in the period, most particularly of the Museum of Roman Art in Mérida (1980–6). While photography and architecture claim, in their different ways, a particular purchase on the real, García Rodero and Moneo are also comparable in the seriousness of their respective projects, marked by an uncompromisingly modern faith in the ability of the artist to intervene in society. The work of both, however, exhibits a temporal simultaneity or anachronism typical of the postmodern. My third artefact is quite different in tone: *Cegada de amor* ('Blinded by Love'; first staged in 1994 by the Catalan performance group La Cubana) is a hybrid film-theatre spectacle that recycles both the glutinous child stars of the Spanish cinema of the 1960s and the glitzy 'moderns' of Almodóvar's 1980s. I contrast it with another tale of a prodigious child: Álvaro Pombo's novel of 1983 *El héroe de las mansardas de Mansard* ('The Hero of the Big House'), set in an equally suffocating and kitsch milieu: a wealthy bourgeois family of the post-War period installed in a lavish house in a northern provincial town. Superficially postmodern (ironic and campy), both *Cegada de amor* and *El héroe* are, I argue, characterized by a serious awareness of the trace of time and of the irrevocability of actions that is essentially modern in tone.

Vattimo[10] argues that postmodernism's 'crisis of the future' not only 'finds in the experience of art a privileged locus of expression' (p. 106), but also 'implies a radical change in our way of experiencing history and time' (p. 107). For Lyotard,[11] on the other hand, the 'crisis of metaphysical philosophy' means that the 'narrative function' (which is now the only source of legitimization) 'is losing its functors, its great hero, its great dangers, its great voyages, its great goal' (p. xxiii). The experience of temporal dislocation may thus lead both to artistic expression and to social and cultural dissolution. Helen Graham and Jo Labanyi argue that in the case of Spain we should be 'careful not to jettison the radical . . . potential which cultural modernism contained [in its] engagement with change'.[12] More sensitive and sophisticated than most of the cultural commentators I cite above, the cultural producers I discuss below betray an engagement with the dynamic force of modernity even as, in their very different ways, they bear witness to the profound historical and temporal crisis that goes by the name of postmodernity.

2. The Future in the Past: Cristina García Rodero and Rafael Moneo

In *Spanish Cultural Studies* Jo Labanyi cites Cristina García Rodero's work as an example of the 'anachronistic survival in contemporary Spain of cultural relics from the past'. 'Freezing time', writes Labanyi, García Rodero 'turn[s] reality into a slick art object' (p. 399). The sense of anachronism referred to here is shown historically in Labanyi's example of the coexistence on the Spanish cultural scene of figures as diverse as García Rodero and Almodóvar. But it is also present within García Rodero's photographs. Thus Labanyi takes 'A las once en El Salvador, Cuenca' ('Eleven O'Clock in El Salvador'), in which an old lady looks at her watch as she stands in front of a line of hooded penitents, as a sign of the 'temporal dislocation and sense of anachronism that characterizes contemporary Spain, where accelerated development . . . has produced a sense

[10] *The End of Modernity: Nihilism and Hermeneutics in Postmodern Culture* (Oxford: Polity, 1988).
[11] *The Postmodern Condition: A Report on Knowledge* (Manchester: Manchester University Press, 1984).
[12] Helen Graham and Jo Labanyi (eds.), *Spanish Cultural Studies: An Introduction* (Oxford: Oxford University Press, 1995), 11.

of living in different time frames at once' (p. 409). Although García Rodero has never to my knowledge been attributed the epithet 'posmoderno', so widely and loosely applied to others in Spain, this 'non-linear temporality' is precisely what typifies for Gianni Vattimo (p. 107) the end of modernity.

Initially, however, García Rodero would appear to be exemplary of the heroic modern artist. Trained as a painter at Madrid's prestigious Academia de San Fernando (graduating in 1972), García Rodero has taught photography at the Complutense since 1983. She was awarded the Planeta Prize for the corpus of her work in 1985 and her best-known collection, *España oculta*, toured Europe and the USA as a government-sponsored travelling exhibition from 1989.[13] García Rodero was also featured, amongst many other photographers, in *Cuatro direcciones*, the official show of contemporary Spanish photography curated for the *annus mirabilis* of 1992.[14] García Rodero's honours are matched by the ambitions of her anthropological project, which is truly global. Over fifteen years she travelled half a million kilometres over Spain in a journey 'against the clock' whose goal was to 'record . . . traditions before they disappeared' (*Cuatro direcciones*, 172). Six thousand photographs have been catalogued at the Getty Centre for the History of Art and the Humanities, 'classify[ing] forgotten places' on the basis of García Rodero's repeated trips in which, we are told, she is recognized and greeted by her subjects (*España: fiestas y ritos*, 9). The very title of her collection suggests the mission of the modern artist (in Lyotard's formulation at least): the revelation of the unpresentable in content (*The Postmodern Condition*, 81).

What is it, then, that is drawn into visibility by these photographs? Foreign critics have no doubt that it is the spirit of Spain itself, timeless and uncontaminated by modernization and internationalism. One French critic[15] comes across García Rodero's exhibition in Houston, the symbol of a United States that is 'as sad and cold as a turkey leg'. The revelation of the show 'change[s] [his] life': it is 'a sensual and irrational whirlwind . . . in which blood, sperm, milk, placenta, and the Mediterranean are

---

[13] I take this chronology from the unnumbered back pages of *España oculta* (Barcelona: Lunwerg, 1989). All references to photographs are to this edition. I have also examined García Rodero's colour collection, *España: fiestas y ritos* (Barcelona: Lunwerg, 1992), introd. William A. Christian.

[14] *Cuatro direcciones: fotografía contemporánea española* (Madrid: Ministerio de Cultura, 1991). García Rodero is placed within the tendency 'Documentary Tradition'. Even within this category, work is very diverse: at the opposite pole to García Rodero's monochrome traditionalism, Marta Sentís documents the domestic lives of African migrants in vivid colour. Another very different 'direction' is the glossy stylization of Pablo Pérez Mínguez and Ouka Lele, photographers associated with the Madrid *movida*.

[15] Claude Nero in *Espagne occulte* (Paris: Contrejour, 1990), unnumbered.

mixed . . . in the mother's womb'. Another[16] claims García Rodero represents the Spain 'which lives outside the tourist traps, concrete beach
resorts . . . the enthusiasm for 1992, and folkloric reconstructions'. The
authenticity of García Rodero's presumed referent thus lies not only in its
archaism, but in its physicality (as immediate as bodily fluids) and in its
femininity (as primal and hermetic as the uterus). However this content is
more problematic to Spanish spectators. Julio Caro Baroja[17] stresses the
ethnographic and anthropological value of the photographs, which constitute a basis for the study of the many regional varieties of folklore. But
he also acknowledges that Spaniards may find the work stereotypical:
clichéd images of a 'black' or 'underdeveloped' nation. He proposes alternative epithets for the Spain they represent: 'traditional' and 'popular'.
But he also concedes that many of the customs depicted will be 'com-
pletely unknown' to contemporary urban Spaniards, perfectly familiar
although they are with the equally rarefied, but better distributed, photographic chronicles of 'bankers and liberated women of the moneyed
classes'.

García Rodero's global project is thus paradoxical: what can it mean to
replay a past which is unknown to the nation for whom it is preserved?
García Rodero raises two postmodern concerns familiar from Vattimo:
the dissolution of the subject/object binarism when hermeneutics confronts anthropology (*The End of Modernity*, 145); and the 'crisis of the
future' (p. 104) when historical memory is evacuated. Ironically, García
Rodero's archaism serves as just another novelty on the art market, as
prone to dissolution and obsolescence as any cultural product. What I will
argue, however, is that García Rodero's referent is more problematic than
photography's ontological status as trace of the real would have us believe,
embodying as that referent does contradictions between the past and the
present, the festive and the everyday, and the mask and the costume and
the face and the body. Such contradictions coalesce around the question
of typology: that is, of Christian iconography as precursor for contemporary social practice. Secondly I suggest that García Rodero's composition
is more complex than has hitherto been supposed, posing as it does the
formal status of photography as art object. While one of the few critics to
have considered the compositional form of the photographs claims the
framings are 'simple' and the 'perspectives reduced to foreground and
background' thus heightening a 'space of emotion' (*Cuatro direcciones*,
172), the work in fact stages complex pictorial relations between vertical
and horizontal, frontal and diagonal, figure and ground. García Rodero
also exploits the strictly photographic relation between tonal contrast and

---

[16] Christian Caujolle, *Espagne occulte*, unnumbered.
[17] *España oculta*, unnumbered.

sharpness of focus and spatial planes and movement. Revealing the unpresentable in content, García Rodero gestures towards the unpresentable in form, Lyotard's definition of the postmodern (*The Postmodern Condition*, 81).

One Spanish critic[18] suggests just such a relation between time and landscape, chronology and locality. García Rodero documents not the primal or essential Spain adored by foreigners, but rather a country in which 'culture after culture has laid down its particular varnish over the eternal cycles of the peasant'. It is 'the complexity of the network that has thus been produced, mixed with the [contemporary] crisis of rural society [that] has provided Cristina García Rodero with the possibilities for her study' (*Cuatro direcciones*, 172). Unlike 'linear and closed' anthropological description, then, García Rodero stages the 'interaction' between individual and tradition, photographer and subject. Such a vision of the past will only become clear in the future: it is a 'summary of how twenty-first-century man feels and seeks his future in the traditions of his ancestors'. This motif of the 'future anterior' or 'future in the past' is shared also by postmodern theorists Vattimo and Lyotard. But there is no doubt that some of García Rodero's works memorialize, even fetishize, the past in the plainest of manners. Thus a barefoot girl, face half hidden by hair, holds on to the neck of the donkey in a field at harvest time (*España oculta*, no. 43); a woman, face partly concealed by a scarf, looks into the camera from behind a horse grazing with a foal (no. 75); or again a younger, barefoot woman, apparently asleep, reclines on sheaves of corn, while behind her an older couple sieve and winnow using traditional implements (no. 78). Such photographs promote a decorative, ruralist nostalgia in which the subjects are physically de-faced and ideologically suspended outside time. Similarly a landscape of the Rocío or Andalusian pilgrimage serves (in Vattimo's words) to 'eliminate any historical dimension' (*The End of Modernity*, 104) by (in Labanyi's words) 'turning reality into a slick art object' (*Spanish Cultural Studies*, 399): a line of wagons recedes diagonally into the distance while, blurred by dust and silhouetted by the sun, a single sombreroed horseman turns to face us (*España oculta*, no. 65).

The collection as a whole sometimes works, against the avowed particularizing goal of the anthropological survey, to homogenize and abstract. Thus formal similarities between pictures mask the fact that they were taken at a distance of some twenty years apart in time and/or hundreds of miles in space. Or again the captions, exiled to the back of the book where they cannot easily be read in tandem with the photographs to which they belong, will remain opaque even to Spanish viewers who (as Caro Baroja

---

[18] In the uncredited notes on García Rodero in *Cuatro direcciones*.

reminds us) may be as unfamiliar with García Rodero's content as foreigners. Moreover, while we are given the place and date of each shot (although most of the locations are recondite in the extreme), no explanation is given for the picturesque local names attributed to the frequently masked celebrants: the 'pricked man' barefoot and hooded in a desert ('El picao'; no. 2) and the 'stick man' dressed as a bride and bound to a bough in an alley ('El empalao'; no. 3) remain anonymous and anomalous even after we learn the names of the traditional figures they impersonate.

Purely ruralist or pictorialist nostalgia is, however, infrequent in García Rodero; and the brutal otherness of these last two examples might well serve, in Vattimo's postmodern style, to shock the spectator into 'consciousness of modernity as such' (*The End of Modernity*, 106), a consciousness that can only be achieved when modernity itself is coming to an end and is thus coming into focus. Vattimo calls this process 'secularization', a modern impulse which destabilizes itself. And if we look once more at the content of García Rodero's work, frequently based on religious festivals, we can see how Christian typology or iconography is dissolved as it is replayed, subject to implicit but persistent secularization. Thus past and present are juxtaposed but not resolved or synthesized: a black-clad *beata* prostrates herself before an outdoor altar, while behind her a line of younger heedless spectators stand by and look on (*España oculta*, no. 26); another widow walks towards us on her knees in the rain, while a car approaches in the road behind her (no. 59); a Virgin, garlanded with flowers, is shielded from the rain by a plastic mac (no. 105); and a young man in traditional festive garb scans a cemetery with his camcorder while another tiny black-clad widow looks not at him but somewhere out of frame (no. 124).

Past and present overlap with festivity and everyday life: five proudly plumed *colinegros* face the camera in a new Last Supper, but on the table in front of them are slices of *chorizo* stuck with toothpicks (no. 18); coned *nazarenos* recede to vanishing point in a pedestrian precinct, while a harassed waiter (white jacket, black string tie) walks against and across their ranks carrying a tray of chocolate and *churros* (no. 22); black-robed men trek towards us diagonally across a barren landscape, while a child in light clothing in front and to the side of them smirks shyly at the camera (no. 28); and two elderly men in top hats and cloaks stand outside a house at whose window we see the face of an old lady above a transistor radio (no. 41). The festive and the everyday (the past and present) are also imaged in the mask and the face: a sullen young girl in modern dress is surrounded by hooded older women (no. 8); a bizarrely masked figure at a café door is echoed by a face gazing out from the window next to it (no. 53); and a man in a grotesque Moorish papier-mâché head holds a baby in his hands (no.

96). The cohabitation of such contradictory elements is taken for granted, presented as everyday. Yet to the modern, urban spectator such scenes remain enigmatic and troubling.

Most disturbing perhaps is the landscape format shot of three children in modern dress recreating the Crucifixion on full-scale wooden crosses (no. 25) (Plate 3). Shot from a low angle which stresses the rocky, tactile texture of the earth, the photograph encourages us to take up the position of the child witnesses within it: two boys and a solitary girl who gaze up, their faces hidden, to the new, bespectacled and callow Christ. Such a picture escapes rural or traditional stereotype by exploiting types or typologies. The Christian iconography fuses form and time, aesthetic similarity and temporal equivalence. But the incongruity of children as actors in the scene remains unresolved, an example perhaps of Vattimo's 'secularization' which avoids nostalgia for the past while 'ungrounding' our position in the present (*The End of Modernity*, 107).

It should be clear from my descriptions of these photographs that, in another characteristic of the typology, composition is inseparable from signification. Typically vertical lines (thrusting poles or crosses) disrupt horizontals (bleak expanses of meseta); frontal compositions (the *colinegros'* Last Supper) are contrasted with diagonals (the processions across the plain); and finally foregrounds (unmasked women and children) are superimposed on contrasting backgrounds (hooded penitents). Although a few images are wreathed in haze or smoke, García Rodero generally prefers a clinically sharp focus in which multiple spatial planes are visible. At its most extreme a masked transvestite in the foreground, all bikini, body stocking, and maracas, is contrasted with the tiny figure of a conventionally dressed man on a motorcycle in the far distance behind her (no. 51). Freezing the moment, focus remains sharp even in scenes of rapid movement: a man is held suspended above the mattress over which he is jumping and on which six babies lie oblivious (no. 38); or again, in the image which graces the cover and concludes the collection, a young skipping girl in white is apparently floating, legs and arms apart, in front of the gates of a cemetery overcast by looming storm clouds (no. 126). There could be no clearer example of the vertigo induced by García Rodero's work, an ungrounding which, following Vattimo, can only be described as postmodern in its appeal to an unsettling of subjectivity and a disruption of linear time that are not simply dissolutive (*The End of Modernity*, 107). Contrary to initial appearances, García Rodero's photographic project is no 'retro scenario'. Rather it is a productive replaying of form and content that we will also find in the modest monumentality of Moneo's architecture.

In the 'prodigious decade' that followed the election of the Socialists in 1982, Rafael Moneo was responsible for some of the greatest architectural projects that changed the face of the nation.[19] Already celebrated for his Bankinter building on the Castellana in Madrid (1973–6), which established his eclectic style as one in the modern tradition but with 'learned citations' and in the 'local mode' (*Oteiza-Moneo*, 62), he subsequently built the massive Museo de Arte Romano in Mérida (1980–6), the discreet Previsión Española headquarters by the Guadalquivir in Seville (1987–91), the yellow brick mosque-like airport in the same city, the great red brick forecourt and clock tower of the restored Atocha Station in Madrid, the Palacio de Villa Hermosa renovated to house the Thyssen Collection, also in Madrid (1989–92), and the as yet uncompleted Kursaal twin auditoria on the beach front in San Sebastián-Donostia. Showered with honours in Spain as abroad (for some years he headed the School of Architecture at Harvard) Moneo most recently received the first prize for the Third Biennial of Spanish Architecture (1993–4)[20] for his L'Illa project in Barcelona: a massive commercial centre 300 metres long and filling an entire block in the nineteenth-century Ensainxe, L'Illa was praised for its modesty and discretion and for Moneo's use of the 'sculptural control [of] mass' to modulate 'changes in scale' (p. 36).

The committee writes of this project that 'at a time when post-modernism can be said to have run its course' and 'neo-technological alternatives' are also exhausted, Moneo invents an architecture 'dedicated to city building' ('crear ciudad'). It is a stress on the delicate third way between modern and postmodern and on a continuing faith in the ability of the artist to make social interventions that is typical of Moneo in particular and of much contemporary Spanish architecture in general. Thus the editors of a collection called *Building in a New Spain* (published to coincide with the commemorations of 1992)[21] stress both the newness of the great wave of public commissions that followed the death of Franco and the importance of 'historic architecture': 'the preservation and adaptive reuse of historic buildings [was] a regional and national priority'

---

[19] I take the following chronology from Antón Capitel's introduction to *Oteiza-Moneo: Pabellón de Navarra, Esposición Universal de Sevilla* (Pamplona: Caja de Ahorros Municipal, 1992). One of the first commissions of the Navarran Moneo had been the bull ring in the regional capital Pamplona (1967).

[20] Javier Frechilla Camoiras (ed.), *III Bienal de Arquitectura Española 1993–4* (Madrid: Ministerio de Obras Públicas et al., 1995).

[21] Pauline Saliga and Martha Thorne (eds.), *Building in a New Spain: Contemporary Spanish Architecture* (Barcelona: Gustavo Gili and Art Institute of Chicago, 1992). Ignasi de Solà-Morales argues in 'The Prodigious Decade' (pp. 91–9) that the case of Spain proves that 'cultural activity on the periphery' can be as creative as in the 'great cultural centres [of] London, Milan, and New York' (p. 91).

(p. 15). The transformation of cities through public works such as the Seville airport and the commissioning of 'monumental new buildings' (often by Moneo) served an unapologetically modernizing agenda: 'transforming Spain into one of the leading countries of twenty-first-century Europe'. If here we find one of Vattimo's paradoxes of modernity (the dependence of the present on a future time from which contemporary developments will be retrospectively visible), the great modernizing project is also reliant on the past. While one characteristic of Spanish architecture is the 'continued use of canons of the modern movement', another is the 'extensive use of brick and native materials' and the 'respect [for] existing historic architecture and environment'. The general 'rejection of postmodernism' by Spanish architects is linked to a pragmatism that has little time for the 'theoretical exercises' of foreigners (who generally lacked the massive public commissions that proliferated in Spain) when local energies are directed towards the 'goal of construction'.

The practice of building a new nation, however, is by no means untheoretical; indeed, as we shall see, just as the celebrated engineer Santiago Calatrava is as preoccupied by aesthetics as he is by technology, so Moneo the creator of cities is also one of the subtlest and earliest Spanish theorists of the crisis of modernity. And two of the most important commentators on Spanish architecture situate it and Moneo in that same conflict between temporality and tradition. Kenneth Frampton, a theorist known in a postmodern context for his proposal of the term 'critical regionalism',[22] stresses the particularity of a Spanish architecture that mediates between tradition and modernity, just as Spanish history moves between retardation and modernization (p. 19). 'Spanish architects', he writes, 'have had the fortune to encounter neo-capitalist modernization rather late and to do so in a retroactive manner' (p. 45). Granted 'the chance to become wise both before and after the event . . . history seems to have empowered them . . . with a detached creativity that has enabled them to mediate a volatile reality in a manner that is simultaneously radical and conservative'. Working, we might say, in Lyotard's 'future in the past' and Vattimo's 'crisis of the future', Spanish architects are, Frampton writes, both 'profoundly aware of all the pitfalls that unavoidably attend modernization in a postmodern age' and 'convi[nced] as to the capacity of their craft to intervene effectively in the production of an environment'. For Frampton this theoretical awareness registers in a practice of building that exhibits 'eclecticism' and a 'knowing recourse to the syntax of the modernist heritage', while remaining 'grounded . . . not only in respect of its literal anchorage in the ground, but also with regard to the expressivity of its material [and] sensitivity towards both topographic and construc-

[22] 'Homage to Iberia: An Assessment', in *Building in a New Spain* (pp. 19–46).

tional form'. Unlike in other countries where the 'free standing object' overwhelms the site, in Spain the topographic intersects with the tectonic in a way that resists 'media consumption' and 'still holds against a global condition in which cultural form becomes progressively reduced to a commodity'.

As we shall see, this hostility to the singular building unable to interact with the general environment in which it stands is addressed by Moneo himself in his theory of typology. But Antón Capitel, another major critic of Spanish architecture,[23] also treats a 'new modernism' and 'eclecticism' which resists postmodern appropriation. Tracing 'the force of history' (p. 47), Capitel cites Moneo's career as exemplary: at the Barcelona School of Architecture in the late 1970s Moneo had 'experienced the final stage of the "modern adventure" but had reacted with exceptional lucidity and agility to the "crisis of modern thought"' (p. 49). For Capitel, Moneo's first major building, the Bankinter in Madrid, at once 'broke with the development of modernity' and revealed a 'relative continuity' with it (p. 51). Capitel names Moneo's style as 'eclectic rationalism', citing its characteristics as 'reason, discipline, composition, construction, city, diversity' (p. 65). On a pie chart of architectural styles it is opposed to Calatrava's 'neo-organic figurativism' (characterized by 'formalism, naturalism, biological analogy') and wedged between 'modern tradition' and 'traditionalism'. As a teacher, Capitel writes, Moneo's contribution is that he 'transcend[ed] the crisis of the modern tradition' (p. 49), thus inspiring generations of pupils. But the precarious equilibrium of Moneo's architectural practice, caught as it is between modernization and retardation (innovation and tradition), suggests rather Vattimo's definition of postmodern culture as that which is 'free from the logic of overcoming' (*The End of Modernity*, 105). A modest monumentalist, who rejects the heroic role of architects of the past and constructs massive buildings masked by subtly modulated scale, Moneo does not transcend modernity but rather extends, preserves, and distorts it.

Like García Rodero, then, Moneo has not been identified with a postmodernism generally associated in Spain with the culture of the spectacle and the architecture of the façade. However, like García Rodero once more, Moneo tends towards anachronism and temporal simultaneity even as he confronts the spectator with work that is radically new. The theoretical foundation for this precarious balancing act is the typology. In 1982 Moneo edited a collection for students at the Madrid School of Architecture on 'the concept of the type in architecture'.[24] His own contri-

---

[23] 'Contemporary Spanish Architecture: From the Foundation of a New Modernism to the Appearance of Eclecticism', in *Building in a New Spain* (pp. 47–65).

[24] *Sobre el concepto de tipo en arquitectura* (Madrid: Escuela de Arquitectura, 1982).

bution to the volume, written as early as 1978, is 'On the Notion of Type'.[25] Moneo defines the type at the start of the essay as 'the true nature of the work' (p. 188). The 'latest tendencies' in architecture, however, reveal both 'the symptom of [the type's] disappearance' and 'the impossibility of retrieving it in traditional terms'. Now that the work has no 'unitary formal structure' and has become 'a series of fragments from which an image is to be recomposed' we should not yearn nostalgically for the unity bestowed by the type on ancient architecture but trust that the type 'will [still] draw the work of architecture out of the isolation to which it is subject if it is considered to be unique and unrepeatable'. Resigned to the loss of the type as object (the loss of a 'shared formal structure' once taken for granted), Moneo does not however give up on the great goal of the modern artist: effective intervention in the social sphere.

A flexible formal category (redefined not as a 'rigid mechanism' but as a 'frame in which transformation and change can be effected'; p. 192), the type is inseparable from temporality. Since the 1960s, writes Moneo, a new theory to explain the formal continuity of the ancient city has been required; for architecture is 'neither an artistic fact nor an industrial product . . . but . . . the result of the action of time on certain formal structures' (p. 201). Architects' labour is thus a 'continuous commentary on the past' in which they 'establish firm links with society'; and time acts on the type 'transforming it in the inevitable process of adaptation [in which] the level of the specific is reached' (p. 203). The type is thus still needed if architecture is to 'elude the void existing between the past . . . and the world in which architecture finally inscribes itself' (p. 205); and this 'new historical dimension of the work . . . helps to situate [the type] in the public sphere not as an autonomous object, but as elements created in the process of the development of the time of history'.

Formal and temporal (the structural inscription of form in time and time in form), the type is also discursive. Moneo writes that it opens a space for 'communication'; and the *OED* gives a specialized meaning of type as 'that by which something is symbolized . . . a foreshadowing in the Old Testament of a persona or event of the Christian dispensation' (s.v. 'type'). Just as García Rodero restages the Last Supper and the Crucifixion using incongruous actors who open up a channel of communication in the void between past and present, so Moneo replays Spanish architectural traditions in new and sometimes ironic garb which gestures towards a unitary world of symbolic plenitude that is now, nonetheless, definitively lost. Bereft of authority and continuity, the artistic and architectural monument still stands; but now (in Vattimo's terms) it is radically temporalized: the putting into work of truth.

[25] 'Sobre la noción de tipo' (pp. 187–211).

Let us return, then, to three buildings by Moneo and, guided by Frampton, Capitel, and Moneo's own theory of the type, reread them for the trace of the postmodern, a term by which they have not hitherto been qualified. Keeping true to the paradoxical temporality of the future in the past I treat them in reverse chronological order. San Sebastián's Kursaal or twin auditoria, uncompleted at the time of writing, is known locally as 'Moneo's cubes'. Prominently placed on the sea front, it would appear to contradict that modesty and respect for the environment that I previously claimed was typical of Moneo's typological symbolization. Although Frampton writes that the auditoria are 'rotated so as to align with the shifting axis of the promontory and the river' ('Homage to Iberia', 27), Capitel reminds us that they do not repeat the urban grid of the nineteenth-century district which they front. Rather it is the case that they violently disrupt that orderly progression to the sea. Moneo himself has stressed the singularity of the great project, which he describes as 'two gigantic rocks launched into the mouth of the Urumea', claiming that they 'do not belong to the city' ('Contemporary Spanish Architecture', 28).

Disrupting the uniformity and conformity of the bourgeois cityscape, still the Kursaal lays itself open to its environment and is not absorbed in its own singularity and autonomy. For in its sculptural form, writes Moneo, it is indeed 'part of the landscape' (*Sobre el concepto*, 28). Interacting with its site, the glass block construction is permeable both inside and out, 'yielding a luminous neutral interior space whose contact with the outside occurs at the spectacular foyer windows overlooking the sea [and] convert[ing] the volume [as seen from the exterior] into a dense opaque mass, which will be reflective and changing during the day and transformed into a mysterious attractive source of light at night'. Here then we see the type in action. Conserving the modernist love of pure geometry even in a vernacular nineteenth-century setting, Moneo has history work on the urban grid just as the maritime climate (sea and sky) interacts with and through his construction. The uncompromising 'value of the new' (Vattimo, *The End of Modernity*, 101) is thus reconciled with a tectonic and topographic reflection on city and time, city and place.

Unlike the Kursaal, Moneo's airport at Seville uses vernacular material: not glass block but yellow brick. Once more Moneo achieves an effect that is, in Frampton's words, 'simultaneously radical and conservative' ('Homage to Iberia', 45). For Capitel this material serves as 'something really present in the context and the image of the architecture' ('Contemporary Spanish Architecture', 76). Studiously combining 'historical principles and modern instruments' and the relationship between place and function, the building avoids 'the superficial stage sets of the "postmodern" without slipping into the technological obsession of the "late modern"'. The figurative sobriety and asceticism of the work (its low and lengthy external walls unbroken by ornament) reflect to Capitel the Spanish 'national tradition'; but they also suggest with their golden brick and bluish roofs 'a strange and unexpected palace, simultaneously ancient and modern' (p. 77). The simplicity of the exterior yields inside to the 'spatial spectacle' of the check-in area, whose columns cite discreetly the type of the mosque (p. 79) (Plate 4). Such a reference may be 'regionalist', but it is for Capitel not clichéd; and just as Moneo subordinates form to function (the airport is admirably simple to use) with similar reticence he draws back from 'personal' statement: here 'theme' and 'place' are the only aims (p. 80).

This sense of temporal simultaneity held in check by typological reserve is displayed yet more keenly in the Museum of Roman Art in Mérida (Plate 5). Here a great project intended to preserve and memorialize the past and mimicking the monumental spaces characteristic of a lost empire tends rather, and paradoxically, towards the temporal and spatial 'ungrounding' typical of Vattimo's post-histoire (*The End of Modernity*, 107). For Frampton this is Moneo's most exceptional achievement revealing as it does a 'subtle stance towards history, both real and imagined' ('Homage to Iberia', 26). Once more Moneo grounds his structure in the topographic and the tectonic: 'the ruined world of the archaic is openly evoked by a building that is situated over the excavation site itself'; and 'built of reinforced concrete and faced inside and out in brick tiles of Roman proportions, it straddles the antique foundations . . . with its piers countermanding the remains of the original Roman city'. Respecting history, still Moneo allows himself 'fantasy', 'irony', and anachronism. For Frampton the museum not only cites nearby Roman monuments but also 'an industrial building from the turn of the century'. Caught between basilica and warehouse, the museum is thus 'suspended' between process and product (the original site below and the artefacts rescued and displayed above). Capitel also calls attention to this paradoxical suspension: Moneo, he writes, 'does not model a space, but analyses it, pulling it apart' ('Contemporary Spanish Architecture', 72). But this analysis is not abstract but rather 'put to the service of a concrete reference . . . the super-imposition of two distinct and diverse spatial schemes'. These schemes, Roman and contemporary in form, correspond to two kinds of material: the concrete is not 'coated' with brick; rather the structure is 'mixed'. The materials thus 'distance the building both from the narrow values of modernity and postmodern tendencies that favour . . . an independent theatrical image'.[26] Built over a void that is the excavation of the historical

[26] For an earlier account of the Mérida museum see Antón Capitel and Ignacio Solà-Morales, *Contemporary Spanish Architecture: An Eclectic Panorama* (New York: Rizzoli,

site, Moneo's museum is, I would argue, exemplary not only of Vattimo's 'ungrounding' of modernity but also of Lyotard's conception of post-modern science as the 'search for instabilities' (*The Postmodern Condition*, 53).

Víctor Pérez Escolano[27] has noted the diverse interventions in Roman theatres by Spanish architects: in Mérida the ruins are protected by fibreglass, while in Córdoba they are incorporated into a new railway station (p. 81). Such experiments, he writes, reveal a 'most pronounced situation of perplexity between preservation and progress' (p. 82). We have seen that in the cases of photography and architecture such a per-plexity can be as productive as it is unsettling. We will now examine how performance and narrative are affected when the unpresentable shifts or slips from content to form.

3. Insubstantial Stories: La Cubana and Álvaro Pombo

Catalan performance group La Cubana are the most commercially successful producers of contemporary theatre in the Spanish state: *Cómeme el coco, negro* ('Soft Soap Me, Black Man') achieved an audience of half a million between 1989 and 1992; its successor *Cegada de amor* ('Blinded by Love') reached a quarter of a million in 1994 in Barcelona alone,[28] before initiating a massive tour which took it throughout Spain and as far as the Edinburgh Festival. In spite of this commercial success the company's origins and history are far from mainstream.[29] Founded in 1980 in the holiday resort of Sitges by Viqui Plana and Jordi Milan (who remains the group's director), La Cubana made its name in street spectacle: *Cubanas Delikatessen* (1983) consisted of twelve 'actions' in public places, as when, for example, a number of brides appear at a church awaiting a single bridegroom who fails to arrive; La Cubana's version of *The Tempest* (1986–7) required the audience's participation in the trans-portation of a giant, inflatable yellow submarine; *Cubana Marathon Dancing* (1992) burlesqued the incursion of foreign capital for the

1986), 134. This collection also contains Capitel's essay 'The Modern Adventure of Spanish Architecture' (pp. 11–20).

[27] 'The Architecture of Democratic Spain', in *Building in a New Spain* (pp. 67–89).

[28] Statistics from Francisco Cerezo, 'La Cubana', *Primer Acto*, 256 (Nov.–Dec. 1994), 86–7 (p. 87).

[29] I take this chronology from the programme for *Cegada de amor* at the Teatro Lope de Vega, Madrid, 1996. The programme also contains lyrics to two of the songs featured in the show. The soundtrack (Barcelona: PDI, 1994) includes all lyrics, plus songs from theatrical production *Marathon Dancing* and Catalan TV3's New Year's Eve special (1991) and sitcom *Teresina S.A.* (1992). Josep Anton Fernández is researching La Cubana's television produc-tions.

Barcelona Olympics by staging job interviews for a fictitious multi-national, lucky applicants to be chosen by their physical endurance. If, as Mercè Saumell writes, La Cubana's 'leitmotif' is the 'confusion of fiction and reality'[30] typical of much street and experimental theatre, then the company is unique for its anachronistic combination of a tradition acting style that 'recover[s] the Mediterranean tradition of caricature'[31] and a meticulous 'technical preparation'[32] that exploits all the resources of modern media. La Cubana, then, stand apart from other groups in Catalunya's rich theatrical life. Founded around the same time as El Tricicle and La Fura dels Baus, they have remained with them outside the main currents of subsidized theatre: Josep Maria Flotats's Teatre Nacional (inaugurated in 1997, projected from 1985) and Lluís Pasqual's Teatro Lliure (the recipient of a smaller amount of public funding for a new space in the second half of the 1980s).[33] While, according to Carles Batlle i Jordà,[34] the 1990s saw a return to text-based theatre in Catalan, La Cubana developed their bias towards visual spectacle and the casting of the audience as the 'true protagonists of the piece'.[35]

One British critic wrote that *Cegada de amor* was both 'the most wanted theatre ticket in Edinburgh and the most lurid and frivolous show ever to grace a major festival'.[36] And opening impressions suggest that the hybrid spectacle will constitute a parodic replaying of the past typical of vulgar notions of postmodernism. Ushered into a large auditorium (Barcelona's Tívoli seats a thousand) by officious staff who prove later to be actors and provided with 3-D glasses in green and pink, the audience is treated to a candy-coloured musical comedy directed by respected veteran Fernando Colomo and projected on a full-sized cinema screen. The star Estrellita is a teenage orphan in a blonde wig with flick-ups and a yellow mini-dress decked with daisies. Falling in love with medical student Jean François (cue the big title ballad) she returns with him to Paris, where she is feted by local youth (cue the 1950s rock and roll parody 'Estrellita mon cheri' [*sic*])

[30] 'Performance Groups in Contemporary Spanish Theatre', in Maria Delgado (ed.), *Spanish Theatre 1920–95*, special issue of *Contemporary Theatre Review*, 7.4 (1998), 1–30 (p. 19).

[31] Mercè Saumell, 'Performance Groups in Catalonia', in David George and John London (eds.), *Contemporary Catalan Theatre: An Introduction* (Sheffield: Anglo-Catalan Society, 1996), 103–28 (p. 125).

[32] María José Rague, 'La Cubana, el gran éxito del teatro catalán en 1989', *Estreno*, 17.1 (Spring 1991), 26–30.

[33] Ibid. 26.

[34] 'Apuntes para una valoración de la dramaturgia catalana actual: realismo y per-plejidad', *Anales de la Literatura Española Contemporánea*, 21.3 (1996), 253–70 (p. 254).

[35] Saumell, 'Performance Groups in Catalonia', 125.

[36] James Christopher, 'This Spanish Director Doesn't Care for Plots: He Prefers Pigeons' (interview with Jordi Milan), *Observer* (London) (17 Aug. 1997).

(Plate 6). It is her birthday and a tragic accident ensues: she is blinded by droppings from a dove placed in the birthday cake by her doting boyfriend. Suddenly the on-screen action stops and the camera pulls back to reveal the crew, headed by Almodóvar clone 'Antonio Valdivieso'. Still on screen, we are introduced to Estrellita's Svengali manager and Antonio's suffocating mother. Some of these characters speak in Catalan. An older, conservatively dressed man rises in the auditorium and in ringing Castilian tones shouts: 'Speak Spanish: we're in Spain'. The audience grows uneasy as other members start shouting back at the screen. Then the characters on screen become aware of the commotion in the auditorium. They step through previously unnoticed slits in the screen and emerge as live actors on stage. In the next two hours the action will flow seamlessly and ceaselessly between auditorium, stage, and screen.

Technically perfect (and financially expensive), La Cubana's 'dazzling, baffling'[37] *coup de théâtre* is not simply a 'gimmick' but rather a fully thought-out strategy for blurring the boundaries between actor and audience, theatre and film, truth and lie. And according to Jordi Milan's programme notes, the spectacle is intended to address one particular paradox of mechanical reproduction, namely the fact that cinema (the colder and more technical medium) is more 'credible' than theatre and thus more easily moves an audience. Milan sets out to 'fuse' the mediatized 'magic' of cinema with the live 'proximity' of theatre in order to produce a 'mixture' he acknowledges to be 'utopian' and names 'three-dimensional cinema'. Such a process raises the postmodern question of legitimization. Breaking the frames of representation (both theatrical and cinematic), frames that he holds to be obsolescent, Milan also destabilizes the relation between authenticating presence (the live voice and body) and alienating absence (the technically mediated image): as the Broadway-style show tune of the finale reminds us, this unclassifiable spectacle is 'neither truth, nor lie'.

Beyond its undeniable and highly pleasurable camp and kitsch, then, *Cegada de amor* also qualifies for the epithet 'postmodern' in Lyotard's technical sense, scorning as it does the legitimizing metanarratives of the past: frames of legibility are dissolved, be they spatial, diegetic, or epistemological. And generic hybridity extends to all aspects of *mise en scène*. Thus the production design is based on two combinations of clashing colours retained throughout the show and its publicity material: pink and green (the twin lenses of the redundant 3-D glasses) and yellow and

[37] Susannah Clapp, 'Catalonia Dreamin'' (Edinburgh Festival review), *Observer* (London) (17 Aug. 1997). Other exceptionally positive British reviews include Dan Glaister, 'Live Cinema!', *Guardian* (12 Aug. 1997) and Robert Butler, 'Love in a Time of Interactive Kitschness', *Independent on Sunday* (17 Aug. 1997).

blue (buttercup gowns with sapphire bows and gloves). Or again the musical idiom is resolutely heterogeneous: from the gravest of traditional Spanish forms (the single unaccompanied voice of the *saeta*) to the chirpy 1960s pop song 'Mancheguita', complete with cheesy organ breaks. If *Cegada de amor* is parody, then, the object of its satire is shifting and unstable, denying itself (in Lyotard's postmodern style) 'the solace of good forms and the consensus of [good] taste' (*The Postmodern Condition*, 81) even as it celebrates the modernity of its own technical accomplishment.

I will return later to this aspect of temporal dislocation or anachronism, more complex than it at first appears. But in the 'intersection of narrative elements that are . . . not necessarily communicable' (Lyotard, *The Postmodern Condition*, p. xxiii) (Catalan and Castilian, *saeta* and pop song) *Cegada de amor* also hints at another postmodern motif: the event. For Lyotard the event takes place when 'the [postmodern] artist and the writer are working without rules in order to formulate . . . what will have been done' (p. 81). In spite of the rigidity of its format (in which live actors must mesh precisely with prerecorded film performances), *Cegada de amor* also suggests this 'paradox of the future anterior'. Thus if a right-wing plant in the audience (identified in the cast list as 'El facha') attacks the Catalan language, the effect will be different in Barcelona and in Madrid. On tour *Cegada de amor* was accompanied by related 'street actions' that interacted with the local environment in unpredictable ways: a blustery autumn day on the San Sebastián sea front was transformed by a small group of actors armed with quantities of blue and yellow confetti. To take a final example, the performances in Edinburgh were framed not only by parallels between Catalunya and Scotland as fellow 'nations without states' but by an induction process staged for British audiences before they entered the auditorium: videos, posters, and souvenirs were used to introduce foreigners to such topics as Semana Santa, Catalunya, and the child prodigies typical of Spanish film under late Francoism.[38] *Cegada de amor* is thus not simply a 'simulacrum' or a 'slick artwork' abstracted from history through aestheticized anachronism; it is also, in the tradition of La Cubana and its fellow Catalan performance groups, an attempt to revitalize public spaces and rescue cultural forms, such as theatre, long since reduced to commodities.

La Cubana itself would be the first to acknowledge the irony that they are themselves complicit in just such commercial depredation. While

---

[38] The ignorance of foreigners and the use of 'Spanglish' in this new version of the production are cited by one Spanish report from Edinburgh, Lourdes Gómez, 'La Cubana la monta', *El País* (14 Aug. 1997). Gómez erroneously gives director Jordi Milan's name as 'Miller'.

conservative critic Francisco Cerezo contrasts their success favourably with publicly subsidized (and often commercially unsuccessful) companies, *Cegada de amor*'s handsome programme lists no fewer than eight major sponsors two of whom are public (the state Ministry of Culture and the Generalitat de Catalunya) and the rest private (chief among them the powerful savings bank La Caixa and the Catalan icons Vichy water and Freixenet cava). Capital intensive and rigidly disciplined, in spite of its air of anarchic improvisation, La Cubana has parodied itself in its solemn recording of the 'Cubana Incorporated Hymn' (i.e. Anthem),[39] an English-language paean to commercial success: 'We are a family of winners I always the best I 'cause for us there is no rest.' Tireless indeed in their pursuit of public and private finance, La Cubana have also been canny in exploiting audiences' mixed and contradictory demands for voyeuristic distanciation and exhibitionistic participation. Thus the 3-D glasses, willingly donned by the audience, are a joke at their expense: such tacky gimmicks will not be needed to see live actors on the stage and, indeed, planted amongst the audience itself. But in an equal and opposite move La Cubana also swoop on audience members, divesting them of their anonymity and having them participate as penitents in a Semana Santa parade that also shifts between stage and screen.

But if, as has been argued, the audience is the true protagonist of La Cubana's multimedia spectacles, then this may suggest a nostalgia for past authenticity and public participation that is no mere frivolous retro scenario. For the absent object or referent here is one that is keenly felt by La Cubana's cast and audience alike. The key here is the chronology of the piece, which is confused. While the film clearly alludes to Almodóvar's prodigious decade of the 1980s, this familiar material shields another and more distant field of interest: the Francoist 1950s and 1960s. Estrellita is provided like the other characters with a backstory in the programme: born (like Almodóvar) in provincial La Mancha in 1947 she is discovered after being taken to a song contest in Madrid by a representative of the Francoist woman's movement, the Sección Femenina. After a first feature *La niña del convento* ('The Girl in the Convent', 1956), she makes (we are told) seventy films before retiring at the implausibly late date of 1982. Just as 'Antonio Valdivieso's' imaginary titles cite Almodóvar (e.g. *Torero Cha-cha-cha* for *Matador*) so the details of Estrellita's fantastic career coincide with the true stories of real-life child prodigies. Thus Estrellita's first film echoes the first and most famous of the orphan melodrama cycle, *Marcelino, pan, y vino* ('Marcelino, Bread, and Wine' (Ladislao Vajda, 1954)) in which a boy lodges in a priests' household. And her chronology

---

[39] Included on the *Cegada de amor* soundtrack CD, composed for *Marathon Dancing*. All music and lyrics are by Joan Vives.

shadows 'the Little Nightingale' and 'professional orphan'[40] Joselito whose first film was also released in 1956. Estrellita's implausibly blond hair invokes rather Marisol, the 'Coca Cola flamenco girl',[41] born in Málaga in 1948 and discovered (like Estrellita again) at a competition in Madrid.[42] The 'sunbeam' and 'angel' of the early 1960s began to falter with *Las cuatro bodas de Marisol* ('Marisol's Four Weddings' (Luis Lucia, 1967)), which like Estrellita's fictional film featured a marriage proposal from a handsome Frenchman and on a film set, no less. Later Marisol posed nude for *Interviú* and confessed to Francisco Umbral that as a child she had been subjected to sexual abuse by her fans. Converted to communism by Antonio Gades she appeared briefly in his dance dramas *Bodas de sangre* and *Carmen*, before retiring in 1985.[43]

Novelist Terenci Moix, perhaps the fondest fan of the 'cinema of [Spaniards'] memory', historicizes the twin prodigies: while Joselito was 'a child of transition, a product of the rural Spain which was firing its last cylinders before the 1960s inaugurated the empire of modernity' (p. 268), Marisol was 'the petit bourgeois modernized response' to the poverty and underdevelopment of earlier flamenco stars, acting as she did as the 'precursor of economic development' (p. 278). In their liminal positions, then, the twin stars were symptomatic of social change even as historicity was rigorously excluded from the vehicles in which they performed. Such symptoms of the *Zeitgeist* would later become as melodramatic as the adult Joselito's conviction for possession of cocaine (Moix, *Suspiros*, 276). Film historian Carlos F. Heredero[44] goes further claiming that the 'defencelessness of childhood is transformed [by Francoist ideology] into a potent appeal to paternalist solidarity' (p. 230). 'Angelical beings', he writes, the prodigies are 'uprooted from any social context' even as they play their ideological role to perfection. Paradoxically, however, the child stars were anachronistic in their own time, out of sync with changing times even as they enjoyed their greatest success. Joselito's settings referred back to the 1940s and to an autarchic and clerical society that audiences of the 1950s sought to escape (p. 232); the middle-class settings of Marisol mirrored Spaniards' material aspirations in the 1960s, but the child's absent parents (typical of the post-War period) did not (p. 233). Heredero even proposes that the 'infantile, musical, and sentimental counterpoint [of the child stars] is strictly parallel to the development of the art house "New Spanish Cinema"' in the same period (p. 234).

[40] The second description is from Terenci Moix, *Suspiros de España: la copla y el cine de nuestro recuerdo* (Barcelona: Plaza y Janés, 1993), 268.   [41] Ibid. 278.

[42] I take chronologies of Joselito and Marisol from Augusto M. Torres, *Diccionario del cine español* (Madrid: Espasa Calpe, 1994), s.v. 'Joselito' and 'Marisol'.

[43] Moix, *Suspiros*, 284, 289, 291.

[44] *Las huellas del tiempo: cine español 1951–61* (Madrid: Filmoteca, 1993).

It could be argued, then, that in their very use of anachronism La Cubana are faithful to the originals they parody; certainly such popular phenomena as Pili and Mili, identical twin blond songstresses of the 1960s, put the fictional Estrellita in the shade. The lurid frivolity of La Cubana (like that of its originals) points to a shift in our reading from the postmodern as unpresentable in form (the gulf between film and theatre) to the modern as unpresentable in content (the nameless horror that cannot be voiced). For the void above which *Cegada de amor*'s flashy structure is constructed is the dictatorship itself, as invisible and as all-pervasive in the nightingales and sunbeams of the past as in the *mancheguita* who so uncannily and perilously persists in the present. The self-proclaimed 'utopianism' of La Cubana's project (a utopianism which also takes the form of economic solidarity: each of the ten performers earns the same wage) thus stages, in Lyotard's words, a modern 'nostalgia for the unattainable' (*The Postmodern Condition*, 81): just as the child star, middle-aged and alcoholic, refuses to acknowledge the passing of time, so La Cubana and their audience at once evoke and erase the forty years of Francoism in which time was suspended and historical process violently expelled to a space just off stage, just out of shot. The most lurid and insubstantial of stories, *Cegada de amor* finally serves (not least in its forceful Catalanism)[45] a fully ethico-political end beneath its gaudy surface.

Like his more celebrated fellow novelist Juan Goytisolo, Álvaro Pombo spent many years in exile. Returning to Spain in the early 1980s he received the First Herralde Prize for the baroquely titled *El héroe de las mansardas de Mansard* (1983),[46] translated into English as the more prosaic *The Hero of the Big House*. Judged by one critic not to 'belong to a Spanish literary "tradition"',[47] Pombo has been compared to foreign authors such as Bulgakhov, Gadda, and Capote.[48] Yet, like La Cubana, his work is also conspicuously frivolous, 'postmodern' in the vulgar sense. What I will argue, however, is that (as in the case of *Cegada de amor* once more) camp or kitsch conceal an implicit engagement with Spanish history. A specialist in 'stories on the lack of substance',[49] Pombo replays the past for a time of 'lost referents'.[50] But if his wilful imprecision is typical of Baudrillard's

[45] Cerezo claims that 'defend[ing] their own Catalan identity' La Cubana stereotype Valencian, Andalusian, and Castilian 'minorities' ('La Cubana', 87).

[46] My edition (Barcelona: Anagrama, 1983).

[47] Lynne E. Overesch-Maister, 'Echoes of Alienation in the Novels of Álvaro Pombo', *Anales de la Literatura Española Contemporánea*, 13.1–2 (1988), 55–70 (p. 55).

[48] See the press notices cited on the dust jacket.

[49] *Relatos sobre la falta de sustancia* (first published 1977) is a collection of stories many of which focus on either the life of an exile in London or the return of an exile to Spain.

[50] In *El héroe* the phrase 'lack of referent' is used to describe a 'divine' actress whose performance is insubstantial (p. 61).

'nebula', still it is traversed by historical currents that reveal to the attentive reader the trace of time.

El héroe skilfully blurs time, space, and subjectivity. Set in a post-War period that is unspecified[51] and in a nameless northern town reminiscent of Pombo's native Santander, the novel's main character is an adolescent of indeterminate age: Kus-Kús the 'prodigious child', so blond that he appears to be foreign (p. 8). While the child protagonist's viewpoint is itself temporally dislocated (migrating between infantile fantasy and adult pragmatism), the perspective of the novel as a whole is yet more unsettling,[52] shifting vertiginously as it does (and generally without warning) between a number of highly coloured characters: Julián, the glamorous butler with a mysterious past; aunt Eugenia, fat, 40, and dreaming of fantastic romances in exotic parts; the dictatorial grandmother Mercedes, installed in her vast estate; and her impoverished and garrulous companion María del Carmen Villacantero. The cast is completed by Manolo, the young stud from the La Cubana grocery store with whom Eugenia embarks on a disastrous affair.

Overesch-Maister has spoken of 'alienation' as the key characteristic of the novel. However, *El héroe* appears to stage, in postmodern style, the abolition of the distinction between self and other, true and false. The only legitimization of such categories is internal: in Lyotard's terms it occurs through language games, narrative function, and performativity (*The Postmodern Condition*, 9, 27, 41). Thus the novel is composed of speaking voices, heterogeneous and often non-communicable, offering mutually conflicting versions of the same events. Such language games as Eugenia's lengthy monologues on duchesses and gigolos in Bariloche (the Argentine ski resort) are impervious to external verification. Kus-Kús himself argues quite explicitly for a third narrative way between truth and lie, game and reality. Announcing to Julián his plan to poison his governess, Kus-Kús claims that it is 'neither playing . . . nor poisoning . . . but something else' (*El héroe*, 36); or again when Kus-Kús hides Julián in the mansard after the latter has stolen from his masters Kus-Kús rejects the 'false distinction [between] playing at hiding a fugitive from justice and [actually] hiding

[51] One critic, misled by 'hazy' time-space coordinates and ignoring references to the Gestapo and the Civil War, erroneously dates the action to the 1920s; Dieter Ingenschay, 'Álvaro Pombo: *El héroe de las mansardas de Mansard*: sobre el problemático hallazgo de la propia identidad y la grácil disolución de la realidad', in Dieter Ingenschay and Hans-Jörg Neuschäfer (eds.), *Abriendo caminos: la literatura española desde 1975* (Barcelona: Lumen, 1994), 65–74 (pp. 69, 71). Ingenschay treats as I do the relation between time, space, and subjectivity.

[52] See José Manuel González Herrán on the 'narrative autonomy' that 'creates its own reality'; 'Álvaro Pombo, o la conciencia narrativa', *Anales de la Literatura Española Contemporánea*, 10.1–3 (1985), 99–109 (p. 107).

one' (p. 90). Like Lyotard's language game, such strategies legitimize themselves, produce a concrete narrative function in the world even as they fail to coincide with other, incommensurable games.

The language game is thus also narrative: the great monologues at once dissolve fixed subjectivity and reinstall it as storytelling. In Kus-Kús's homoerotic fantasy Julián is identified with Eugenia's lost love Giacomo Gattucci and with the heroes of the films whose romantic plots are retold to him (p. 26). While narrative and monologue are primary, action and dialogue are marginal, pushed to the very edge of the fictional stage or screen. Insubstantial anecdotes go on for ever, while momentous events are related with lapidary concision: 'And the police entered the room' (p. 176). The narrative function of legitimization (which marginalizes action) is thus performative, composed of speech acts and played with theatrical props: Julián's dark glasses (fetishistically hoarded by the child) conceal eyes that either water or weep, a 'mask' that may or may not shield 'simulated' tears (p. 9); taking up a position in the somnolent house, Julián finds himself 'unwillingly disguised as a sleeper . . . further from the surface [when he is] closer to the disguise' (p. 33); Eugenia's glittering and fake jewels are 'truer and closer to the skin than skin itself . . . more precious than genuine precious stones' (p. 171). When the depressed Eugenia fails for once to paint and primp herself, the child claims she is 'feigning, lying, playing a great part' (p. 171). In familiar postmodern style, glasses and eyes, mask and face, costume and body are each indistinguishable from the other.

In this aestheticization of affect, time is arrested in an eternal present, determined by the space in which it occurs: within the house 'memory . . . reality yielded . . . all identity [was] suspended' (p. 68); hiding out under the mansards (a location described with minute hyperrealism) Julián feels that 'there were only instants; the present, previous, and subsequent instant, transformed into a pure present' (p. 124). Likewise Kus-Kús oscillates between 'past childhood and future maturity . . . without managing to stop in either of the two ages' (p. 127). Just as space is confined, hermetic, even uterine (the mansard is strangely relaxing and familiar), so time is regressive, ungrounding the subject even as it provides the medium for his or her narrative process.

What we find here, however, in this weakened or evacuated temporality is a resurrection of history in a newly reduced and distorted form. María del Carmen's epic narrative of the transportation of a toy tightrope walker for Kus-Kús from Paris features walk-on parts by the Gestapo (p. 22), the horrors of history sidelined by family trivia; there are passing references to a minor character's father 'shot by the Nationalists' (p. 64) and to ration books and the black market, signs of the famine raging outside the great house and which we are never shown (p. 138). Games and disguises may come and go at random, but we are told they 'inevitably signify something and implacably qualify those who immerse themselves in them' (p. 37). Likewise the narrative function fuses subjective and objective, internal and external in new and discomfiting ways. Aunt Eugenia's life story is told with typical laconism: 'Then her father went into politics; then she met a German boy, then 1936 and then now . . . Now a great silence reigned' (p. 44). Deprived of its grand metanarrative, national history is reinscribed in the tiny, but tragic, stories of the subjects that compose that nation. Typically, however, Pombo chooses the most marginal amongst them: women, children, and homosexuals. Lyotard's 'great hero' of modernity (*The Postmodern Condition*, p. xxiii) is weakened and shrunken in the 'gnome' Kus-Kús, oscillating as he does between infantile innocence and proto-adult malice; and the last of his monologues is a pathetic confession of erotic desire for other boys which must surely exile him from familial and national history. But even here, authentic revelation is predicated on pre-existing narrative: Kus-Kús speculates about the sexual habits of comic book Fascist hero Roberto Alcázar and his youthful sidekick Pedrín (*El héroe*, 201) before he betrays Julián (and Eugenia) to the police.[53]

Language, narrative, and performance may thus be evacuated or rendered insubstantial (typical of the liminal stage of adolescence), but finally they give way to definitive and irreversible acts: Kus-Kús's betrayal produces the singular and irrevocable event of Eugenia's suicide. Where once all was 'antepenultimate' (the 'sign of chic' in Bariloche) now Kus-Kús, who knows little of endings (p. 198), confronts a definitive conclusion. Looking back at the novel, however, the trace of a linear, even fatal, time is everywhere inscribed or secreted in space: the great house of Kus-Kús's family, with its mansards and *miradores*, crisp linen and English marmalade, is the image of the somnolent and corrupt Spain of those who won the War; and the grandmother's asparagus beds are set in ranks 'like tombs' (p. 156). The unspeakable 'other . . . the vice of men' (p. 165) is thus not the only unpresentable content that provokes and resists the 'torrential forgetfulness of the past' (p. 167). If time is arrested and temporal process excluded from the stage it is not without reason, even if that reason is not directly revealed. Nostalgic for the political and social intervention of earlier, more confident novelists, Pombo thus hints at that paradoxical postmodern condition in which the present is dependent on the future: momentarily opening vistas the novel does not care to explore,

---

[53] For comics in *El héroe* and elsewhere see Ana Rueda, 'Entre la fascinación y el descrédito: el superhéroe del cómic en la narrativa actual', *Revista Monográfica*, 7 (1991), 350–63.

the narrator tells us with characteristic reticence: 'Many years later Kus-Kús would remember that night with horror.' (p. 201).

4. The Forest of Forgetting

On 19 September 1995 in the dying days of the Socialist administration, conservative daily *ABC* devoted its editorial to 'Postmodernity or Servile Spirit?'[54] Invoking (but not citing) Baudrillard, Vattimo, and Lyotard, the author pleads confusion as to the nature of postmodernity: does it stress the exhaustion of the avant-garde or rather the emergence of a new narcissism and individualism, a slave to the present moment? Rejecting both tendencies *ABC* claims that what ails Spain is rather an Ortegan 'servility of spirit': 'the corollary of the political degradation which we are suffering.'

ABC is right to distinguish the general 'autumnal' status of postmodernity from the 'specific case' of the Spanish corruption of the public sphere. But perhaps it would have found the coexistence of exhaustion and novelty less confusing had it been aware that both Vattimo and Lyotard state that the postmodern is implicit in the modern: for the former 'progress has a tendency to dissolve itself' (*The End of Modernity*, 104); for the latter the 'incredulity to metanarratives' that defines postmodernity is, once more, a product of progress itself (*The Postmodern Condition*, p. xxiii). If there is little evidence of Baudrillard's 'nostalgia for Fascist violence' in a Spain for which such phenomena were still too close for comfort, then the *desencanto* that followed hard on the heels of the Socialist victory of 1982 might indeed be characterized by Baudrillard's claim that 'the historical stake [was] chased from our lives by a sort of immense neutralization, which is dubbed peaceful coexistence on a global level and pacified monotony on the quotidian level' (*Simulacra*, 43). The prodigious decade of the 1980s would still be full of memorable events in Spain, but with the collapse of any viable opposition, the public sphere would grow neutral and monotonous indeed.

Eduardo Subirats, less pessimistic than other Spanish intellectuals, predicted a 'promise of happiness' in amongst the death and decline of art. And the cultural products I have studied in this chapter generally concur with this optimistic attitude to the contemporary condition. Thus García Rodero and Moneo share characteristics that can be claimed as postmodern in my theorized sense (such as temporal dislocation) even as they reinvent the role of the modern artist who intervenes in society; La Cubana and Pombo, on the other hand, gesture towards the lost historical object of modernity even as they offer the mixed formal

[54] Luis González Seara, '¿Posmodernidad o espíritu servil?', *ABC* (19 Sept. 1995).

pleasures associated with the postmodern in its common sense. All four give the lie to the many Spanish philosophical and cultural commentators who identify postmodernism with irrationalism and irresponsibility. Refusing to reject too soon the positive potential of a modernizing process that remains unfinished, these Spanish artists have engaged in a kind of critical regionalism that has proved popular even beyond the borders of the Spanish state: Moneo's most recently completed commission is the National Museum of Modern Art in Stockholm, a work praised once more for its modesty and sensitivity to the site in which it was built. While Spaniards have not made internationally recognized contributions to the theorization of postmodernism (Juan Luis Cebrián, we remember, contrasts their 'fireworks' with Vattimo and Lyotard's sober 'task of thought'), they have few rivals for a practice that I have defined as postmodern in photography, architecture, performance, and narrative.

Typical of such practice are a modest monumentalism[55] and a qualified heroism. While García Rodero and Moneo embark on great projects fully aware of the conditions that constrain their completion, La Cubana and Pombo focus on the figure of the child prodigy, who embodies the possibility of a social change of which she or he is unaware. If then (in Baudrillard's words once more) 'the historical stake [is] chased from our lives' (*Simulacra*, 43), then in the case of Spain it returns in more ghostly and resonant terms than in the lifeless works lamented by Baudrillard. Vattimo's 'change in the way of experiencing temporality' (*The End of Modernity*, 107) is thus not confined to those 'epoch-making' works he cites (Proust, Musil, and Joyce). A cultural form as popular as La Cubana's can also exploit non-linear time to subtle effect; and the other artists I have treated exhibit the mastery of form of which Lyotard speaks (*The Postmodern Condition*, 87), a mastery that is capable of 'continu[ing] to offer the reader or viewer matter for solace and pleasure'.

Lyotard ends *The Postmodern Condition* by claiming enigmatically: 'it is not our business to supply reality but to invent allusions to the conceivable which cannot be presented' (p. 81). Such an uncanny invention might be exemplified by La Cubana's 'arrival' in the old part of Madrid's Atocha Station: a space devoid of trains but remodelled by Moneo to feature an incongruous, but magical, tropical rainforest. The press release for this event,[56] intended to publicize *Cegada de amor*'s opening at the vast Teatro Lope de Vega on the Gran Vía, told journalists to gather to meet Estrellita

---

[55] I take this phrase from Richard Dattner, *Civil Architecture* (New York: McGraw Hill, 1995), 233. The type of Dattner's modest monumentality is Jefferson's University of Virginia campus.

[56] Victoria Sanz (Barcelona, 18 Dec. 1995). *Cegada de amor* opened in Madrid on 25 Jan. 1996.

and her fictional friends at the 'statue of the traveller' by Eduardo Urculo. It is a statue that consists of a coat, hat, and suitcase with no trace of a human figure. More pragmatic than Lyotard (who asks us to 'wage war on totality') still Spanish artists treat that waning of reality and dissolution of the subject held to be typical of postmodernity. But more optimistic and more historically grounded than their equivalents in some other countries, the texts I have discussed discreetly counter what Pombo calls the 'forest of forgetting' (*El héroe*, 74), an oblivion darker and more terrible than any replaying of the past could be.

PART II
Space

4 | Social Space and Symbolic Power: Fernando Savater's Intellectual Field

Fernando Savater is perhaps the best-known and most representative intellectual of the Socialist era in Spain. Yet his work and persona are characterized by contradictions. Thus he is an avowed internationalist who was until very recently dedicated to teaching in the young university of his native Basque Country; a political activist who has never joined a political party; and an avowed anarchist who claims individualism as a foundation for a non-violent ethics of community.

Often posing as a 'devil's advocate'[1] (in, for example, his ironic apologies for terrorism or cultural imperialism), Savater has also described himself as a 'heretic' (*Contra las patrias*, 17), refusing to subscribe to the doxa, be it institutional, territorial, or philosophical. Thus in a gesture which reveals both his intellectual perversity and his attachment to institutional marginality, Savater engaged in a polemic with Jean-François Lyotard at the University of Vincennes on the necessity of non-violence even in the case of an act widely welcomed in Spain and abroad: ETA's assassination of Carrero Blanco, Franco's nominated successor (*Contra las patrias*, 21). In a Spanish philosophical institution which, according to at least one professional observer,[2] retained much of the nepotism and mediocrity it had exhibited in the Franco era well into the 1980s, Savater is conspicuous not only for his contribution to philosophy proper (most apparent, perhaps, in his work on Schopenhauer), but for his ambiguous position as a professional intellectual, charting and creating a contested space between the university and the more general public sphere.

In this chapter I attempt to address the complex relation between

---

[1] *Contra las patrias* (Barcelona: Tusquets, 1984), 194.
[2] Eugenio Trías, 'La resaca del pensamiento débil', in Rafael Conte (ed.), *Una cultura portátil* (Madrid: Temas de Hoy, 1990), 201–26 (pp. 210–12). Trías mentions Savater on pp. 212 and 217.

literary stances and institutional positions with reference to Bourdieu's analysis of the 'intellectual field'. As a sociologist, Bourdieu claims that the social space of intellectual work has been consistently neglected, or reduced to the (theoretically inadequate) role of milieu, context, or 'background'.[3] He suggests, rather, that there are structural or functional parallells (or 'homologies') between the social, political, and literary spheres. But structural equivalence does not mean identity; and analogous terms have their own specific form in each field: thus literary capital is both the instrument and object of struggle; and (unlike its financial equivalent) cannot easily be inherited or reduced to commercial success or social recognition ('The Intellectual Field', 141). If the work of art (of literature or philosophy) must be placed within the field produced by the totality of works and producers, then naive biographical criticism or internal stylistic analysis will both be rejected as equally reductive. What must be explored is the relational dynamic or homology between the space of works and the space of producers and institutions ('The Intellectual Field', 147).

While the hypothesis of a structural parallel between an academic institution, the cultural life of a nation, and the development of a discipline (say, philosophy) may seem circular, even totalizing, the field is for Bourdieu the site of constant struggle: of both critique and consecration. Moreover, the spatial model of the field (the incommensurability of the objective positions linked by fragile homologies) is also temporal (the simultaneity of successive habitus as subjective dispositions and identifications). It thus follows that at moments of crisis (the 'events' of May 1968 in France; the massification of Spanish universities in the 1960s and beyond), the field will fracture, with positions and stances, social and symbolic spaces, no longer coinciding and thus no longer experienced as natural or taken for granted.

In his introduction to perhaps the most institutionally philosophical of his many books, Savater traces a 'genealogy of the work in the life' which hints at just such a fracture and crisis.[4] Savater cites three significant moments. The first is his imprisonment for anti-Franco activism in 1969. Savater's fellow political prisoners argued they should be separated from the common criminals: while the former's 'crimes' were altruistic, the latter's were simply selfish. To this Savater replies (with 'youthful vehemence') that, as the member of no organized group, he has always acted strictly in his own interest (*Ética*, 15–16). The second moment is a university debate on 'The Left Today' with celebrated philosopher and

[3] 'The Intellectual Field: A World Apart' , in *In Other Words: Essays towards a Reflexive Sociology* (Cambridge: Polity, 1994), 140–9 (p. 140).

[4] *Ética como amor propio* (Barcelona: Grijalbo-Mondadori, 1988).

veteran anti-Francoist dissident José Luis Aranguren, which took place after Franco's death. When Savater proposes that the Left should reject pseudo-Christian altruism and embrace the principle of enlightened self-interest, Aranguren dismisses Savater's proposal as a mere 'boutade'. The final moment is a journalistic skirmish ('necessarily superficial') which took place about a year before Savater's book was published and in which a female opponent was as scandalized as Aranguren by Savater's supposed selfishness.

What interests me here is not so much the overt content of the anecdotes (which serve to establish the writer as devil's advocate, heretic, or free-floating intellectual) as the unacknowledged fusion of geographically and discursively distinct spheres: the strictly political (the prison); the purely academic (the philosophical debate); and the journalistic (the newspaper controversy, a genre in which Savater has specialized). In the very vagueness of its coordinates (no specific times or places are given), Savater's profession of personal commitment to political and philosophical analysis transforms partial interests into the timeless authority which underlies Bourdieu's 'intellectual field', moving from social space to symbolic power as a result. However, the relation between these different spheres remains one of homology, not identity, even as Savater's rhetoric tends to blur them together; and the hypothesis of a homology between the social and the symbolic can be explored in the interstices between such moments of attempted consecration.

In this chapter, then, I explore the gap (blurred but not erased) between the institutional and the intellectual by examining two texts by Savater which (superficially at least) could not be more dissimilar. *Contra las patrias* (published 1984) is a collection of short, mainly journalistic pieces from the early 1980s devoted to the political problem of Basque and Spanish nationalisms. *Ética como amor propio*, on the other hand, is a lengthy and often technical volume of 1988 proposing, in more philosophical mode, a revised version of self-love as a basis for social action and engagement with others. While the first is published in a series whose title ('Cuadernos Ínfimos') and modest format are self-consciously marginal, the latter is much better produced and appears with the multinational house of Grijalbo-Mondadori. The difference in the physical appearance of the two books not only points to their relative positions in the hierarchy of social space; it also permits a point of entry for the exploration of the literary field as, in Bourdieu's terms, the homology between the space of works and the space of producers and institutions. What I will argue, then, is that Savater comes to occupy the finely balanced position of what Bourdieu calls the 'consecrated heretic' or 'heresiarch';[5] and that

[5] *Homo Academicus* (Cambridge: Polity, 1988), 105.

Savater's political and philosophical analyses are underwritten by unacknowledged movements from the social to the symbolic and back again. We can thus read Savater's works as an 'allodoxia': 'an alternative system of taken for granted assumptions, running counter to the implicit consensus.'[6]

However, internal analysis of this kind must (as Bourdieu recommends) be supplemented by external, even biographical, analysis if the concept of the field as relational matrix is to be preserved. How, then, does Savater's institutional position interact with his intellectual stance? One characteristic of Savater is the privileging of geographical place over genealogical identity. Thus in the introduction to the 'personal commitment' of *Contra las patrias* Savater performs what he calls an 'ideological and biographical striptease' (p. 11), proclaiming that his childhood quite simply 'is' the San Sebastián and Guipúzcoa which were oppressed by the Francoism of the 1950s (p. 15); and that, even without 'Basque blood', he is as jubilantly *donostiarra* as his *madrileña* mother and Andalusian father, who were resident in San Sebastián for some thirty years (p. 16). Savater says he suffered as a child a double persecution for his accent (held to be excessively Castilian in Euskadi and excessively Basque when the family moved to Madrid) (p. 16), a privation which rhymes with his subsequent 'heretical' political position (too supportive of Basque self-determination for the *españolistas*; too attached to the Castilian language for the *abertzales*) (p. 17). And he goes on to describe the new Zorroaga campus of the University of the Basque Country where he gives classes on ethics: it is an institution which both encourages foreign visitors (such as Derrida) and promotes Euskera as a philosophical language (p. 22); an institution which in spite of its vigorous and open intellectual atmosphere is wholly neglected (Savater claims) by the Basque government. The latter's officials prefer to patronize its more established rival, the Jesuit University of Deusto, where a local worthy has been canonized as an official intellectual of the *autonomía* (23).

The twin marginalizations of the personal and the institutional are thus aligned: a Spaniard in the Basque Country and a Basque in Spain, Savater is also a philosophical prophet who is without honour in his own, contested country: a cultural dignitary of the ruling Partido Nacional Vasco, ignoring or dismissing the contributions made by Savater and Zorroaga, laments the fact that philosophy has put down such shallow roots in the newly autonomous nation. What I will argue, however (following Bourdieu's analysis of the intellectual field), is that this logic of double privation is implicit in the fragile status of humanities professors in

[6] Pierre Bourdieu and Jean-Claude Passeron, *The Inheritors: French Students and their Relation to Culture* (Chicago: University of Chicago Press, 1979), 156 n. 3.

general, most particularly when they participate in the rival symbolic power of journalism.

In Bourdieu's analysis of Parisian universities in the 1960s we find two mutually incompatible 'axes of inertia': the intellectual capital of the arts and social science faculties and the social capital of law and medicine (*Homo Academicus*, 48). The conflict between intellectual independence and social integration cuts across the faculties in the form of another homologous but distinct opposition: that between professors who specialize in research and those dedicated to teaching and administration. This second opposition itself recreates, in Bourdieu's words, 'the structural opposition between [non-academic] writers and professors, the freedom and audacity of the artist's life and the somewhat circumscribed rigour of *homo academicus*' (*Homo Academicus*, 109). Pointing out the disparity between the intellectual prestige and the institutional impotence of such very visible figures as Derrida, Barthes, and Foucault, Bourdieu traces the negative correlation between symbolic power and social space in celebrated, but marginal, institutions such as Vincennes, the post-1968 campus where Savater crossed swords with Lyotard on the emblematic theme of political violence. Such institutions not only 'condense in the social being [of their teachers] the tensions and contradictions inherent in marginal academic institutions'; they also attempt 'to convert a two-fold opposition, often linked to a double privation, into a willed transcendence' which may take the form of theoretical 'fashion' or of 'a critical liberty in the [double] crisis in intellectual and social foundations' (*Homo Academicus*, p. xxii).

Clearly the conditions of Paris in the 1960s and the Basque Country in the 1980s are very different; but the principle of double privation applies to both Vincennes and Zorroaga, at least in Savater's description of the latter's twin attempt to transcend political and geographical marginalization through institutional and academic innovation. And 'condensing in his social being' institutional tensions and contradictions, Savater is the nearest Spain has to the intellectually rich but temporally impoverished heroes of other countries. Moreover the massification of French universities, which Bourdieu sees as the hidden social motive of the symbolic violence of 1968, had also occurred in their Spanish equivalents, which had suffered structural fractures since the 1960s with the influx of socially diverse staff and students whose subjective ambitions could no longer be matched by objective expectations of career development. Too intellectual to be bourgeois and too bourgeois to be intellectual,[7] Savater thus occupied, like consecrated heretics elsewhere, an increasingly contradictory position.

---

[7] For this 'double disqualification' see *Homo Academicus*, 119.

One apparent solution to this disparity between *homo academicus*'s social space and symbolic power, and one exercised by Savater on a weekly basis for some twenty years, is journalism. For Bourdieu, journalism offers the objective power of criticism and consecration and the subjective aura of a 'symbolic capital of renown' (*Homo Academicus*, 79). However the specific nature of academic capital is that, unlike its financial homologue, its value is always contested. Thus while some academics see journalism as a 'dubious compromise', others view it as an 'opening up to the world and to "modernity"' (*Homo Academicus*, 111). It is hardly surprising to see Savater himself argue against those scholars who view an engagement with contemporary issues ('actualidad') as 'vulgar' (*Ética*, 255). Moreover, with the increasing intrusion of journalistic criteria into the once autonomous space of the university, the prestige of frequent collaboration with the predominant newspaper (in Savater's case *El País*) may serve as both a way out and a short cut: the attempt to purchase a 'minor form of renown' analogous to that of great scholars who remain strictly within the institution may also lead, with the increased heteronomy of that institution, to increased status within the academic world itself (*Homo Academicus*, 111–12). Where Bourdieu traces the 'convergence [in Paris] between the most intellectual journalists and the most journalistic intellectuals' (exemplified by the essayists of *Le Nouvel Observateur*) (*Homo Academicus*, 119), Savater stakes out a unique career in both the local and the national press, which both substitutes for the international intellectual fame he is unable to achieve (lamenting as he does that Spanish intellectuals are not granted by foreigners the right to speak on universal concerns) (*Contra las patrias*, 57) and is reconverted into strictly academic capital on his accession to a Chair of Ethics in the late 1980s, at a time when the Socialists' Ley de Reforma Universitaria had sought both to rationalize career structures and to open up the university to outside influences.[8] Savater's public figure thus acts out in a single body the hidden complicity between modernists and authoritarians (writers and professors), mixing as it does in an unstable combination the former's intellectual audacity and the latter's institutional gravity.

Bourdieu tells of one unlucky candidate for a university post, held to be overactive in journalism, who was told by a distinguished professor: 'You are not unknown enough'(*Homo Academicus*, 321 n. 12). Excessively visible (or more properly, too little invisible) because of his journalism, Savater's intellectual capital is always in danger of being compromised by his overwillingness to engage in undignified polemic. Journalism thus raises problems of dependency and legitimization for academics: for while the charismatic aura of the professor (most particularly in Spain where the

[8] John Hooper, *The Spaniards* (Harmondsworth: Penguin, 1987), 103.

press is more deferential than elsewhere) renders academic discourse more respected than the more ephemeral journalism, still the former is dependent on the latter for access to that space which the presence of the professor serves, in turn, to legitimize; and phenomena such as the 'hit parade' of French intellectuals testify to the circularity of consecration in the media, whereby journalists honour intellectuals for the high media profile that both have been complicit in creating (*Homo Academicus*, 79, 120).

Moreover, if the notion of the intellectual field (the articulation of the space between works, producers, and institutions) requires the scholar to think in terms of not empirical but epistemic individuals (that is, according to subjects' specific locations in the social and symbolic space) (*Homo Academicus*, 22), still those locations are disproportionately affected for those 'constructed' individuals with a high media profile by what Bourdieu calls 'hexis': the mode of physical being or bearing (*The Inheritors*, 157 n. 6). For many Spaniards, Savater's familiar and unprepossessing appearance (short, fat, and bearded), with which he has himself expressed public dissatisfaction,[9] is not easily separable from the experience of his role in the Spanish media world. However, if (as Bourdieu recommends) we break with the subjective or pre-theoretical viewpoint of those agents who are fully located in the field, we may discern the social structures masked by the symbolic interactions they subtend. More specifically, we will be able to test Bourdieu's counterintuitive hypothesis that, in the case of *homo academicus*, 'it is not . . . political stances which determine people's stances on things academic, but their positions in the academic field which inform the stances they adopt on political issues' (*Homo Academicus*, pp. xvii–xviii).

In the journalistic and academic pieces collected as *Contra las patrias*, Savater stresses the marginal political stance he takes up, which is analogous to what we have seen of his personal and institutional positions. Thus in the introduction he insists that he is neither centralist (rejecting the manifesto recently signed by Castilian-speaking intellectuals in Catalunya), nor blindly regionalist (scorning the 'cheap folklore' of Basque separatism). Offering himself to one US academic audience as the witness to the concrete and varied reality of Spanish modernity ('junkies and terrorists, homosexuals and trade unionists, pacifists and feminists') (p. 81), Savater insists throughout on the deadly materiality of violence. Thus he runs the double risk of being shot by the very terrorists for whom

[9] See the interviews by Marcos-Ricardo Barnatán, collected as *Contra el todo* (Madrid: Enjana, 1984). Savater claims that his bodily appearance pleases neither himself nor others (p. 93). Barnatán's title mimics Savater's own *Panfleto contra el todo* (Barcelona: DOPESA, 1978).

others accuse him of being an apologist (p. 23). Or again the abstractions of 'theory' are contrasted with the localized space ('sitio') in which Savater hears the voices of terror: the screams of those tortured by the 'lovers of truth of all stripes' (p. 122). Savater insists that social violence cannot be confused with its symbolic equivalent: the explosion of a real bomb is not the same as the phone call which gives rise to a false bomb scare (p. 176).

Yet Savater also analyses violence within its institutional context: the state implicitly appeals to a monopoly of terror within its frontiers (p. 13), a monopoly which is experienced by most of its citizens as 'natural' (p. 80). And violence has unpredictable effects, encouraging ideological conformism (of different kinds) and the complicity of deadly opponents: institutional and anti-institutional violence feed off one another (p. 97); macro- and micro-nationalisms are co-dependent in their mutually exclusive, but ideologically identical, claims (p. 62). Thus the new Basque government has wasted no time in institutionalizing culture: promoting education as a means of fixing identity; and subsidizing those arts (such as cinema) which will most visibly promote a culture held to be self-evident (p. 70).[10]

Yet if the social cannot be reduced to the symbolic (if the deaths of so many young men are in no way comparable to 'cultural genocide'), still there is a persistent connection between the two. Thus Savater fears a 'militarization'[11] of language in the symbolic discourse of cultural struggle and artistic polemic (p. 110); and if he breaks with the subjective viewpoint of actors in the national field (insisting that neither side transcends their own limited point of view) still the logic of his argument shifts imperceptibly from the social to the symbolic, from the objective to the subjective. For example, he holds violence to be 'indifferent' (in both senses of the word), unable to distinguish between the objects it obliterates; love, on the other hand, is the principle of differentiation itself (p. 173). Or again, the violent totalization of nationalisms derives from the aggrandized identification which subjects project onto national leaders (p. 14). For Savater identity (national, and perhaps, personal) should be non-identical, unreproducible, based not on the fossilized past but on the unpredictable promise of the future (pp. 66–7).

The grand narrative of nationality is thus founded on the little narratives of locality and subjectivity: we must consider the meaning of proximity with others; and understand the confrontation between inside and outside (self and other) on which political solidarity and exclusions

[10] For a later proposal of independent thought in the Basque Country, see Savater and Javier Sádaba, *Euskadi: pensar en el conflicto* (Madrid: Libertarias, 1987).

[11] For more essays on pacifism, see Savater's *Las razones del antimilitarismo y otras razones* (Barcelona: Anagrama, 1984).

are based (pp. 25–6). Tracing the historical definitions of *patria*, Savater shows how the word shifted its meaning from the strictly territorial or geographic ('the place in which one is born') to the emotional and personal ('belonging to a nation, with all the affective ties thus implied') (p. 28). And rejecting the naive perspectivism of the patriot (noting sarcastically that the supposed 'variety' of Spanish topography would not strike a visitor from the United States or China) (p. 85), Savater claims that the self-determination of a state is achieved not by the affirmation of an identity presumed to pre-exist it but rather by a demystification of the same (p. 36).

Breaking with immanent subjectivism, Savater's model of the state is thus performative (p. 19). Just as the affirmation of statehood produces the nation which it claims merely to reflect (p. 35), so the quest for national heroes actually produces figures, however mediocre, appropriate to that purpose (p. 65). It is a hermeneutic circularity which Savater satirizes in two anecdotes: that of the Basque who laments he lost his 'mother tongue' even before he was born; and the Andalusian who claims to be yet more deprived than the Basques or Catalans: he lacks a language the enforced loss of which would legitimize the claim to nationhood which his region is denied (p. 38). Here the witty Savater uses humour further to objectify the political and cultural field of nationalisms, even as he encourages his reader to adopt for a moment the multiple and mutually exclusive perspectives of which that field is composed.

If, then, Savater breaks with subjectivism in order to present his new critically denaturalized vision of violence and nationalism, then we too must operate a second break with his own point of view. For Savater's polemical style acknowledges that the field in which he operates is, like Bourdieu's intellectual field, one in which struggle is a constant; and it is not to minimize the courage and the importance of Savater's engagement with the most vital and dangerous political issue of the time to suggest that his essays (even at their most directly political) are also homologous with struggles in the academic arena. Indeed the motifs and arguments of Savater's polemic recur in Bourdieu's analysis of *homo academicus*. Thus the intellectual field is a 'battle field' or 'force field' ('The Intellectual Field', 143) in which the state claims a monopoly on legitimate violence.[12] Or again the nation state can be read (like the academy) as a 'legitimized social space', a 'world' whose legitimization must remain tacit if it is to be effective: 'not the product of deliberate and purposive action' ('Social Space', 135).

As a 'freelance intellectual installed within the university system' Savater is (like his French equivalents) 'more or less totally deprived of, or

---

[12] 'Social Space and Symbolic Power', in *In Other Words*, 122–39 (p. 135).

liberated from, the powers and privileges, but also the tasks and the responsibilities of the ordinary professor' (*Homo Academicus*, p. xix).[13] Likewise in the political arena, Savater's lack of allegiance to a fixed position (to a party or group) offers him freedom of movement, but deprives him of practical efficacy: the Non-Violence Group which he co-founded is strangled at birth by the existing (consecrated) political interests against which Savater's 'independents' have no power.[14] Moreover it could be argued that there is in this political field a tacit collusion between opponents, homologous to that which we have already seen in the academy: thus the extremity of Savater's stance is counterbalanced by the marginality of his position, that of the consecrated heretic for whom media visibility is a poor but strictly proportionate compensation for his powerlessness in the world.

The circularity of legitimization of the academic and political fields thus coincides in a mirroring of subjective and objective conditions. In Bourdieu's words: 'The specific regularities that constitute the economy of the field [are] immediately filled with sense and rationality for every individual . . . hence the effect of communal validation which is the basis of collective belief in the game and its fetishes.'[15] Even in his tireless demythification, then, as a player in the national and academic game, Savater cannot wholly avoid that collective belief in the fetishes of the state and the university. To exile oneself from such a belief would be to refuse to participate in the game at all and thus to be rendered invisible and inaudible.

Savater thus moves from the socio-historical to the subjectively symbolic, a move exemplified in *Contra las patrias* by a piece which contrasts unfavourably the supposed contemporary reality of the state of Israel with the romantic myth of diaspora Jewry as eternal exile and expectation (pp. 197–202). But if Savater is disposed in his political journalism to find 'salvation through the Jews' (that is, in an ideal of spatial and temporal indeterminacy), what, then, of his professional performance as a philosopher, licensed to comment on and to judge abstract thought? Savater's position in *Ética como amor propio* seems at first sight typically heretical, invoking as he does in support of his argument for self-interest such figures as Kant, generally held to be in the vanguard of altruistic ethics (p. 40). Moreover his argument appears to display the bourgeois voluntarism of which Marxist opponents have accused him: Savater

[13] Savater's account to Barnatán of a 'typical day' makes no reference to university duties (*Contra el todo*, 61–2).

[14] For Savater's account of bilateral hostility to his 'Movimiento por la Paz y la No Violencia' see 'Violencia y conformismo', in *Contra las patrias* (pp. 95–9).

[15] *The Logic of Practice* (Cambridge: Polity, 1992), 66.

argues that man is a 'self-invention' (p. 25) and ethics a universalization of the subject's will (p. 33).

Ethics is thus inseparable from affectivity (p. 39) and aesthetics (p. 91). Marshalling a Nietzschean critique of altruism which identifies morality with 'style' (pp. 67, 91), Savater invokes a string of fashionably heterodox French authorities from Foucault on the classical 'souci de soi' (p. 49) to Barthes on the supposed necessity of the choice between egoism or terrorism (p. 83). It is not surprising to see in this self-consciously hedonistic context a reference to Freud's account of the role of narcissism in the constitution of identity (p. 102) followed by a defence of the 'scandal of pleasure', understood as the world's assent ('asentimiento') to our positioning ('asentamiento') in it (p. 136). Historically, also (claims Savater), the development of social individuation has led to an increasing interiorization of subjectivity, with the space of ethics now located firmly in personal choices and will as opposed to archaic social strictures imposed from the outside (p. 179).

However, if self-love is 'the foundation of values' (p. 23) it is inextricable from homologous fields such as law and politics (p. 23). The self-affirmation which defines the human (and which prescribes the impossibility of disinterest) is always based on reciprocal recognition in the other (p. 30). And if the 'individualizing society' may lead, as Savater believes, to autonomy, it also gives rise to atomization (p. 165). Thus Savater's argument against self-denial has clearly political implications: abnegation of self may be complicit with an identification with the totalitarian ideal ego of the dictator (p. 37); and if Savater cites Freud on narcissism, he also cites Bettelheim on ethics as the best mode of surviving the Holocaust (pp. 84–5). The second half of *Ética* (essays described as 'direct complements' of the first, theoretical half) extends the philosophical analysis to address such contemporary issues as the Heidegger controversy and the defence of individual drug use. And here Foucault is cited for his late turn or return to the Enlightenment as 'rational universalism' not as 'normalizing uniformity' (p. 282). If self-love is the foundation of ethics and if virtue is individualism (pp. 329, 333), then, walking the fine, heretical line once more, Savater proposes the 'active recognition of human rights' as a safeguard against the terror of both the Left (who see human rights as a mask for bourgeois privilege) and the Right (who view them as a cover for the Communist attack on nationalist *raison d'État*) (p. 337).

But the clearest acknowledgement of this move from the symbolic to the social (from subject to institution) is to be found not in the dense and voluminous text of *Ética* but in its short prologue. Here Savater reveals that the essays on self-love as the foundation of values and on human rights were written for and delivered as a lecture ('discurso magistral') at a professorial competition at which he was awarded the Chair he currently holds. Thanking the distinguished scholars of the panel who, he says, transformed this tiresome academic parade ('paso de armas') into a 'day of stimulating and lively reflection' (p. 19), Savater notes, not without irony, that this is his first book to appear *ex cathedra*. In a typical gesture of negation, however, he at once affirms and denies his institutional position: the book carries minimal critical apparatus, since, unlike most academic works, it deals not with the commentaries of other scholars, but rather with the thing itself (p. 18).

Savater thus positions himself, in Bourdieu's terms, as an *auctor*, not a *lector*: a creative intellectual whose task is production, not a worthy pedagogue whose duty is reproduction (*Homo Academicus*, p. xxii). Indeed the disavowal of the properly academic (of the dutiful display of footnotes and references) is part of what Bourdieu sees as the rhetoric of 'brilliance' internal to the academy: the originality of the *auctor*, as opposed to the commendable but unexciting 'reliability' of the *lector*. However if we see here the logic of circular causality particular to the intellectual field (in which positions and dispositions fall effortlessly into line) (*Homo Academicus*, 99), then we must also read *Ética* in its institutional context as a professorial performance. For Bourdieu the inaugural lecture bears witness to:

the properly magical efficacy of the ritual [which] rests upon the silent and invisible exchange between the new entrant, who publicly offers his words, and the assembly of scholars who attest . . . that such words, by being thus accepted by the most eminent masters, become universally acceptable, that is, in the full sense of the word, magisterial.[16]

The spectral audience of Savater's professorial peers (absent from the text of his book, listed by name in the prologue) bear mute witness to this assumption of magisteriality, which is tacitly attested by the effortless parade of (albeit unfootnoted) textual authorities in the work itself and its uncharacteristically abstract mode of discourse. Savater here comes closest to Bourdieu's 'official point of view' in which social space is fused with symbolic power in a moment of disembodied authority. From this sovereign position the speaker can make an assertion as to the present state of affairs, a prescription directed to the future, and give an authorized account of the past ('Social Space', 136). However the magisterial moment (of 'official nomination') is also, for Bourdieu, an instance of symbolic state violence in which the 'spokesperson [is] invested with the power to speak in the name of a group which he or she produces' through that same

---

[16] 'A Lecture on the Lecture', in *In Other Words* (pp. 177–98), 177.

speech ('Social Space', 139). It is a circular logic we have also seen in the case of the charismatic national or cultural leaders, whose sudden eleva-tion Savater ridicules. Here he himself assumes that '*mysterium* of the *ministerium*', in an alchemical transformation of the social into the symbolic, a transformation which cannot be explicitly alluded to even as it transforms Savater's institutional position and his intellectual stance in the academic field.

In a study of student life called, significantly, *The Inheritors*, Bourdieu writes that the academic world is a 'game, a field of validity of rules [which] proposes or imposes on those who play it . . . by persuading them that their whole being is at stake in it' (p. 45). The vehemence of Savater's polemics bear out this sense of life or death struggle, whether it takes place in the spectacular but ephemeral realm of journalism or the less visible but equally unpredictable space of academic controversy. It may be that Savater's ability to move between the two fields is eased in Spain by the match between a newspaper readership which is much more socially restricted than in other countries (the upmarket *El País* is the most commercially successful daily in the period) and a newly massified audience of graduates of higher education.[17] But if Bourdieu warns us that the logic of the intellectual field means that 'oppositions between internal and external, hermeneutics and sociology, text and context [are] fictitious' ('The Intellectual Field', 148) this does not imply that the rela-tions between institutional positions and subjective dispositions are mechanical or hermetic.

Savater's career is exemplary in this respect in its triple development: institutional, territorial, and philosophical. Thus his stances as academic-journalist, Basque internationalist, and ethical egotist are accommodated by an institution increasingly open to the heteronomy of non-academic forms of discourse, a nation in which separatist terror loses what legiti-macy it may have claimed in the time of Carrero Blanco, and an intellec-tual sphere in which the decline of the Marxist values of solidarity and collective struggle renders Savater's anarchist individualism increasingly attractive. But if the field accommodates itself to Savater, then Savater accommodates himself to the field, most spectacularly in his emergence, after years of sexual heterodoxy, as a *père de famille*, dedicating his newly *ex-cathedra* texts to a nominated successor or inheritor: his young son.[18] The line between audacity and reliability, between intellectual indepen-

---

[17] For the close relation between journalism and the universities in Spain see John Hooper, *The New Spaniards* (Harmondsworth: Penguin, 1995), 292.
[18] In an interview with Barnatán, Savater both refuses to be sexually pigeon-holed (claiming to desire 'men, women, and post boxes') and speaks on the new-found pleasures of paternity (*Contra el todo*, 92, 94).

dence and embourgeoisement, thus becomes increasingly fine. And the consecrated heretic with his new Chair and high media profile is doubly in tune with the Socialists' much debated Ley de Reforma Universitaria, which both upgrades a proportion of untenured university teachers (PNNs) and opens up the academy to outside influences.[19]

Bourdieu writes in his inaugural lecture that this kind of analysis of the intellectual field 'tears us from the state of innocence which enables us to fulfil *with felicity* the expectations of the institution' ('A Lecture', 177). What he suggests, however, is that this lack of felicity is not paralysing but enabling: a first step in the acknowledgement and the exploration of the movement between social space and symbolic power. It is a lesson also borne out by the many and varied works of Savater whose common aim is to denaturalize (strip away the innocence from) such fetishes as the university, the nation state, and the academic discipline. If Savater's 'enlightened self-interest' seems suspiciously close to the self-interest *tout court* typical of the consumerist 1980s and if he sometimes seems closer to reproducing theoretical fashions than exercising his own critical liberty, still he testifies to a time which (like the May 1968 which he invokes as a utopian movement)[20] reveals a twin crisis in the intellectual and social foundations: a critical moment in which the subjective and objective slipped out of sync and, in sympathy with the forces fragmenting and renovating the Spanish state, the intellectual field fractured to reveal its constituent and contradictory spaces.

[19] *The New Spaniards*, 270.
[20] *Contra las patrias*, 13.

5 | Between Land and Language: Locating Bigas Luna

1. Local History, Local Space

Bigas Luna is generally thought to be a film-maker of the body, who focuses on 'the line of the stomach'.[1] But it could also be argued that his main concern is place or space. Thus the so-called 'Iberian trilogy' of the early 1990s exploits the varied and picturesque locations of the Peninsula: the arid and empty plains of Monegros in *Jamón, jamón* (1992), the thrusting skyline of Marbella in *Huevos de oro* ('Golden Balls', 1993), and the streets, beaches, and ancient monuments of Barcelona and Tarragona in *La teta i la lluna* ('The Tit and the Moon', 1994).

This concern for geographical place in the trilogy is echoed at the levels of time and subjectivity. In a lecture inaugurating the academic year at the new Universitat Pompeu Fabra in Barcelona just two weeks after the première of *La teta i la lluna*,[2] Bigas Luna proposed a 'triangular' relation of time in which the 'real time' of preproduction and the 'fictional time' of shooting (in which the actors are taken over by their roles) give way to the 'life time' ('tiempo vida') in which the fiction escapes the control of its originators. Similarly the trilogy has been presented as a triangular movement that is at once temporal and subjective: *La teta i la lluna* treats the first love of a child, *Jamón, jamón* the erotic pleasures of young adults, and *Huevos de oro* the rawly sexual exploits of a phallocrat doomed to an impotent middle age.[3] Or again the press kit to *La teta i la lluna* features a schematic diagram by Bigas Luna in which a central vaginal lozenge representing the main female character Estrellita (Plate 7) is surrounded by a triangle whose three points are marked by numerals standing for the

[1] I take the phrase from Antonio Weinrichter, *La línea del vientre: el cine de Bigas Luna* (Gijón: Festival de Cine, 1992).

[2] 24 Oct. 1994. The university website ('Formats 1') also reproduces some of Bigas Luna's photographic collages from the *Jamón, jamón* shoot; see www.iua.upf.es/formats/mem/m06et.htm.

[3] Esteve Riambau, 'La teta de Tete y la luna de Bigas', *Dirigido Por*, 228 (Oct. 1994), 38.

three men who compete for her affections: '2' is for Tete (Plate 8)(the child who is the generation of 2000), '7' for Maurice (the French *gavatxo* of the 1970s), and '9' for Miquel (the Andalusian *xarnego* of the 1990s).[4]

Bigas Luna's claim that *La teta i la lluna* is a romantic and innocent conclusion to the trilogy is somewhat contradicted by the fact that *Interviú* magazine, a scandalous survivor of the *destape* period of the 1970s, offered a video copy of the film as part of its series 'Classics of Erotic Cinema', billing it as 'Bigas Luna's most arousing film'.[5] And *Interviú*'s special edition features on its cover an image that did not appear in the original promotion for the film: a close-up of a breast from which a stream of milk appears to gush.[6] Beyond such exploitation, however (characteristic of much of Bigas Luna's career), the significance of *La teta i la lluna* lies rather in its explicit attention to a theme absent in Bigas Luna's previous nine features: Catalan nationalism. Marvin D'Lugo has recently given an excellent account of the film focusing both on the question of *catalanitat* and on the dynamic relation of time, space, and subjectivity.[7] D'Lugo stresses how 'the narrative of the community and that of the individual are woven into a national, allegorical text' (p. 198). Beginning as the film does with 9-year-old Tete (Biel Durán) trembling at the top of a human tower ('castell'), a traditional Catalan sport, it goes on to reveal that the child's 'precarious position' is emblematic of 'the unstable space of a national community in the throes of reshaping itself around a series of radical economic, social, and political changes' (p. 198). For D'Lugo the 'regional chauvinism' exemplified by such traditions as the *castell* is, like Tete's childish fantasies, a 'transitory stage to be superseded' (p. 198) by insertion into a 'regional/national/global interface' (p. 199). The 'eccentric instability of Tete's point of view' is thus also emblematic of Bigas Luna's 'market driven' quest for access to the 'commercial space of transnational European cinema' (p. 200). Just as Tete's 'psychic growth' (p. 206) will lead him beyond his immediate family and into the wider world, so Catalunya's development as a 'creative frontier in Iberian social space' (p. 209) will lead to the 'integration of Spain into Europe [a process in which] borders necessarily dissolve' (p. 212).

---

[4] London: Metro Tartan, 12 July 1996. The press book also has a lexicon translating these and other Catalan terms.

[5] Advertised in *El Mundo* (8 Feb. 1998). Features in this issue of *Interviú* include 'The Most Spectacular Spanish Underwear Models' and 'Sixty Ways to Avoid Being Assassinated by ETA', a characteristic mix of sexual and political sensationalism.

[6] The most frequent promotional still was that placed on the British video cover: the child opening his mouth to receive the stream of milk.

[7] '*La teta i la lluna*: The Form of Transnational Cinema in Spain', in Marsha Kinder (ed.), *Refiguring Spain: Cinema/Media/Representation* (Durham, NC: Duke University Press, 1997), 196–214.

D'Lugo's is the most developed reading of the film of which I am aware and certainly the only one to take seriously Bigas Luna's interrogation of *catalanitat*. And the director clearly shares D'Lugo's scepticism towards cultural nationalism. The problem of location remains, however. For even as he addresses Catalan cinema (and D'Lugo is one of the few foreign scholars to have studied the field[8]) he employs terminology that is clearly offensive to local sensitivities. Thus the first paragraph repeatedly invokes the adjective 'Spanish' to qualify the film itself, its audience, their identity, and culture ('*La teta i la lluna*', p. 196). Catalunya, meanwhile, is described as 'regional', 'provincial', even (following Marsha Kinder[9]) as a 'micro-region' ('*La teta i la lluna*', 199). As we shall see in a moment, Bigas Luna's own position in the cultural politics of Catalunya is as precarious as that of Tete on the top of the *castell*; but it remains the case, however, that *La teta i la lluna* (shot in Catalunya and in Catalan with the financial support of the Generalitat's Department of Culture) cannot be read as a 'Spanish' film without reconfirming those fears of *españolista* assimilation which may appear exaggerated to foreigners but remain keenly felt by many Catalans. It is characteristic that the official websites of the central government's Ministry of Education and Culture offer no means of identifying Catalan productions such as *La teta i la lluna*, invariably citing Castilian film titles as 'original' and claiming all features are '100% Spanish'.[10]

D'Lugo draws on anglophone theorists of cultural identity such as Benedict Anderson, Fredric Jameson, and (most recently) Homi Bhabha. Such theories were evolved to respond to and account for the emergence of nineteenth-century nation states (Anderson), the fractal geometries of the postmodern metropolis (Jameson), and the tragedies and ironies of postcolonialism (Bhabha). In such contexts the weakening of frontiers and the dissolution of boundaries are often to be celebrated; but the critique of the nation state, however urgent, cannot necessarily be extended to nations without states such as Catalunya. One foreign critic of *La teta i la lluna* uses 'patriotism' and 'intolerance' as synonyms,[11] an attitude unintelligible to many Catalans. What I argue in this chapter, then, is

[8] 'Catalan Cinema: Historical Experience and Cinematic Practice', *Quarterly Review of Film and Video*, 13 (1991), 131–47.

[9] *Blood Cinema: The Reconstruction of National Identity in Spain* (Berkeley and Los Angeles: University of California Press, 1993), 389.

[10] Ministerio de Educación y Cultura: Secretaría de Estado de Cultura gives the 'original title' of Bigas Luna's film as *La teta y la luna*; the website giving statistics on 'Producción Española de Largometrajes en 1996' (the most recent year available at the time of writing) also lists such Catalan-language films as Ventura Pons's *Actrius* ('Actresses') and Joaquín Jordá's *Cos al bosc* ('Body in the Forest') only under their Castilian titles; see www.mcu.es/cine/index.html.

[11] The critic is Annelie Bojstad in her 'Commentary' on the film for the Stockholm Film Festival website.

that any analysis of the work of a director such as Bigas Luna whose career has coincided with the rebirth of self-government should pay attention to what Catalans themselves have written on nationalism, however contradictory it may be. I thus take the strongest and most populist model of nationalism (that of long-time President Jordi Pujol) and contrast it with the more theorized versions of Catalan academic historiographers. While Pujol explicitly locates the 'common ground' of national identity in language and culture, still his texts are marked by a return to land and to physical place. Similarly the historiographers' polemic, which concentrates on chronology, also reverts to space and to a re-evaluation of locality. While Bigas Luna presents a mythical 'Iberia' in his trilogy as a geographical third term transcending states and nations, Catalan nationalists turn or return to the 'lived space' of the locality. Neither dissolution of boundaries nor chauvinistic retrenchment or reterritorialization, such locations combine the 'third spaces' of anglophone theorists with the respect for Catalan sensitivities I mentioned above.

Bigas Luna shot the scenes set in Tete's family flat in an abandoned hospital scheduled for demolition in the port district of Barceloneta.[12] And throughout his career Bigas Luna has shown a concern for the rehabilitation (or more simply, rehabitation) of everyday spaces, however temporary they may be. Thus in his early career as a conceptual artist, Bigas Luna transformed domestic locations, recreating an abandoned, Fascist dinner party, suspending chairs in mid-air, or having actors harangue unsuspecting visitors to an otherwise empty art gallery.[13] Screenings of *Angoixa* ('Anguish', 1986), winner of the Generalitat's cinematography prize, were accompanied by disturbances staged by actors in the cinema itself, a mirroring of the on-screen action which took place in a movie theatre.[14] Finally the completed trilogy was itself complemented by an illustrated book featuring Bigas Luna's polaroid collages of the varied locations in which shooting took place.[15] The still photographs frequently focus on topographical, even geological, detail: the texture of boulders in Monegros or of sand on Barceloneta beach. The multiple viewpoints of the collages (similar to David Hockney's work of the same period) testify once more to an instability of perspective (like that of Tete on the *castell*) even as they draw our attention to the concrete materiality of the location.

Clearly enamoured of the sensual experience of land (and most particularly of his native province of Tarragona), Bigas Luna is at best pragmatic

[12] Bigas Luna and Cuca Canals, *Iberian Portraits* (Barcelona: Lunwerg, 1994), 125.

[13] Ramón Espelt (ed.), *Mirada al món de Bigas Luna* (Barcelona: Laertes, 1989), 33, 29, 7.

[14] Ibid. 78, 275.

[15] *Iberian Portraits* also contains schematic drawings by Bigas Luna.

and at worst disingenuous when discussing Catalan nationalism. Thus he has frequently attacked the cultural policy of the Generalitat, claiming that 'subsidized art' is 'shat art';[16] yet this did not prevent him taking TV3's funding to direct a most unlikely project intended to promote Catalan identity in child viewers, the extraterrestrial drama series *Kiu i els seus amics* ('Kiu and his Friends', 1985).[17] In promotional interviews for *La teta i la lluna*, Bigas Luna proclaims to the Barcelona *Vanguardia* that his cinema is 'supercatalan' and that the film is a 'homage to Catalunya beyond nationalisms'.[18] The nationality of a film, he says, is located not in its language but in the identity of its director, who is in this case 'rooted' in the 'land' of Tarragona. In Madrid's *El País* Bigas Luna also draws attention to the film's location: it is a 'portrait' of the place in which he was born and the 'landscape' he has known since childhood.[19] He stresses, however, the film's hybridity ('mestizaje'), as shown by the soundtrack's fusion of flamenco and Piaf; and to the conservative *ABC* he claims that although *La teta i la lluna* is 'very Catalan' it will appeal to the most traditionalist *madrileño* ('un chulo de Chamberí').[20] As far as reviews are concerned, Catalans were untroubled by Bigas Luna's parodic intentions: *Avui* wrote blandly that *La teta i la lluna* 'internationalize[s], through ironic distancing, the archetypical Catalan image repertoire'.[21] Castilians tended either to erase the specificity of the film's Catalan setting or loftily to patronize the Catalan audience whose pretensions it was thought to mock: thus *Ya* reported of the *La teta i la lluna*'s première at the Venice Film Festival that it was the only 'Spanish' film to be shown that year;[22] and *El País* wrote that Bigas Luna's 'self-directed irony' might not please the 'nationalist authorities' but was 'the healthiest and most radical vindication of Catalunya in our cinema in recent years'.[23]

---

[16] Weinrichter, *La línea del vientre*, 15.

[17] See the exemplary website 'La producción de ficción de Televisió de Catalunya S.A. (1984–1995)': www.iua.upf.es/~laura/WEB_TVC/serie85.htm. Seventeen half-hour episodes were made of this hugely expensive programme. The then head of TV3 explained that the rationale for the project was to 'see our own [Catalan] identity reflected back to us', a perhaps unusual goal for a science fiction series.

[18] Santiago Fondevila, 'Bigas Luna apunta con su cámara a Cataluña', *La Vanguardia* (7 Mar. 1994); Diego Muñoz, '*La teta y la luna* es mi homenaje a Cataluña por encima de los nacionalismos', *La Vanguardia* (6 Oct. 1994).

[19] Josep Palou, 'Bigas Luna: "Sólo el adolescente es capaz de matarse por amor"', *El País* (26 Mar. 1994).

[20] María Güell, 'Aunque *La teta y la luna* es un filme muy catalán puede emocionar a un chulo de Chamberí', *ABC* (6 Oct. 1994).

[21] Núria Bou, 'A la recerca del pit perdut', *Avui* (9 Oct. 1994).

[22] Antonio Pelayo, 'El cine español presenta hoy su único filme a concurso en Venecia', *Ya* (8 Sept. 1994).

[23] M. Torreiro, 'Dulce Cataluña', *El País* (9 Oct. 1994).

El País's positive review has only one complaint: the 'confusion' of the two perspectives of the adult director and the child protagonist. The latter frequently describes scenes which he could not have witnessed. This flaw in the verisimilitude and 'narrative logic' of the film is not solved, the reviewer writes, by the insertion of 'oneiric details' drawn from 'the territory of dreams'. I return to these imagistic inserts when I discuss the film itself later. But this precarious point of view (also cited by D'Lugo) recurs in a most unexpected place: the texts of the figure who has embodied Catalan nationalism for some twenty years, Jordi Pujol. Shifting from language to land, Pujol's conception of national identity is unstable; but institutionally, also, his position is precarious. Many Catalans resent the identification of 'Pujolism' and 'Catalanism'; and Pujol's lengthy tenure as President (he was elected for a fourth consecutive term in 1992) has required continual negotiation with not only the central state government in Madrid but also the Socialist mayoralty in Barcelona.[24]

Pujol has consistently stated in speeches[25] that Catalunya is defined not by race but by language (p. 38). A land of 'passage, hybridity, and frontiers' (p. 44), it is articulated by its 'proper tongue': the 'nerve of our nation' (p. 176). It is language and culture that form the 'personality' of Catalunya (p. 177), a personality that is implicitly transhistorical. While Catalunya remains, Pujol says, an 'open and permeable society' (p. 189), any people requires a 'collective mystique to give it a backbone and a meaning' (p. 140). The celebration of the supposed millennium of the nation in 1988 thus serves to 'ensure the continuity' of a people (p. 45) who enjoyed sovereignty long before an entity known as 'Spain' had come into existence (p. 46). But national identity, however immemorial, remains fragile. Hence Pujol's concern for education and immigration, twin challenges to a nation without a state. First the policy of 'linguistic normalization' (which provoked protests from Castilian-speaking intellectuals in 1981) is simply part of an attempt to restore the dignity of 'the language proper to Catalunya' (p. 180). Secondly and more controversially, Andalusian migration (massive since the 1950s) is a terrible warning to Catalans: the Andalusian is 'incoherent', 'anarchic', 'destroyed' by Spanish assimilation (p. 214). The 'great mission of Catalunya is to give migrants back their [mental] form . . . to make the uprooted take root once more' (p. 217). Such 'integration', Pujol insists, is not 'assimilation' (p. 55); but to be Catalan it is not enough to live and work in Catalunya, one must 'want to be Catalan' (p. 56).

---

[24] For the vicissitudes of Pujol's minority Convergència i Unió Party see Albert Balcells, *Catalan Nationalism: Past and Present* (London: Macmillan, 1996).

[25] Collected in Castilian translation by Ramón Pi as *Cataluña España* (Madrid: Espasa Calpe, 1996).

In spite of their stress on the historicity of language and culture then (and their implicit mistrust of a land that has always been a place of passage for other, larger nations), Pujol's texts appeal to an ahistorical mystique of national identity that is 'rooted' in an idealized earth. His speeches, composed for an oral audience, frequently invoke territorial fables: unlikely to see Catalunya's full independence in his lifetime, Pujol compares himself to the 'child of the tribe who wanted to cross the desert to the sea' (p. 117). The child died in a ditch, but left tracks in the sand pointing the way to freedom. Or again, his generation who came to man-hood under Franco lived in a 'barren land, a cursed land, a land of sterile men' (p. 122). Yet he describes a childhood idyll whose sensuality is equal to Bigas Luna's: a summer sunset seen from a cornfield (p. 130), the smell of damp earth and mown alfalfa (p. 131). Catalunya under the dictator-ship may have been a 'sick' world, but it was a 'unitary' and 'virginal' one which did not distinguish between agricultural and industrial workers and was therefore 'capable of making men' and 'form[ing] characters' (pp. 131–2). Such 'dense social texture' (p. 162) is laid down archaeo-logically in the land: Pujol proposes that each village should have its own tiny museum because beneath that village lies an 'Iberian settlement' where locals can search on Sundays for 'combs' and 'amphoras', precious relics of the past (p. 173). Yet such rootedness, however ancient, is fragile, ever vulnerable to the ravages of modernity and migration. Once more the metaphor is spatial: 'Since we have no container, we are at the mercy of interference . . . we have no walls to defend us' (pp. 152, 154). Unprotected by the invisible but unquestioned privileges of a universally recognized state (such as Spain), Catalans may not see the dissolution of borders as a blessing, nor identify integration into Europe (as Bigas Luna and D'Lugo do) with 'psychic growth'.

This is a point Pujol shares, surprisingly perhaps, with academic historians proud to proclaim themselves 'nationalists' even as they historicize the national character Pujol tends to mythify. Albert Balcells has collected texts documenting the bitter polemic between nationalists and self-styled 'anti-mythists' in a volume published in the same year *La teta i la lluna* was released.[26] The sceptics fired the first volley in a text titled 'The Myths of the History of Catalunya', written by Miquel Barceló, Borja de Riquer, and Enric Ucelay. The position attacked here is seen in spatial terms: nationalists attempt to 'capture and delimit a territory in which Catalan nationality can be produced' (p. 11). Mimicking Castilian historiography, Catalan nationalists proclaim their own 'reconquest' (of Lleida, Valencia, and the Balearics), a 'romantic' or 'epic' historiography in which Jaume the Conqueror displaces the Cid he merely shadows

[26] *La història de Catalunya a debat: els textos d'una polèmica* (Barcelona: Curial, 1994).

(p. 13). Both subject and object of history, this 'organicist vision of Catalunya' is based on 'the Catalan character' that has 'lived through the centuries' and whose continuity is to be demonstrated by the historian (p. 14). The 'neo-Hegelian ascent of a people to freedom and civilization' is reinforced by self-government: with the coming of the Generalitat, the authors write sarcastically, 'the tumultuous romantic epic could now be calmed, since the fullness of self-realization would soon be felt' (p. 14). Accused of 'demobilizing history' by leftist historians still influenced by a once hegemonic Marxism, the heretics claimed that 'to demythologize is not to demobilize', adding: 'It may be that demythologization is at a given moment the symbol of progressive nationalism … what the country needs is a critical Catalanism, ready to confront the inertia of conservative and *barretina* Catalanism' (p. 25). The traditional red cap will also be ridiculed in *La teta i la lluna*, incongruously placed as it is on the tiny head of Tete's newborn brother.

In the mid-1980s the sceptics continued their attack, attributing to nationalist historians a 'nostalgia for originary essences and … a search for an ancestral identity [that implies] a localist self-immersion [that rejects] other peoples and other cultural influences' (p. 38). But the following year three nationalists (Casimir Martí, Josep Termes, and Balcells himself) replied, rejecting 'totalizing ideology and the organic personalization of the nation' (p. 45) but also claiming that there was a third way between 'self-determinationist voluntarism' and 'antinationalism disguised as cosmopolitanism' (p. 55). Catalan nationalism is thus not to be reduced to Pujolism (p. 73); yet, they write, 'peripheral nationalisms [are] much more vulnerable to antinationalist critique [than Spanish nationalism, given the former's] political and institutional weakness' (p. 94). By 1992 nationalists felt obliged to counter claims that the avowed aim of 'national formation' in Catalan education was identical to that of the Franco period, which had been expressed in similar terms: there could be no neutral pedagogy. The alternative to promoting 'national consciousness' can only be the promotion of 'national unconsciousness' (p. 165); 'demythification' is but a 'new myth': that of the historian who stands 'outside' historial conflict. Nationalists should not 'instrumentalize' history for social and political ends, however noble; but nor should they be 'indifferent' to politics (p. 168). But in 1994 (the year of *La teta i la lluna*) such tortuous double negatives gave way to a positive proposal from fifty teachers of history in a manifesto entitled 'The history of Catalunya, an indispensable element of cultural normalization': 'A knowledge of its own history', write the teachers, 'is for any people an element of national identity and cultural normality, and the way to wipe out both of these is to instil in a people contempt for or forgetfulness of its own history' (p. 184).

Pointedly evading such controversies over the teaching of Catalan culture and language, Bigas Luna shows us only one of Tete's teachers: 'La Caballé', a monstrous English mistress. But one nationalist historian proposes a third way between anti-mythist deconstruction and self-assertive normalization that I will suggest is particularly appropriate for the sceptical yet nostalgic vision of Bigas Luna. Agustí Colomines proposes a return to 'Local Space in the Context of National History' (1993). Colomines does not deny that local history has served since the nineteenth century as a 'discourse promoting unity and uniformity' and a 'perfect refuge for antiquarians', occupying as it has a position somewhere 'between archeology and folklore' (p. 146); and he admits that local history has served to affirm one's own 'personality' and 'principle of identity'. This 'minor history' ('història menuda') remained disconnected, lacking any global perspective (p. 147). But this does not mean (as denationalizers claim) that all such history is out of date: positivist and historicist (p. 149). Rather 'microhistory' can be used to investigate 'the virtuality of local history, of local space': it is 'the reconstruction of the relations that join men and environment in a lived space which often does not correspond with economic or administrative [boundaries]'. If 'lived space' is defined as the 'representation of forms of life by those who act in them', then 'local space' is the interaction of lived space with a concrete environment, a concept of 'little history' which does indeed open out on to general and national history (p. 150). 'Local space' thus goes beyond mere geographical limits to address the 'necessary interconnection between historical process and place' (p. 145).

2. Spatializing Time

I will argue that it is in this spatial dimension of social form, proposed by Colomines, that Bigas Luna's engagement with *catalanitat* is to be found. But let us look first at the opening sequence of the film. The unpublished script gives a slightly different version from the final cut. I transcribe omitting the Catalan dialogue.[27]

1 INT. NOCHE. CABARET. (TÍTULOS DE CRÉDITO)
Sobre la tapa de una caja aparecen los títulos de crédito.
Una mujer a la que no vemos la cara está situada en la parte inferior de un escenario. Dos hombres la aúpan para introducirla dentro de un agujero que comunica con el escenario.
La caja empieza a abrirse y aparece ESTRELLITA, se despliega abriendo sus brazos,

---

[27] 'La teta y la luna (On parle français)/Guión cinematográfico de Cuca Canals–Bigas Luna' (Barcelona: Lolafilms, 1994).

es una mujer muy atractiva, de unos 25 años, vestida de bailarina, que recuerda las bailarinas de Degas.

2 EXT. DÍA. PLAZA STA. MARÍA DEL MAR

Plaza llena de gente, ambiente festivo. Los balcones de las casas adornados con banderas catalanas. Vemos dos grandes manchas de color . . . son las dos collas de castellers que van a competir . . . También hay un grupo de músicos preparándose para tocar, afinando los instrumentos etc. . . .

Vemos en primer término varias fajas negras moviéndose y descubrimos a el [sic] PARE de Tete dando vueltas sobre sí mismo y dando instrucciones a MIGUEL [sic], un joven de 25 años . . . Junto a ellos está un joven corpulento, STALLONE . . .

Dos músicos afinan las grallas. Junto a ellos uno toca el tamborilet. TETE un niño de unos nueve años está junto a su MADRE, una mujer visiblemente embarazada de unos 35 años, su padre le habla con mucho entusiasmo, y se lo sube a los hombros. . . .

La colla de Tete está ahora colocada . . . con el padre de Tete en el centro dando instrucciones. . . .

Stallone y Miguel empiezan a subir. La NOVIA de Stallone también sube . . . Tete empieza a subir. Pasa por detrás de Stallone y de la novia de Stallone y le toca las tetas. . . .

El castell empieza a tambalearse . . . Vemos desde arriba el interior del castell, tal y como lo ve Tete. . . .

Tete tiene miedo, mira hacia abajo, el castell tiembla. . . .

El padre de Tete está desesperado, aún grita dando ánimos a su hijo. . . . Finalmente el castell se derrumba.

(fos. 1–5)

1 INTERIOR. NIGHT. NIGHTCLUB. (OPENING CREDITS)

The opening titles appear over the top of a box.

A woman whose face we don't see is placed under the stage. Two men lift her up to fit her through a hole leading to the stage.

The box starts to open and ESTRELLITA appears, uncurling her body as she opens her arms, she is a very attractive woman of about 25, dressed as a ballerina and recalling the ballerinas of Degas.

2 EXTERIOR. DAY. SQUARE OF STA MARÍA DEL MAR [IN BARCELONA]

A square full of people, a festive atmosphere. The balconies are hung with Catalan flags. We see two great splashes of colour . . . they are the two *collas* [teams] of *castellers* who are to compete . . . There is also a group of musicians getting ready to play, tuning up their instruments etc. . . .

We see black sashes moving in close-up and find Tete's PARE [father] rushing round in circles giving instructions to MIGUEL, a young man of 25 . . . Next to them is a hefty young man, STALLONE . . .

Two musicians tune up their *grallas* [cornets]. Next to them another plays a *tamborilet* [small drum]. TETE a child of about 9 is next to his MOTHER, a women of about 35 visibly pregnant, his father speaks to him very forcefully and lifts him onto his shoulders. . . .

Tete's *colla* is now in place . . . with Tete's father in the middle giving instructions.
. . .
Stallone and Miguel start to go up. So does Stallone's GIRLFRIEND . . . Tete starts
to climb up. He goes behind Stallone and Stallone's girlfriend and feels her
breasts. . . .
The *castell* starts to sway . . . We see from above into the middle of the *castell*, just
as Tete sees it. . . .
Tete is afraid, looks down, the *castell* shakes. . . .
Tete's father is in despair, still shouting out to encourage his son. . . .
Finally the *castell* collapses.

In the credit sequence Bigas Luna omits the men placing Estrellita
(Mathilda May) on the hidden mechanism below the stage: we are
presented simply with the magical apparition of the dancer, spiralling out
of the box. The graphic dissonance between this sequence and the *castell*
scene which follows it (the delicate pink and white of tutu and box contrasting with the bright red of the *castellers'* costume) is heightened by a
filmic element unmentioned in the script: music. Nicola Piovani's
plangent soundtrack, with its haunting flute motif, gives way to the
strident sound of the Catalan cornets and drums. The *castell* scene economically and unambiguously introduces some of the main characters,
with Tete's voice-over prompting the spectator: first comes Miquel
(Miquel Poveda), the *xarnego* from the south, and then Stallone (Genís
Sánchez), the native muscle man. But the way the sequence is actually shot
is more disruptive than the script suggests. First there is constant cross-
cutting between long shots from an overhead position of the great crowd
in the square and extreme close-ups of overlapping body parts: hands,
feet, and faces confused together. As specified in the script, one shot
even gives us Tete's precarious point of view, looking vertiginously and
vertically down the inside of the *castell*. Secondly (and unlike in the script)
the human tower collapses more than once, with jump cuts suggesting
repeated and frustrated action. The graphic contrast is thus not only
between the credit and the opening sequences (with the first abstracted
and feminine and the second concrete and masculine), it is also within the
castell sequence itself where the phallic tower is undermined by the
cinematography and editing as they attempt to reproduce what D'Lugo
calls the 'eccentric instability' of Tete's point of view.

The *castell*, as festive performance, suggests a temporary transformation or rehabitation of an everyday space: the town square. Such spatial
practices might seem to reconfirm Pujol's ideal of popular continuity
through time: indeed the vertical *castell* could be read as precisely the
'backbone' which Pujol recommends to spineless Catalans. But the
sequence also addresses Pujol's twin concerns of education and immigra-

tion. By 1994, with the 'normalization' of Catalan in schools, it would be implausible for a child of Tete's age to speak anything but his 'proper tongue', the 'nerve of [his] nation'; and with the *xarnego* joining native-born Catalans in quite literally supporting the cultural structure, there could be no clearer visual example of the 'integration' of Andalusians uprooted from their native soil. Indeed in crowded close-up it is impossible to tell where Miquel's body ends and those of his comrades begins. Pujol's childhood idyll is recreated in the voice-over of Bigas Luna's child protagonist, with its naively sensual commentary (Tete mentions the smell of Miquel's feet and the hardness of the breasts of Stallone's girlfriend). But this density of sensation and sociality is fragile: formed by nothing other than the human body (lacking a physical 'container') the Catalan tradition repeatedly trembles and falls, the tower losing its structure and dissolving into an undifferentiated mass of bodies.

But if the scene echoes Pujol's praise of and fear for *catalanitat*, it also reworks the motifs of the historiographers. For the *castell* itself is a historical myth of Catalunya, originally practised in just a few regions and only recently exported throughout the nation.[28] And just as the demythologizers claim romantic Catalan history is but a substitute for an equally mythic Castilian chronicle of national formation, so one commentator has claimed that the *castells* were promoted by TV3 as a substitute for bullfighting, the Spanish *fiesta nacional* which is not carried by the Catalan channel.[29] The phallic tower can thus be read not only as a competitive masculine sport contrasted with the decorative feminine display of the title sequence, but also and yet more ironically as the 'ascent' of the Catalan people in an era of self-government, a process held by critics to be little more than the fetishization of conservative folklore. By repeatedly demolishing the tower (and by adopting Tete's eccentric point of view) Bigas Luna could be seen as undermining *barretina* Catalanism, based as it is on a voluntarism that is, finally, impotent: for all his father's urging the child does not have the will (does not have the 'balls') to reach the top.

Yet if Bigas Luna is sceptical then he is also nostalgic. Identifying with the child's fears and fantasies we are distanced from the contemporary reality of Catalunya in which Bigas Luna has no interest (or so he has professed in interviews). Claiming to stand outside historical conflict, the director and his proxy the child protagonist inhabit or rehabilitate a newly intense and sensually saturated local space: the history of a minor, *La teta i la lluna* will also prove to be 'minor history' in the academic sense. Its

[28] Balcells, *Catalan Nationalism*, 191. The *castells* originated in Valls and Tarragona.

[29] Arcadi Espada, *Contra Catalunya* (Barcelona: Flor del Viento, 1997), 190. Espada, a journalist at *El País* and professor at the Universitat Pompeu Fabra, is a vitriolic campaigner against what he sees as the claustrophobia and immobilism of *catalanista* cultural policy.

elements may be disconnected and its access to the global obscure, but still it exploits the virtuality of locality by privileging social forms (such as the *castell*) that are based on the relation between people and their environment, examples of lived space that need not coincide with economic or administrative boundaries.

As *La teta i la lluna* develops from this opening sequence the oscillation between criticism and nostalgia, disjunction and identification, is played out in filmic form. Thus, exploiting graphic contrast once more, Bigas Luna cuts from the bright and noisy town square to the dark and solitary beach, where Tete and his grandfather share another folkloric fetish: the traditional Catalan bread rubbed with tomato. And in an ironic echo of Erice's *El espíritu de la colmena*, Bigas Luna has his own dark-eyed child swear allegiance to the moon. Typically, however, this naturalistic, albeit lyrically illuminated, sequence segues into the first fantasy insert: Tete as a child astronaut planting a Catalan flag on the lunar surface. The romantic ambitions of nationalist 'reconquest' (a motif ridiculed by the demythologizers) are here replayed in a form that is at once ironic and nostalgic, traditional (the ancient flag) and modern (the silver suit of the spaceman). Subsequent inserts (the local women baring their breasts to the lovelorn Tete, his hated brother replaced by a baby pig) also exploit critical disjunction even as they promote nostalgic identification with the inner fantasies of the child protagonist, fantasies that are formally indistinct from his perception of the outer world. Like the historian's model of 'local space' once more, the film's mode of representation stresses the interaction between subjective or abstract forms of life and objective or concrete environments.

Graphic contrast and dislocation are also exploited in such bravura action sequences as the death of Stallone in a motorcycle accident. Here Bigas Luna cuts rapidly and impressionistically between an extreme close-up of a shoe cracking a walnut on the ground, a long shot of the speeding bike, a glass *porró* or spouted jug shattering on the floor, an approaching car, a speeding train, and (finally) the blue wreckage of the Kawasaki flying through the air. Elsewhere dislocation is achieved through the unhinging of image- and soundtracks: when Tete first confronts his beloved Estrellita he reaches out to squeeze her breast, while telling us in voice-over that she offers it to him herself. And if the art design repeats not, as D'Lugo claims, the Catalan colours of red and yellow, but rather those of the *gavatxos'* tricolour (thus encouraging us to identify the varied locations with one another), more often elements of *mise en scène* are used critically for contrastive effect: thus Tete sees his father filling cars at the service station, but dressed as a Roman legionary; or again, the father, dressed in the same uniform, marches towards Tete over the Tarragona aqueduct, but holding the lacy red bra the child has stolen from Estrellita's washing line. The classical pretensions or archeological ambitions of nationalists are thus at once mocked and preserved, recycled as a new kind of cultural continuity grounded in local space.

This leads us to the most important of Bigas Luna's techniques and one inseparable from the use of a child's viewpoint: the spatialization of time. Bigas Luna exploits a number of locations at some distance from each other in reality and whose relation to one another is not established in the fiction: the communal space of the town square (shot in Terrassa) gives way to the familial space of flat and street (Barceloneta), and the elemental, cosmic space of the beach and moon. The *gavatxos'* camping site (Castelldefels), a nomadic, frontier space, is contrasted with 'Cava Park' (Barceloneta once more), the beach front restaurant where Estrellita and Maurice (Gérard Darmon) perform to drunken revellers waving Catalan and European flags, a fully territorialized space. Finally the Roman ruins cited above and the prehistoric monolith of Mèdol are contrasted with the alienating and deracinated modernity of planes, trains, and cars, modes of transport that suggest the abolition of concrete location in the quest for pure, abstract motion. What is important about this spatialization of time, then, is the simultaneity of different temporal levels of development in both the infantile psyche of the protagonist and the dense and multilayered landscape of Catalunya.

If time is presented as space, then this is in part determined by the regressive nature of the medium: in the visual syntax of cinema, image must take precedence over idea. However the spatialization of time is not only typical of a director celebrated since his days as a furniture designer for his visual style and of a child narrator who chooses imagistic fantasy over the constraints of the real. It is also characteristic of a narrative that favours location over progression and *mise en scène* over plot. Thus in the final sequence Tete returns to the beginning and once more ascends the *castell*; but he also regresses to childhood, passing from Estrellita's breast to that of his mother. This regression, at once spatial and psychic, can be read as an implicit rebuke to the neo-Hegelian ascent narrative of the nationalists, who seek personal and national self-realization in the teleology of historical progress.

We return then to *catalanitat*. If the time of history is reduced to the space of national geography and the formation of the subject to the persistence or insistence of the object, then this is because Bigas Luna is fascinated by the frozen moment of fetishism. Just as his characters settle for substitute sexual objects (the red bra), so they fixate on symbolic national icons (the red cap). Reducing, in accordance with Marx's diagnosis of fetishism, a relation between people to a relation between things, Tete's parents appear indifferent to their son's anxiety, even as they enforce his participation in the phallic and national rivalry of the *castell*. What the theory or theories of fetishism (both Freudian and Marxist)[30] offer a reading of *La teta i la lluna*, then, is a structural relation between Bigas Luna's twin concerns of sex and politics. Both result in immobilization: the arresting of libidinal and national dynamism when contained within excessively restrictive borders. Beyond, then, any simple and finally undecidable debate as to whether Bigas Luna's fetishization of the image subverts or reconfirms stereotypes of women and of Catalans (and there is no doubt that his authorial touch is often heavy-handed in both areas), the psychic and narrative inertia or regression of *La teta i la lluna* suggest that nostalgia and parochialism cannot gain access to general history, cannot open out onto the wider world.

However Bigas Luna's cosmopolitan hybridity (his blend of flamenco and Piaf, *xarnegos* and *gavatxos*) could be read in a Catalan context as an alibi for antinationalism and as indifference to the particularity of Catalunya. But what I have argued is that Bigas Luna is indeed faithful to local space, in the restricted sense, in so far as he focuses on the 'microhistorical' relations between people and their environment, relations which cannot be reduced to economic or administrative terms. And if we turn to the anglophone theorists of postmodernity and postcolonialism cited by D'Lugo we find an emphasis on the problematic intersection of time, space, and subjectivity that is also comparable to Bigas Luna's exploitation of film form. In *The Location of Culture*,[31] Homi Bhabha cites Benedict Anderson on 'the disruptive temporality of enunciation [that] displaces the narrative of the Western nation . . . written in homogeneous, serial time' (p. 37). The subject of enunciation is a 'Third Space . . . unrepresentable in itself [which] ensures that the meaning and symbols of culture have no primordial unity or fixity: that even the same signs can be appropriated, translated, rehistoricized and read anew' (p. 37). Or again in an essay in the same volume entitled 'How Newness Enters the World' (pp. 212–35) Bhabha cites Jameson on the anxious 'narratives of the borderline' in 'a world [that] reveals itself as caught up in the space between frames' (p. 214). This fractal space is also 'the breakdown of temporality . . . engulfing the subject with undescribable vividness . . . this present of the world [that] comes before the subject with heightened intensity' (p. 214). For Jameson the 'transnational attenuation of local space' (p. 216) leads to a 'third space' of radically discontinuous subject-

---

[30] For a brilliant extension of the twin theories of fetishism to erotic cinema, see Linda Williams, *Hard Core: Power, Pleasure, and the Frenzy of the Visible* (London: Macmillan, 1991).

[31] (London: Routledge, 1994).

ivity. Bhabha argues that this third space is in Jameson both positive and negative: on the one hand, the recognition of such disjunctive spaces is crucial for the emergence of new historical subjects; but on the other, the containment of disjunctive social time is necessary for historical process to occur at all (p. 217).

Now I argued at the start of this chapter that the anglophone bias towards the weakening of frontiers and the dissolution of borders may not coincide with the interests of nations without states such as Catalunya, nations which (as Pujol says) have no 'container', no walls to defend them. But Bigas Luna does indeed coincide with aspects of the critique of the nation state in Anderson, Jameson, and Bhabha. Thus *La teta i la lluna* focuses from the very beginning on a problematic space of enunciation: the child's viewpoint and narration, which in its discontinuities and ellipses disrupts the homogeneous, serial time of national formation, even as it appropriates, translates, and rereads the signs of that same nation. The instability of enunciation, then, attacked by Spanish critics of the film, points rather to the constitutional (and not simply empirical) hybridity of cultures which have no meaning outside the stories told by those subjects that enunciate them and thus locate them in the world. As Bigas Luna reveals in his equally disruptive use of film form (of clashing *mise en scène*, cinematography, and editing) the world of such borderline narratives is caught between frames, fraught with psychic and national anxiety. But the vividness of *La teta i la lluna*'s imagery and the heightened intensity of its representation of everyday life testify to the sensual pleasures afforded to the subject (and most particularly to the child) when the smooth sequence of temporality breaks down. It has long been acknowledged that Bigas Luna is more successful as a director of isolated moments than of continuous narrative. Postmodern or postcolonial theory would suggest that such temporal disruption is both positive and negative: it both provides the opportunity for new subjects such as the cosmopolitan and supercatalan Tete to emerge and prevents those subjects from becoming truly historical, from inscribing local space in a global perspective.

It is instructive to compare Bigas Luna's response to this dilemma with another cultural reworking of national image repertoire, the Museum of the History of Catalunya ('Museu d'Història de Catalunya') which opened in Barcelona in 1996. Claiming to offer a 'journey through time' the museum combines temporal linearity with spatial containment. Thus the eight rooms of the permanent exhibition suggest the organicist development of a Catalan personality (from 'Birth of a Nation' to 'Defeat and Revival') and the territorial positioning of that entity (from 'Our Sea' to 'Edge of Empire'). Using history to promote national identity and cultural normality, the museum traces the trajectory of the emergent nation and of the child visitor through a sequence of geographical locations and spatial practices intended to promote identification with the past: the child is encouraged to grind corn with prehistoric Catalans and to build an arch with the Roman colonists. And a 'time line' on CD Rom accompanies visitors throughout their journey. In spite of the linearity of this progression, however (with visitors moving up the building as they go forward in time, physically mirroring the spiritual ascent of the nation), the museum is cinematic in style. For, acknowledging the impossibility of literally embodying historical process, it contains no original objects. Rather each room (each epoch, each location) is a set: tastefully decorated, dressed with appropriate props, and peopled by mannequins dressed in 'period' costumes. And there is a final irony. The museum inhabits a reconverted space (the old General Stores or 'Magatzems Generals' of the Port) in that same Barceloneta where Bigas Luna situated Tete's family home, an area from which the working-class inhabitants nostalgically celebrated in *La teta i la lluna*'s Felliniesque street scenes were evicted in the urban developments preceding the Olympics of 1992. The smooth surfaces of the museum, both inside and out (so different to the distressed texture of the buildings in the film), signal the elimination of the trace of time from a location that seeks, nonetheless, to celebrate time and to promote national memory.

Of course many cities contain such virtual museums; and Barcelona itself boasts two recently redeveloped or opened institutions that a cultural critic could use to draw quite different conclusions about *catalanitat*: the Museu Nacional d'Art de Catalunya, high on Montjuïc, contains impressive collections of Romanesque and Gothic painting, including a large number of graphic 'Mothers of God of the Milk' that are clearly precedents for *La teta i la lluna*; and the high tech Museu d'Art Contemporani, an uncompromisingly modern structure inserted into the old heart of the city, is devoted to the international avant-garde. When set against the MHC's orderly succession of tableaux, however, Bigas Luna's disruptive time and disjunctive space (his juxtaposition of Roman legionary and petrol service station) promotes national consciousness with markedly greater pictorial vividness and sensual intensity. Certainly the film is truer than the museum to the dense and rich social texture that is produced by the interaction in Catalunya of historical process and place. For, as Pujol knows, it is in the superimposition of archaeological strata (the presence of the Iberian village beneath the contemporary town) that the cultural wealth of location is to be found.

Bigas Luna describes his Iberia in terms of this overload of sensual gratification: it is a place where 'you can order a coffee in a thousand different ways'.[32] Nationalists have also used the coffee metaphor, but to more ironic effect. A joke told at the time of the drafting of the Constitution which transformed Spain into the State of Self-Governing Areas or Autonomías tells of five customers in a café (Pujol, *Cataluña*, 48). One asks for black coffee with no sugar; the second for a small espresso with a little cold milk; the third for *café con leche* in a large cup, etc. After listening to their orders the waiter calls out 'Coffee all round!' ('¡Café para todos!'). The clients are, of course, the *autonomías*, the waiter is Madrid. The sensual diversity of the Peninsula (in which gastronomy serves as an index of the rich particularity of local space) is here frustrated by the boorish inflexibility of assimilationist central government. In such a context the urge towards the weakening of frontiers and the dissolution of borders will have differing effects according to the locality in which it is expressed. While Bigas Luna's 'Iberia' promotes a fantastic erasure of boundaries, even that which is longest legitimized by history (the frontier between Spain and Portugal), the narratives of the Iberian trilogy themselves suggest that the blessings of letting go or letting loose are at best mixed: *Jamón, jamón* ends in death and *Huevos de oro* in abject impotence. Even *La teta i la lluna*, more youthful and optimistic, ends (*pace* D'Lugo) not with Tete's 'psychic growth' but with his regressive return to the maternal breast. The final fantastic scene after Tete's successful return to the *castell* competition is of Estrellita ('the Queen of Stuttgart'), Maurice, and Miquel harmoniously chorusing Piaf in an unestablished European location. Tete, however, has no access to this scene; and as Estrellita returns once more to her box (under the scrolling of the final credits) it is unclear whether Tete has made the transition claimed for him by D'Lugo from phallic to feminine, and from regional chauvinism to global interface.

Bigas Luna himself did not achieve the expected success with this the final film of the trilogy. Official figures show that the number of spectators in the domestic market fell from 673,242 with *Jamón, jamón* to 204,879 with *La teta i la lluna*.[33] Given the similarity of the production team that worked on all three films (screenwriter Cuca Canals, cinematographer José Luis Alcaine, producer Andrés Vicente Gómez, and composer Nicola Piovani) it seems likely that it was the Catalan theme of *La teta i la lluna* that proved unattractive to a 'Spanish' audience. Certainly the fact that the film was shot in Catalan (albeit released in a Castilian version in Madrid) prevented the casting of bankable stars such as Javier Bardem and Penélope Cruz who had proved so attractive to audiences in the previous films. It had been the experience also of Catalan historians that there was

---

[32] *Iberian Portraits*, 5.
[33] Website of the Ministerio de Educación y Cultura.

no market for their product outside Catalunya itself. But in spite of the psychic failure of the protagonist and the commercial failure of the film, *La teta i la lluna* has much to offer the spectator. For if Catalunya is a nation without a state, then 'Spain' is perhaps a state without a nation. The visual brilliance of *La teta i la lluna*, no less than its disruption of filmic form and narration, testify to the third space in which a nation is caught between frames (between land and language) and in which locality is lived with uniquely sensual vividness and graphic intensity.

6 | Cross-Cut: City

1. The Production of Urban Space

Since Jane Jacobs's influential *The Death and Life of Great American Cities* of 1961, theorists have not ceased to predict the end of a specifically urban mode of experience. The loss of the centre and of sociality; the decline of density and festivity; the disappearance of the public sphere: these are the common coinage of a debate which sets the intricate and intimate 'sidewalk ballet' of Jacobs's Greenwich Village[1] against the social and spatial dislocations of Mike Davis's 'fortress LA'.[2] Any visit to a Spanish city in the 1980s or 1990s would appear to contradict such commonplaces. Relatively dense and sociable, still centred for the most part around historic cores, Spanish cities have also managed to repeat and to reinvent spatial practices of public celebration: from traditional *tertulias* and *paseos* to the modern *movida* (exported beyond Madrid to such unlikely sites as Vigo)[3] and the *ruta del bakalao* (the technoclubs of Valencia).[4]

The significance of the city, however, is not merely phenomenological, and cannot be reduced to the observation or the experience of such very visible practices.[5] Indeed professional Spanish urbanists writing on their own country have spoken, like their US counterparts, of the 'empty metropolis'[6] and the 'destruction of the city'.[7] Sociological sources of the

[1] *The Death and Life of Great American Cities* (London: Cape, 1962), 50. For Jacobs the uses of sidewalks include safety, contact, and 'assimilating children'. A selection is reprinted in Richard T. LeGates and Frederic Stout, *The City Reader* (London: Routledge, 1996), 103–8.

[2] *City of Quartz: Excavating the Future in Los Angeles* (London: Verso, 1990), 221–63. A selection is reproduced in LeGates and Stout, *The City Reader*, 158–63.

[3] José Luis Gallero, *Sólo se vive una vez: esplendor y ruina de la movida madrileña* (Madrid: Ardora, 1991), 79.

[4] John Hooper, *The New Spaniards* (Harmondsworth: Penguin, 1995), 208.

[5] Donald J. Olsen's *Town Planning in London* (New Haven: Yale University Press, 1982) is an excellent example of how invisible forces (in this case, the leasehold system of land tenure) shape the social and spatial practices of a metropolis.

[6] Antonio Fernández Alba, *La metrópoli vacía* (Barcelona: Anthropos, 1990).

[7] Antonio Fernández Alba and Carmen Gavira, *Crónica del espacio perdido: la destrucción de la ciudad en España* (Madrid: Ministerio de Obras Públicas y Urbanismo, 1986).

period tell a tale of alienation and polarization (due to unemployment, drugs, and AIDS); atomization and violence (most particularly the rise of racism); and the privatization of leisure and domestic space.[8] If, in a much quoted statistic, Spain boasts more bars than the rest of the European Union countries put together,[9] its population also tops the league for homeownership and is second only to the British in television viewing.[10] The Spanish city is thus not immune to the global 'flows' which have dislocated and evacuated urban life. It is symptomatic that the 'dream home' promoted in a recent Sunday supplement of *El País*[11] is not a glamourized version of the apartments in which the overwhelming majority of Spaniards live, but a free-standing 'chalet' in its own private plot, whose smooth maquette conceals the temporal and social implications of the lifestyle demanded by its architecture: the necessity of a lengthy commute to the workplace and the loss of the city street as a site of encounter. In spite of its architect's claims to ecological and climactic sensitivity (the ideal positioning of the house in relation to the sun; the recommendation of indigenous, water-efficient plants for the yard), *El País's* dream home embodies an abstraction of space, in which the purely architectonic is strictly isolated from any social geography.

In this chapter I treat this theme of the death of urban space by looking not at the work of Spanish town planners but, more obliquely, at emblematic figures from such fields as literature, art, architecture, and sociology. These figures are marginal in relation to both their respective disciplines and geographical locations: Juan Goytisolo (b. 1931) is a novelist and essayist, resident in Paris and Marrakesh; Santiago Calatrava (b. 1951) is an engineer and architect, who practises throughout Europe and has offices in Zurich, Paris, and Valencia; and Manuel Castells (b. 1942) is a sociologist and urban theorist, trained in Paris, who recently returned from the University of California at Berkeley to head the Institute of Sociology of New Technologies (IUSNT) at Madrid's Autonomous University. Antonio López (b. 1936) might appear to be the odd man out: trained as an artist in Madrid at the Real Academia de San Fernando, he has always been based in Spain. But, as we shall see, he has worked in a great variety of media (easel painting, drawing, and sculpture in bronze and painted wood); and his vision of the city is inflected by an ironic and critical provincialism. Licensed heretics and nomads, these

---

[8] The best-documented social survey is Carlos Alonso Zaldívar and Manuel Castells, *España, fin de siglo* (Madrid: Alianza, 1992). Discursive chapters on modernization, the economy, social inequality, regionalization, new technologies, and foreign relations are backed up by a full statistical analysis.

[9] See ibid. 17.

[10] Hooper, *The New Spaniards*, 282, 307.

[11] 'Una casa para soñar', special issue, *El País Semanal* (30 June 1996).

four figures (acknowledged leaders in their respected fields, even as they blur the boundaries of the conventional discipline) offer a privileged perspective on the urbanism of contemporary Spain, critically removed from both the professional concerns of town planners and the immediate personal experience of lifelong residents.

The analysis of multiple media requires a general theory of urbanism, which I take from a former teacher and colleague of Castells, Henri Lefebvre.[12] At this point a few brief axioms are sufficient to suggest the implications of Lefebvre's account of 'the production of space'. First, Lefebvre addresses a wide variety of cultural phenomena in their interconnection (art and architecture, literature and town planning) in a bid to remedy both the globalism and the fragmentation of late capitalism. Second, Lefebvre stresses both the necessary link between different spheres (the architectonic and the social) and the difficulty of moving between them (the mental and the physical conceptions of space). Finally, Lefebvre laments and contests that abstraction of space which we saw in *El País*'s 'dream home'; indeed he sees the evolution of the city, historically, as the violence of 'abstraction in action' (p. 269). Broadly speaking, then, Lefebvre rewrites Marx's history of political economy in spatial terms, tracing a new genealogy from the 'absolute' space of Antiquity and feudalism through the 'abstract' space of mercantile and bourgeois capitalism to the 'contradictory' and 'differential' spaces of the early and late twentieth century. It is important to stress, however, that for all its ambitions, Lefebvre's theory of the production of space is not systematic; rather it throws up multiple and overlapping analytical categories: from the dyads of 'dominated' and 'appropriated' space to the more characteristic triplets of 'spatial practice', 'representations of space', and 'representational spaces' (referring respectively to space as it is perceived, conceived, and lived).

The richness and complexity of Lefebvre's arguments may arise, as has recently been argued,[13] from a continuing but often implicit dialogue with other French theorists of the time. Thus against structuralism, psychoanalysis, and discourse analysis (Barthes, Lacan, and Foucault) Lefebvre argues for a return to the history and agency which he claims have been violently excluded from both the sanitized *mise en scène* of the Haussmanian city and the aridly linguistic intellectual territory of his theoretical

[12] Unless otherwise stated, all references to Lefebvre are to *The Production of Space* (Oxford: Blackwell, 1991; French original, 1974). I have also referred to the anthology edited by Eleonore Kofman and Elizabeth Lebas, *Writings on Cities* (Oxford: Blackwell, 1996).

[13] Kofman and Lebas argue throughout their introduction that Lefebvre has been improperly appropriated by English-speaking scholars ignorant of the French context of his work. Ironically they describe the Spanish Castells as a 'French Marxist urban sociologist' (*Writing on Cities*, 3).

rivals. Lefebvre does not, however, simply reinstate such Marxist fetishes as the working class as revolutionary agent. Rather he conceives space as a third term, beyond the philosophical binary of subject and object. Space is thus at once produced (by particular and economic causes) and productive (of specific, but unpredictable, social and subjective effects).

Perhaps the most pertinent of Lefebvre's conceptual tools for urban purposes is the distinction, always perilous and provisional, between work (*œuvre*) and product. Lefebvre writes that his approach:

tends to surpass separations and dissociations, notably those between the *work* (which is unique: an object bearing the stamp of a 'subject', of the creator or artist, and of a single, unrepeatable moment) and the *product* (which is repeatable: the result of repetitive gestures, hence reproducible, and capable ultimately of bringing about the automatic reproduction of social relationships). (p. 422)

Lefebvre's prime example here is Venice: a unique site of artistic creation (a work), inconceivable without those technological and mercantile practices (the repeatable gestures of the product) without which it could never have come into existence (pp. 73–4). What I shall argue is that the cultural object, like the city which it represents, is also at once work and product, both bearing the single stamp of a subject or creator and giving rise to automatized social reproduction.

The themes treated by my Spanish nomads are those of US urbanists and of Lefebvre: the loss of sociality and monumentality; the irruption of violence and the body; the uncanny persistence of reference to nature and history. But they also confront a theme only glimpsed by Lefebvre in an earlier period: the progressive disappearance or dematerialization of both subject and object, citizen and city. All four figures thus confront us with the death of urbanism, prophesied by Jacobs; but they do so with quite different emphases. Moving from work to product, Goytisolo and López contrast the uniqueness of high art and urban experience with the impossibility of aesthetics and the desolation of the city; moving from product to work, Calatrava and Castells propose, implicitly or explicitly, a remedy to the ravages of mechanical reproduction in the reconstruction of a new, lighter monumentality and a new community of social meaning in the dislocated space of flows. As we shall see, the dead city may thus be revitalized by the very technological means which have abolished its sense of history and demolished its sense of place.

2. The Evacuated City: Juan Goytisolo and Antonio López

The title of Juan Goytisolo's experimental novel of 1982, *Paisajes después de la batalla* ('Landscapes after the Battle'),[14] announces from the very beginning its apocalyptic theme: the death and life of the global city. However it also suggests the relation between space and representation (landscape) and violence and history (the battle). Moreover *Paisajes'* vision of a dystopian Paris anticipates both the future of Spanish metropolises, which would only later become subject to a substantial flow of immigration, and the internationalization of Spanish narrative in the coming decade, the increasing appeal to rootless or nomadic characters and settings by younger novelists such as Javier Marías and Soledad Puértolas. Goytisolo's position is thus at once marginal and symptomatic, pointing forward to emerging trends even as he holds himself rigorously aloof from contemporary Spain.

Paisajes consists of fragments whose setting alternates apparently at random between the chaotic street scenes of Le Sentier and the hermetic garret of its anonymous narrator. Thus the first fragment 'Hecatomb' (or 'sacrifice') stages what Lefebvre calls an urban 'moment': a 'point of rupture . . . somehow revelatory of the totality of possibilities contained in daily existence'.[15] To the consternation of its indigenous residents (the 'drinkers of Calvados'), the neighbourhood is progressively 'invaded' by unintelligible graffiti until one morning residents awake to find all the familiar street signs ('Rex', 'McDonald's', 'L'Humanité') have been replaced by others written in Arabic script (p. 46). A dark-haired, laughing youth offers himself as a guide to the confounded French inhabitants of the transformed metropolis (p. 48). From the ground zero of this 'catastrophe', the perspective shifts in the second fragment to the 'suspicious character's' eyrie above the urban chaos of which (we are told) he is the instigator. We are treated to a cityscape from his perspective: over grey slate roofs to the ornamental dome of the Opéra and the high tech towers of the Défense. Indifferent to this spectacle, the solitary citizen busies himself with the care of his body: filing his nails and peeing in the sink (p. 50).

What *Paisajes* savours above all is the sociality of the street: the 'texture' (p. 43) of the neighbourhood is described in terms of taste: it is a 'cake' composed of successive layers of immigration: Jews, Spaniards, Turks, Arabs, and Bengalis (pp. 53–4). Unplanned geographically, the neigh-

---

[14] My edn. (Madrid: Espasa-Calpe, 1990).
[15] The quotation is from David Harvey's 'Afterword' to *The Production of Space*, 425–32 (p. 429).

bourhood is also overdetermined temporally, an 'urban palimpsest' (p. 108) characterized by inscription and erasure: the violence of repeated movements and gestures, the abolition of the divide between private and public (p. 108). More of a sidewalk scrum than a ballet, here the physical encounter recreates a social 'fabric' (p. 113) in which there can be no secrecy or privacy. The density and complexity of this fabric (composed of 'smells, colours, gestures, a halo of menacing proximity'; p. 147) marks the new permeability of both city and nation, when 'Africa begins in the boulevards' (p. 203) and space is no longer a rigid grid, but a spontaneous 'fold'. The map of this 'future, bastard city' is also the plan of the protagonist's life, the 'megalopolis' his 'Byzantium', a revenge on the ordered classicism of the Franco-Roman empire.

The opening graffiti thus mark, in Lefebvre's terms, the triumph of appropriated space over dominated space. But the renaissance of sociality is also the decline of monumentality. The spatial ambitions of the bird's eye or 'world' view of the capital, described indifferently yet obsessively by the narrator, are repeatedly undermined: the narrator contrasts his vital 'territory' of Belleville and the Goutte d'Or to the tourist quarter of the Palais Royal and the Place de la Concorde, rigorously designed to exclude 'disorder' (pp. 104, 204). His 'temple of the Muses' is not the despised Opéra, but a public lavatory decorated, once more, with the gestural palimpsest of graffiti (p. 125). The grandiose 'perspectives' of Bourbon and Napoleonic Paris are dismissed as 'cardboard',[16] the 'neutralization' of 'space in movement' (p. 146); and drawing a connection between urbanist and philosophical representations of space typical of Lefebvre also, the narrator calls Haussman's ordered perspectives 'Cartesian' (p. 188). Beneath the oppressive weight of the Arc de Triomphe lies (in the narrator's fantasy) the corpse of an Unknown Soldier of African origin (p. 154): the reverse of the monument is the unspeakable violence of colonial racism, a violence at once expressed and concealed by the abstraction of space imposed by the imperial metropolis on all of its subjects, both near and far.

But if the narrator proposes a new model of the city as a living body (a representational space) which pushes him 'through its veins and arteries [with its] incessant rhythm' (p. 187), then abstract representations of space still hold their attractions for him. Thus he confesses his 'addiction' to the metro map (p. 75) whose 'spatial simultaneity' makes him forget the 'narrow, one-way street of time' (p. 134). This nostalgia for a geometric order dismissed elsewhere (by both Goytisolo and Lefebvre) as the alibi

[16] In an essay lamenting the intellectual and social 'void' of Paris in the 1980s, Goytisolo uses the same image to describe the emptying of the monumental city; see 'París, ¿capital del siglo XXI?', in *El bosque de las letras* (Madrid: Alfaguara, 1995), 177–90 (p. 179).

of statist violence is complemented by an ambiguous attitude to the unmediated sociality and unsynthesized difference hymned at the start of the novel. Thus the urban spaces once dedicated to social interaction (cafés and parks) are now given over to silent *tertulias* and abortive attempts to seduce underage girls (pp. 91, 99); and the atomization of politics gives rise to random urban violence: the terrorist *otekas*, protesting against centuries of oppression, push randomly chosen citizens under metro trains (p. 62); or again, the narrator is inexplicably held hostage by a group calling themselves the 'Red Queers' ('los maricas rojos'; p. 215).[17] As Lefebvre argues, in contradictory space the loss of the monument leads inevitably to violence: 'inasmuch as sites, forms, and functions are no longer focussed and appropriated by monuments, the city's contexture or fabric . . . unravel . . . Indeed space as a whole becomes prone to sudden eruptions of violence' (*The Production of Space*, 223). If the 'world view' was oppressive (with the city, as Lefebvre puts it, 'putting itself in perspective, like a battlefield'; p. 273), then it is not clear that this atomized violence is an improvement on the global abstraction of terror which preceded it.

For all its love of difference, then, *Paisajes* fails to recognize a vital paradox of the modern metropolis. This is the interdependence of representations of space and representational spaces; that is, space as it is conceived and as it is lived. The narrator's critique of the spatial discipline of modernity (of the dead hand of French rationalism) is combined with an archaic and incompatible view of the city as an image of the world. In Lefebvre's words: 'The way citizens [of ancient Rome] "thought" their city was not as one space amongst others but . . . as their representation of space as a whole, of the centre of the world. Within the city, on the other hand, representational spaces could develop [as] the order of the world spatially embodied and portrayed in the city' (*The Production of Space*, 244). Goytisolo's narrator takes this identification of the city as *imago mundi* a stage further, arguing in his contempt for the country that only the city contains the idea of space and that 'nature is formless' (*Paisajes*, 75).

The problem is that (as *Paisajes* itself clearly shows) by the 1980s the city was less a world than the world was a city: the global market had long since erased the borders between town and country, between one nation and another. Paradoxically, then, *Paisajes* is dependent on the preservation of

---

[17] As Brad Epps notes of this passage's twin attack on communism and gay liberation, '[Goytisolo] remains unambiguous in his celebration of ambiguity and all but univocal in his praise of polyvocality'; *Significant Violence: Oppression and Resistance in the Narratives of Juan Goytisolo* (Oxford: Oxford University Press, 1996), 375–6. It is an ideological contradiction similar to that between Goytisolo's twin incompatible models of the metropolis.

boundaries to integrate a formless space (that of the city and of the novel), a space that is repeatedly fractured and evacuated by its own narrative. In its nostalgia for the *imago mundi Paisajes* is thus indifferent to the true spatial scandal of the period in which the novel was written: the expulsion of ethnic minorities beyond the beltway or *periphérique*, spatially and socially distant from the impoverished but vibrant inner city celebrated by Goytisolo. And having abolished the grand history of the metropolitan monument, the text also erases the little narratives of its nameless immigrant heroes: African and Arabs, glimpsed in subway corridors or squalid lodgings, are returned through their music and magic (tom-toms and clairvoyance) to a utopian, premodern space: the rural village (pp. 65, 88). Such rhythmic, bodily gestures, however, cannot replace the technical abstractions of the West even as they inscribe themselves over them: finally, graffiti can be no match for the metro map.

A late fragment of *Paisajes* portrays a nameless catastrophe: an empty city without traffic, its citizens sheltering at home (p. 228); a vast perspective of empty streets, barred gates, deserted buildings, wrapped in dense and threatening silence (pp. 230–1). It is the 'City of the Dead' in which the 'tyranny of time' is ended (p. 233). There is, however, a disturbing homology between the city and the novel. For the fragmentation of the urban tribes is echoed in Goytisolo's narrative form of fragments which also resist integration; the impersonality of the city is reinforced by Goytisolo's refusal to grant his fictional characters names; and, finally, the expulsion of time from city space effected by town planners and terrorists alike is reinforced by the novelist who revels in the destruction of ancient monuments, but can offer no alternative reinscription of temporal forms into space.[18] The avant-garde form of Goytisolo's novel (its fragmentation and aestheticization of character, plot, and theme) thus implicitly proclaims the end of both the novel and the city as 'works', unique and unrepeatable creations of a privileged subject (author or urbanist). As a product of the urban condition it seeks to explore, *Paisajes* thus rejects the tyranny of totality, whether subjective or objective, but only at the cost of deadly dispersion. In Lefebvre's resonant image of the city, the novel is 'like a fist clenched around sand' (p. 320).

In 1985 Goytisolo was awarded the Europalia Prize for his collected works, the same year that Antonio López exhibited as the Spanish representative

---

[18] As Randolph D. Pope notes, one 'momentous event in historical reality' (the failed coup or 'Tejerazo' of 23 Feb. 1981) is noted and parodied in the novel: 'the postmodern celebration of fragmentation is tempered with the suspicion that . . . individuals never cease to be dependent on vast forces beyond their control'; *Understanding Juan Goytisolo* (Columbia: University of South Carolina Press, 1995), 138. I would argue, however, that *Paisajes* remains unable to integrate historicity and fragmentation.

at the Brussels art show which bears the same name. Just as the translation of *Paisajes* had been acclaimed abroad as 'the voice of a new Spain',[19] so López's artworks were one of the means through which Socialist Spain represented itself to Europe and to itself. Moreover just as Goytisolo the exile had previously been relatively neglected in his place of birth, so López the native son had not hitherto been promoted abroad by a Spanish government which had since Franco exported local avant-garde art (from abstraction to conceptualism) as testimony to its own fragile modernity.[20] While López's anachronistic representation of space (the meticulous academic virtuosity often branded 'hyperreal'[21]) could hardly be further from the experimental technique of a Goytisolo, both share an allegiance to the high work of art or *œuvre* which is extremely marketable abroad.

Like *Paisajes*, López's urban artworks shift between the public and the private sphere: from monumental exteriors or cityscapes (Plate 9) to intimate interiors or still lifes. Let us begin with the former, which constitute perhaps his best-known works. *Madrid* (1974–82)[22] is an aerial view of a wide, empty boulevard lined by dull, blank façades. No distinctive historical or modern landmarks are visible. A digital clock above one building reads '21.40'. *South Madrid* (1965–85)[23] is also an aerial panorama or 'world view': brown and grey roofs recede to a flat, hazy horizon. Two-thirds of the canvas are devoted to an opaque, dully luminescent sky. Once more no landmarks are visible: no mountains on the horizon and no distinctive buildings in this unfashionable part of the city. Only a railway line bisects the picture from left to right, shadowing the picture frame. Finally, the celebrated *Gran Vía* (1974–81)[24] takes up a low

---

[19] H. Eyres, 'Modern Spain Finds a Voice', *The Times* (London) (14 Oct. 1989).

[20] Edward J. Sullivan, 'Deserted Streets and Silent Rooms: Contemporary Spanish Realists', in *Contemporary Spanish Realists* (London: Marlborough Fine Art, June–Aug. 1996), 2–8 (p. 4). While Sullivan is clearly anxious to promote the figurative artists showing in this exhibition, his claim that the Spanish government continues to export avant-garde styles which are easily digested abroad is borne out by the official catalogue for the exhibition in the Spanish Pavilion of the Seville Expo which, with the exception of López himself, is overwhelmingly dedicated to conceptual and minimal artists; see *Pasajes: Spanish Art Today* (Seville: World's Fair, 20 Apr.-12 Oct. 1992).

[21] Francisco Nieva denies López is a hyperrealist, claiming rather that he is 'Baroque', concerned with the fugitive nature of time, the presence of death, and the cruelty of the objective; 'Introduction', *Antonio López García: Paintings, Sculptures, and Drawings, 1965–86* (London: Marlborough Fine Art, 9–31 May 1986), 4–5 (p. 4). Nieva is one of those who detects 'provincialism' in López's 'sullen, ironical, harsh, and distant urban landscape' (p. 5).

[22] No. 8 (pp. 36–7) in the 1986 Marlborough exhibition and catalogue.

[23] No. 10 (p. 20).

[24] No. 7 (p. 27). Contrast López's deserted street with Rosa Montero's description of the Gran Vía as a great urban highway, dense with people and traffic, the very image of the multiplicity and simultaneity of contemporary urban life; 'La vida caótica', *El País Semanal* (17 Nov. 1996), 12.

1. Fernando Fernán Gómez (Fernando, far right) in Víctor Erice, *El espíritu de la colmena* ('The Spirit of the Beehive', 1973)

2. Ana Torrent (Ana, left) and Isobel Tellería (Isabel) in *El espíritu de la colmena*

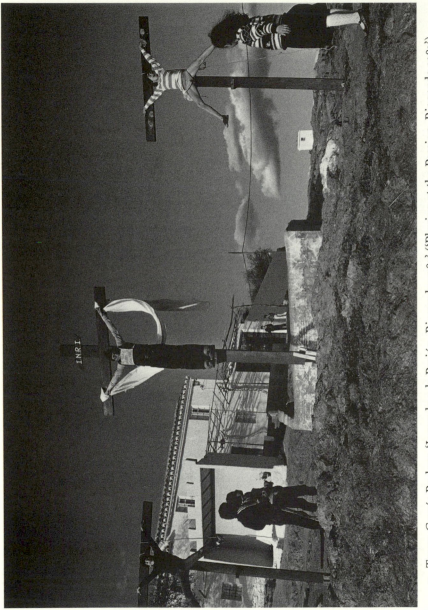

3. Teresa García Rodero, 'Jugando a la Pasión, Riogordo 1983' ('Playing at the Passion, Riogordo 1983')

4. Rafael Moneo, Airport, Seville (1987–91)

5. Rafael Moneo. National Museum of Roman Art, Mérida (1980–6)

6. La Cubana, *Cegada de amor* ('Blinded by Love', 1994)

7. Mathilda May (Estrellita) in Bigas Luna, *La teta i la lluna* ('The Tit and the Moon', 1994)

8. Biel Durán (Tete) in *La teta i la lluna*

9. Antonio López García, 'Madrid visto desde Capitán Haya' ('Madrid seen from Capitán Haya', 1987)

10. Santiago Calatrava, Bach de Roda Bridge, Barcelona (1985–7)

11. Emma Suárez (Ángela) and Carmelo Gómez (Angel) in Julio Medem, *Tierra* (1995)

12. Silke (Mari) and Juan José Suárez (Manuel) in *Tierra*

13. Laura del Sol (Carmen) and Antonio Gades (Antonio) in Carlos Saura, *Carmen* (1983)

14. Antonio (Pedro Alonso) and Lucía (Amara Carmona) in Chus Gutiérrez, *Alma gitana* ('Gypsy Soul', 1996)

point of view in the middle of the deserted street. From this perspective what was once the most glamorous boulevard in the metropolis (the life-line of the entertainment district) looks dusty, drab, and provincial, its grandest building, the great tower of the Telefónica, partially obscured in the distance. The shops are shuttered, their signs ironically offering absent consumers the promise of Parisian luxury: 'Crassy', 'Piaget', 'Baume et Mercier'. Once more a digital clock is frozen: at 06.30, precisely.

As art critics have noted, there is an implicitly ironic contrast here between the monumentality of the size and format of these oil paintings (the largest measuring some 96 inches or 244 cm across) and the banality of their subject matter.[25] The anonymity of the first scene, the wilful perversity of the second (any direction other than the south would have resulted in a more picturesque panorama), and the deadpan satire on metropolitan pretensions in the third, each of these suggests a divorce between the conception and the experience of urban life, between the lovingly or jealously preserved Renaissance representation of space (of the perspective of façades, of the vanishing point, of planes receding to the horizon) and representational spaces which can no longer support such grandiose ambitions. For López's cityscapes are wholly uninhabited. What remains unclear at this point is whether López's dogged academi-cism constitutes a conservative reaction to the dislocations of modernity (of the modern art and the modern city) or an ironic repetition of those same dislocations (a parody of that desocialization or dematerialization which artists and urbanists have so frequently deplored).

The evacuation of the city thus makes visible the hidden violence of abstract space: in painting, in urbanism, and even in economics. As Lefebvre puts it: 'The fact of viewing from afar, of *contemplating* what has been torn apart, of arranging "viewpoints" and "perspectives" can . . . change the effects of a strategy into aesthetic objects' (*The Production of Space*, 318). If we choose to read López's monumentalism as social critique (and so it was read in the last years of the Francoist dictatorship), then these paintings could be viewed, in Lefebvre's words once more, as a demonstration of 'the illusory clarity of space . . . the illusory clarity of a power that may be glimpsed in the reality that it governs, but which at the same time uses that reality as a veil' (pp. 320–1).

That privileged insight into the texture of everyday urban life 'behind the veil' recurs in López's equally uncanny and unpopulated interiors, which are treated once more with the false but diagnostic transparency of the academic draughtsman. For if civic monumentality is (as in Goytisolo) destroyed, then urban domesticity is similarly dissolved or

---

[25] Nieva notes a further irony: López's 'immense anachronistic purpose' of 'objectify[ing] reality as if photography . . . were not yet in existence' (*Antonio López García*, 4).

dissipated (as in Goytisolo once more). For López's interiors depict not so much dwellings as housing. The early oil painting *Washbasin and Mirror* (1967)[26] registers in microscopic detail the toothbrush, tweezers, and scissors, the razor, brush, and shaving stick left on a bathroom shelf. But the mirror above the objects (the viewpoint of the top half of the picture) reveals no reflection. Similarly the oil painting *Toilet Bowl and Window* (1967–71)[27] reproduces the cracked and stained tiles and the brush poised against the wall in the corner, but these tools and traces of habitation are independent of any human body or subject. Finally the pencil drawing *Remainders from a Meal* (1971)[28] shows a table from an invisible diner's point of view: three plates recede from the picture plane on a soiled white tablecloth; indistinct remnants of food persist on the nearest, on which an upturned spoon also leans. Mimicking that most symbolic social practice of the meal, López depicts the aftermath of eating as a battlefield, strewn with random traces left by absent bodies and completed gestures.

Hence the importance of tools (of razors and spoons) in López and in Lefebvre. For the latter, tools are 'separate from nature . . . but extensions of the body and its rhythms' (*The Production of Space*, 213). Being closely bound up with 'gestural systems' they serve to 'connect representations of space to representational spaces' in places of residence (p. 215). 'Organized gestures', Lefebvre continues, 'are not simply performed in "physical" space [rather] bodies themselves generate spaces which are produced by and for their gestures' (p. 216). Hence, just as in his urban exteriors López divorces the city from the citizen, so in his domestic interiors he separates the tool from the gesture, the gesture from the body, and the body in turn from the space which produces and is produced by it. The invisible violence of abstract space thus substitutes for gestural spatial practice in the home, as in the city.

But one technique in these early interiors which is not shared by the later urban panoramas is worth stressing here. This is the interiors' lack of consistent point of view. Thus in the twin bathroom oil paintings the top half of the picture (the mirror or window) is seen from straight on, while the bottom half of the picture (the basin or toilet bowl) is seen from above. There is thus a horizontal fracture in the perspective, reinforced by the consequent break in the regular rhythm of the wall tiles. In these pictures, López calls attention to the false transparency of abstract space by introducing into that space a visual analogue of those contradictions which are for Lefebvre inseparable from late modernity. In Lefebvre's words: 'The evanescent space of images and signs does not . . . manage to attain consistency. . . . It even seems at times that this world is about to disappear . . . into some cleft that, with just a little widening, would swallow it up' (pp.

[26] No. 2 (p. 14).   [27] No. 3 (p. 15).   [28] No. 20 (p. 26).

389–90). López's breach in perspective is just such a cleft, one which seems already to have engulfed the phantom family at his dinner table, like the ghostly pedestrians of his Gran Vía.

But central to López's academic training is life drawing. And the human body does indeed appear in his work. *Man and Woman*, an unfinished sculpture in painted wood (1968–86),[29] consists of two disconnected and life-size naked figures in frontal pose and gaze, their arms hanging limply at their sides. The flaky texture of the paint mimics the trace of time in ageing skin. Or again in a series of life-size pencil drawings of male nudes from the mid-1980s, younger figures adopt the same frontal pose.[30] The only semblance of gesture is that while some are equally balanced on both feet (like archaic *kouroi*), others are slightly animated by the shifting of weight onto one leg (like classical athletes). The vacuous monumentality of the city is here reassigned to the idealized male figure, whose anonymity is reinforced by teasingly abbreviated names ('J. Enrique', 'L. Fernando') and by vestigially sketched or even absent heads (as opposed to generously detailed and proportioned thighs, torsos, and genitals). But if the figures are abstracted, then the space they inhabit is not rendered at all. Just as the city is without citizens, so the citizen is without a city: deprived of those clothes, tools, or residence which render him human. The body in the void thus hints at the possibility of the body as void: as empty as the receding plains of south Madrid, sketched with equally ironic precision. For Lefebvre, 'the enigma of the body . . . is its ability to produce differences out of repetitions—out of gestures (linear) or out of rhythms (cyclical)' (p. 395). It is this paradoxical productivity of the repetitive and the differential which is erased by López's life studies and cityscapes, whose abstraction intensifies the conflict between the conceived and the lived which is so violently performed by the city. Deprived of both gesture and rhythm, López's nudes are unable to produce difference out of repetition, unable to integrate conception and experience.

The reinventor of cityscape and life study, López is also a master of a traditional Spanish genre, the still life. In repeated pencil works of the 1980s minute draughtsmanship gives back to nature the monumentality of which the city has been stripped: iconic quinces (consecrated by Víctor Erice's film)[31] and massive pumpkins are stripped of their organic origin and lent architectonic form and volume.[32] But once more, this academic petrification of the real can be read as critique, as much as celebration. For the function of López's fruit and vegetables (one incompatible with the

[29] No. 15 (pp. 10–11).

[30] Nos. 8–11 (pp. 20–1) in the *Contemporary Spanish Realists* exhibition and catalogue.

[31] *El sol del membrillo* (UK title 'The Quince Tree Sun'; US title 'Dream of Light'), 1992.

[32] Nos. 5–6 (pp. 17–18) in *Contemporary Spanish Realists*.

loving intensity with which they are delineated) is, in Lefebvre's words, simply to '[be] in space and [to occupy] a location' (p. 341). Rather than objects they are commodities:

The commodity asks for nothing better than to *appear*. . . . Self-exhibition is its forte. . . . And yet, once it has appeared, its mystery only deepens. . . . The commodity does not answer questions, it is simply *there*, exposed to the gaze of passers-by. (p. 340)

Like Lefebvre's commodities, López's painted objects occupy a contradictory space of 'homogeneity made up of specificities' (p. 341). In other words, the imposition of violent abstraction (of universal exchange value in economics, of unitary perspective in art) erases but does not abolish the material particularity of the object. Just as the empty city remains a unique and unrepeatable work (*œuvre*) even as its desolation pays witness to the horrors of the production process that has destroyed it, so the monumental quince or pumpkin testify mutely and obliquely to the fact that the commodity is both an abstraction and '*qua* "thing" it is endowed with a terrible, almost deadly power' (p. 342). In a pencil drawing of 1988 (*Antonio López García*, no. 5, p. 17) the organic profusion of the vegetables is juxtaposed with a recurrent motif: the skinned head of a rabbit, raw and abject as an aborted foetus.

It might be excessive to read López's artworks as testimony to that Marxian commodification and alienation in which, as Lefebvre puts it, 'what is dead takes hold of what is alive' (p. 348). It remains the case, however, that critics of the 1970s did read such pictures as 'testimony to the conditions of [man's] life and labour';[33] and that López's practice over some thirty years reveals an irrevocable cleft or rift between subject and object: for the two are rarely depicted together within the space which they have jointly produced through gesture, ritual, and residence.[34] The last moral of López's evacuated metropolis is (like Goytisolo's 'city of the dead') that citizen and city are mutually constituting, even as the relentless

[33] Raúl Chávarri, *La pintura española actual* (Madrid: Ibérico Europeo, 1973), 79. Chávarri places López between the twin trends of 'social testimony' and 'avant-garde realism', claiming López and similar artists are dedicated to 'their personal vision of social problems' (p. 66). Juan Antonio Gaya Nuño praises the hidden meanings ('intención') behind López's ironic provincialism ('catetismo'); *La pintura española del siglo XX* (Madrid: Ibérico Europeo, 1972), 430.

[34] Compare the oil paintings of equally uninhabited shuttered shops and graffitied façades by fellow 'Madrid realist' Amalia Avia; *Contemporary Spanish Realists*, nos. 1–2 (pp. 11–12). The depopulation of these Spanish cityscapes contrasts with the bustling Boulevard Saint Michel and busy Fifth Avenue of another Marlborough artist, Raymond Mason; see the ink drawings in *Works on Paper by Contemporary Artists* (London: Marlborough Fine Art, Mar.– Apr. 1988), 30–1. López exhibited two pencil drawings of quinces and pomegranates in this show.

logic of exchange value eliminates the use value of festivity on which the economy and geography of the city were first founded.[35]

The final irony, then, is that the López who is celebrated as the master of the 'Madrid school' of realists and is marketed as such to wealthy buyers in the global cities of New York, London, and Tokyo,[36] the López who is a uniquely skilled figurative artist is also a master of 'abstraction' in Lefebvre's sense, in that his art evacuates time (as movement, duration, or historical change) from urban space. The ironic arresting of the digital clocks so prominent in the cityscapes points up the absence of some twenty tumultuous years of Spanish history: the period during which López worked on his 'world views'. López's reinvention of the heroic and monumental mission of the artist (his vain ambition to capture the totality of the real) points inevitably and anachronistically to the work, even *chef-d'œuvre*, that even in its unfinished state remains haloed by the aura of the artist's touch. However the expulsion of time from López's Madrid (as from Goytisolo's Paris) betrays in spite of itself the violent abstractions and repetitions through which the product is produced and in which the producer of art is necessarily complicit.

3. Healing the Urban Wound: Santiago Calatrava and Manuel Castells

In the mid-1980s and early 1990s Zurich-based engineer-architect Santiago Calatrava designed some of the most spectacular structures in Spain. From his signature bridges in Mérida, Seville, and Ripoll to the Montjuïc Communications Tower at the Olympic site in Barcelona and the project for a massive Science Museum in Valencia, Calatrava's designs are at once recognizably his and unique to their site. Exploiting what Lefebvre has called the 'uncomfortable position' of the architect, caught between the demands of the client and his own imagination (*The Production of Space*, 396), Calatrava has bridged the gap between repetition and difference, knowledge and creativity, product and work. One recognition of his official status and popularity was a record-breaking one-man show at the Royal Institute of British Architects in London in the *annus mirabilis* of 1992, sponsored significantly by the Valencian regional government in collaboration with the British Cement Association.

Calatrava has thus been conspicuously successful in what Lefebvre calls the 'trial by space' through which a designer's ideas are tested by the tricky transition into 'morphology' (p. 416). Moreover the modernity of his

---

[35] For the city as work, use value, and festivity, see Lefebvre, *Writings on Cities*, 66.

[36] Marlborough has galleries in each of these cities, as well as in Madrid and Santiago de Chile.

design (its unapologetic exploitation of the most recent building technologies) is echoed by the novelty of Calatrava's professional position: a 'new
internationalist or European' or 'universal designer [whose] practice is
sustained by international competition and by the international technical
press'.[37] Yet if there is no doubt as to the scale of his achievement, there is
some controversy as to its nature. While architectural scholars agree that
his work is synthetic or dialectical (fusing architecture and engineering)
and frequently draw on Calatrava's structural vocabulary for their own
conceptual framework (lending their essays such titles as 'Crossing
Boundaries' and 'Bridging the Gap'),[38] they disagree radically as to the
relation of that synthesis and innovation to urbanism and a sense of place.
Thus while one critic proclaims Calatrava's indifference to the city core
and attraction to the 'no man's land' of the urban/rural periphery (pp.
18–19), another states unambiguously that Calatrava is a 'place-maker',
citing his Bach de Roda bridge (1985) (Plate 10) in a reclaimed sector of
Barcelona (p. 26);[39] and while one claims that Calatrava's designs have
'nothing to do with the organic' (p. 22) another writes that Calatrava's 'eye
for the curve' echoes the nature that abhors straight lines (p. 25). Finally
one critic maintains Calatrava is indifferent to the 'context' of the urban
site, devoted rather to its 'dynamic development' (p. 16); another writes
that Calatrava does indeed respect context: 'Calatrava's buildings don't
impose on a cityscape. They are respectful of the fact that the world was
there first. They don't fill space, they give it meaning' (p. 28).

Calatrava is typically reticent and oblique when asked to verbalize his
intentions. But critics have offered varied readings of his interventions
into urban space. Thus writing of Calatrava's fragmentary restoration of
Lucerne Station after it was destroyed by fire (Calatrava left what had been
the entrance to the old building isolated as a new Triumphal Arch, disconnected from the new station), Bernhard Klein writes that in the era of
the Nebulous City, 'Calatrava's buildings correct an underdeveloped or
failed social space by the architectonic means of real or virtual connection'
(p. 16). Contrary to the monumental appearance of its Arch, the station,
he claims, is an 'anti-place'. But that negativity is the only honest response
to the erosion of city space that has already occurred: Calatrava's 'subjectivity of feeling about mechanical principles' lends a 'possibility of over-

[37] Dennis Sharp, 'Santiago Calatrava: Building Cultural Bridges', in his edited volume
Santiago Calatrava, 2nd edn. (London: E. and F. N. Spon, 1994), 8–13 (p. 10). All references
to Calatrava follow this volume, which includes essays by Bernhard Klein, 'Santiago Calatrava and the Nebulous City' (pp. 14–23); and Anthony Tischhauser, 'Santiago Calatrava: An
Eye for the Curve' (pp. 24–9).

[38] Sharp gives a selected bibliography, ibid. 94–5.

[39] For the Bach de Roda bridge as 'creator of urban spaces', see also Xavier Güell (ed.),
Spanish Contemporary Architecture: The Eighties (Barcelona: Gustavo Gili, 1990), 52.

coming the urban grievance' in its implicit move from the individual to the collective (p. 23). Such a collectivity has nothing to do with the senti-mental or commercially motivated attempts by conservationists or developers to restore the so-called 'heart' of the city. Calatrava thus participates in a new production of urban space which aims to reconstruct lost social meaning, but without nostalgic recreation of the past.

Central to this reconstruction and renovation of social meaning is a new vision of the monument. The Bach de Roda bridge is at once func-tional (establishing a connection over a railway line and from the interior to the sea) and aesthetic (its great arches serving, in the words of one critic, to 'achieve the status of dominant landmark in its setting in the urban landscape').[40] But this monumentality is also lightened or weakened in the service of the citizen: ample pedestrian walkways, distinctively separated from traffic flow, swell into central cantilevered protuberances offering a view of the newly created park: ambiguous floating spaces ('hanging piazzas'), suspended above and in the urban site. For Klein, once more, this architectonic form represents a 'new kind of monumentality' partly in response to grass-roots campaigners such as Jane Jacobs (p. 17), one more suited to a 'post-industrial society' in which the intricacy of the Beaux Arts façade yields to an 'overall view of urban reality' (p. 17). Where nineteenth-century monumentalism was reactionary and nationalist, the dynamic structural form of Calatrava's bridges (the reliance of massive structure on thin tensioned cable) proves that monumentalism can serve, to the contrary, as 'an expression of social change' (pp. 21–2).

In the new monument, then, material, form, and function (steel, curve, and traffic flow) are held, dialectically, in tension, a dynamic equilibrium which rhymes with the strains of the urban site, caught as it is between technology and history. Thus the massive steel arch (spanning 189 metres) of the Lusitania bridge in Mérida (1988), strung with delicate cables, at once repeats and reverses the curves of the Roman bridge upstream. The La Devesa bridge in Ripoll (1989) also employs a steel arch from which the wooden walkway is cantilevered, but this time tilted or pivoted to one side. Finally, and most dramatically, the Alamillo bridge in Seville (1987–92) is supported by thirteen pairs of cables strung from a single massive concrete pylon 142 metres high and inclined at a gravity-defying angle of 58 degrees: a giant harp joining historic Seville to the northern fringe of the Expo site La Cartuja. In such landmark structures the unique and unrepeatable aura of the work is married to the production brief of the public client. Sensitive to the topography of the site, yet refusing to blend in with the existing urban context, Calatrava's bridges seek to 'recover the whole' of city experience by expressing the 'quality of

[40] See ibid. 52.

the individual object' (p. 23). Calatrava thus avoids what Lefebvre calls the 'urbanism of maquettes and overall plans', the 'fake lucidity . . . presiding over the spectacle, and forging the unity into which all the programmed fragments must be integrated, no matter what the cost' (*The Production of Space*, 318). For although he is famous for the translucent beauty of his models (constructed by a Swiss colleague), Calatrava resists the tyranny of abstract space by reinscribing difference into repetition, in both the characteristic asymmetry of structures such as the Alamillo bridge and the family resemblance of his projects, which are similar enough to be the work of a single creator and diverse enough to respond to multiple commissions and competitions.

The restoration of sociality to the city (the overcoming of urban grievance) is thus inseparable from a lightened or weakened monumentality which tends towards tension, movement, and festivity. The Calatrava whose doctoral thesis was on 'The Foldability of Space Frames' (*Santiago Calatrava*, 9) is also the Calatrava who perceives structure as arrested or contained movement, the unfolding of a flow. The utopian end of such a tendency is an ephemeral, kinetic architecture: the unbuilt project for a floating platform in the form of a flower in Lake Lucerne (1989) or the delicate concrete ribs of the Kuwaiti Pavilion at the Seville Expo, hydraulically raised or lowered according to atmospheric conditions, and compared by critics to both 'scimitars' and 'a prehistoric skeleton' (p. 66).

The anatomical reference is apt. For, integrating high technology and aesthetics, Calatrava cites bodily forms even as his work takes modern materials to their technical limits. Calatrava has filled notebooks with life drawings, reminiscent of Leonardo and Michelangelo; and, spurning computer design, he begins always with anachronistic, even archaic, freehand drawings of his projects, drawings which are intertwined with organic forms: the curve of an eyelid or the interconnection of vertebrae. Calatrava's sculptures analyse and abstract the 'equilibrium in the human body . . . figures in tension . . . the gesture of the hand unfolded [as] movement drawn out into form' (p. 29); his projects and plans have been exhibited alongside the whitened skeleton of a dog. Prestigious public projects for Spanish cities such as Sondica Airport in Bilbao or the Concert Hall intended to reclaim the harbour area of Santa Cruz, Tenerife (both 1990), are compared to 'huge bird[s] poised in flight' (pp. 55, 71). Apparently evacuating massive structures, Calatrava balances a vertical javelin on the crowning element of his inclined Montjuïc Communications Tower (1989–92); the even taller tower project (327 metres) for the Valencia Science Museum (1991) has another weightless javelin float inside a 'monumental tripod' (p. 57).

But just as Calatrava uses nature not as an image repertoire to be plundered but (as in Lefebvre's description of Andalusian architecture) a 'pedagogy of space', inducing and producing endless differences (*The Production of Space*, 397), so he evacuates his very visible urban monuments, transforming them into elegant and fragile pointers to the invisible space of flows (to the electronic communications it is their function to emit and receive). The formal references to the bodily and the organic, always fully abstracted and integrated into the architectonic design, suggest not nostalgia for the premodern past but rather a future reintegration of the human and the spatial through technology. Calatrava's structures are thus 'grand creations' in Lefebvre's sense of 'gestural space[s] which [have] succeeded in mooring a mental space . . . to the earth' (pp. 216–17). While Lefebvre's example here is a medieval cloister, Calatrava's bridges and towers also testify to the conjunction of gestural spaces (held in tension 'like a hand') and symbolic systems (in which new transport and communications technologies substitute for older theologies).

Delicately poised between engineering and architecture, technology and aesthetics, Calatrava is also balanced between the historical residue of the city site and its dynamic development. Frequently commissioned to rebuild outside Spain in such historically loaded locations as Berlin, Calatrava has pointedly refused the task of national or nationalist reconstruction, producing indeterminate or intermediate structures: the Kronprinzen bridge (1991–5), built on the site of an original demolished to prevent escapes from the East to the West, boasts apparently floating piers 'shaped like river barges' (*Santiago Calatrava*, 63); the sheet glass Spandau Railway Station (1991) is 'suspended between office blocks' by 'organic, tree-like supports', shunning the 'big structural statement' that might be expected in such a site (p. 64); finally, Calatrava's project for the Reichstag (1993; one of three which won 'first prize' in the international competition) is pure transparency: a glass dome spans the historic shell, shielding four successive glazed inner courts, allowing light into the very heart of government (p. 77). Capable of the grand gesture in historic Spanish cities (the spectacular bridges of Mérida and Seville), Calatrava's mission to overcome the urban grievance does not allow him the reassuring remedies of conservationism. Settling for smallness in Berlin, his aesthetics of disappearance shows sensitivity towards the terrible history of that metropolis. Some urban wounds should not be allowed to heal.

According to Lefebvre's diagnosis of the fractured and contradictory urban space in which Calatrava was to build:

The balance of forces between monuments and buildings has shifted. Buildings are to monuments as everyday life is to festival, products to works, lived experience to the merely perceived, concrete to stone etc. [The problem is] how to reinstitute monumentality within the sphere of buildings. (*The Production of Space*, 223)

I would argue that it is Calatrava's achievement to have realized this 'dialectical transcendence'. Dignifying everyday urban life, enlivening abstract perception of the city, Calatrava produces animated, gestural locations in which technology is rendered festive (Valencia) and modern concrete compared and contrasted with classical stone (Mérida). And if Calatrava does not always bridge the gap between representations of space and representational spaces (if the great harp of the Alamillo bridge leads only, as it does, to a deserted and evacuated technocity), then we must proceed to examine the complex positioning of architecture as just one urban element caught in the cleft or rift between the nomadic flows of global technology and the place-based policies of local government.

Like Calatrava, Manuel Castells left Francoist Spain (for Paris and Berkeley, rather than Zurich) only to return to make substantial interventions in urban projects funded by the Socialist national state and regional *autonomías*. Castells was the consultant for an ambitious project to transform the site of Expo 92 into La Cartuja 93: the centre of high technology for southern Europe. It was for this site, we remember, that Calatrava designed the Alamillo bridge, intended to be one of a pair crossing the Guadalquivir twice as it twisted round the San Jerónimo bend, thus forming a monumental gateway to and from Seville and its hinterland. Moreover if Calatrava is the 'new European man' who owes his career to international competitions and commissions, Castells is the global intellectual, travelling the world in the search for remedies to the urban grievance, that violent abstraction of space which has dislocated society and evacuated the citizen from the city.

Typically global is the 1994 study by Castells and collaborator Peter Hall: *Technopoles of the World*.[41] For Castells the technopole (a coinage he borrows from the French) is a new form of urbanism: 'a planned development [drawing on a] partnership between the public and private sectors ... generat[ing] the basic materials of the informational economy' (p. 1). Sited typically on the periphery of established urban areas, studiedly anonymous in its landscaping and architecture ('a campus-like atmosphere'), and dedicated to the production of ideas not things, the technopole would seem to embody a *non plus ultra* of that abstraction of social space and destruction of local specificity which urban commentators have lamented since the 1960s: parachuted in at random, Castells writes,

[41] Manuel Castells and Peter Hall, *Technopoles of the World: The Making of Twenty-First-Century Industrial Complexes* (London: Routledge, 1994).

observers would be hard put to tell which country they were in, let alone which city. As the late twentieth-century equivalent of the mines and foundries of the industrial revolution, the technopole is the result of three simultaneous economic transformations: the rise of new technologies; the emergence of a real-time global economy; and the precedence of information over commodities as a generator of wealth (p. 3). But technological change has social effects, generating a 'variable geometry' of decentralization (of the city and the corporation) (p. 4) and new social divisions of labour: just as nineteenth-century industrialized England dominated the Portugal whose fine wines rich Britons consumed, so (prophesies Castells) East Asian electronic supremacy may soon ensure that the language of the London stock exchange switches to Japanese, or perhaps Korean (p. 5). Cities or nations too inflexible to innovate in their technical and social frameworks and locked into declining industries, will become 'industrial ruins' (p. 7).

This global catastrophe is expressed in terms of space: the transformation of the world's 'economic geography' and the loss of the 'old logic of spatial divisions of labour' (p. 8). Yet if the invisible flows of the informational economy have reworked the world, indifferent to the particularities of place, then, paradoxically, cities and regions have re-emerged as 'new economic actors', 'critical agents of . . . development' (pp. 6–7). Travelling the world, Castells and Hall discover, to their surprise, that the old metropolises of Paris and London are as productive 'milieux of innovation' as such celebrated technopoles as Silicon Valley (p. 9). As Lefebvre had predicted in the 1970s, in spite of increasing deterritorialization, 'urban space, though it has lost its former [dominant] role, nevertheless continues to ensure that links are properly maintained between the various *flows* . . . of energy and labour, of commodities and capital' (*The Production of Space*, 347). As we shall see, the reconciliation of flows and places will be a priority for Castells, also.

Thinking globally once more, Castells contrasts two technocities being built at the time of writing: Seville's La Cartuja 93 and the Japanese-Australian Multi-Function Polis (*Technopoles*, 193). Just as Expo 92 was reorientated by the Socialists from the celebration of Discovery to a shop window for the new Spain (from historical commemoration to the new frontiers of science and technology) (pp. 196–7), so the technopole project was proposed as an 'enduring monument' (p. 196), redeploying the infrastructure of the largest World's Fair in history (p. 193). The 'spectacular site' also heralded a reinscription of history into modernity: La Cartuja is the location of the monastery where Columbus was first buried before it was transformed into a ceramics factory, now derelict (p. 199). The ghostly traces of colonialism and industrialism would thus be renewed by the flow of new technology, new productivity, in a typically dematerialized fashion: planning regulations stipulated that there could be no manufacturing on site.

Summoned as consultant by the Andalusian regional government, Castells devised an ideal project design: as a technopole La Cartuja would be dedicated to research and development and funded jointly by the public and private sector. Formal links would be established between research teams within the technopole and local firms outside it; and the prime location would also draw incoming investment from European Union and global bodies (pp. 200–1). Management would be devolved to an autonomous public corporation (p. 202). What followed was, in Castells's own words, a 'high tech soap opera' (p. 205). In May 1991 the newly elected conservative mayor of the city opposed the plans of Socialist regional and national authorities, stressing short-term profiteering and services at the expense of long-term investment in research and training (p. 203). According to Castells, such a policy appeared to have immediate advantages: not only did it supply unskilled jobs, desperately needed in a notorious black spot for unemployment; it also connected more closely than the vision of a twenty-first-century technopole with the Andalusian tradition of public amusement and leisure (p. 203). In Lefebvre's terms, the mayor triumphed with a representational space whose lived expression confounded the representations of space of his opponents which were conceived to transform, and not simply to complement, existing conditions.

Ironically, however, it is just that spirit of the place which led Castells to promote Seville and Andalusia as loci for new technology, the 'California' of Europe. For just as established cities and regions can indeed compete as milieux of innovation with technocities established *de novo*, so it is the very historicity of Seville (Castells cites its Roman, Judaeo-Arab, and Renaissance strata) and its dense texture of spatial practices (jasmine and orange trees, fountains and mosaics) which lend it cultural capital as a location on a global market which is supposedly indifferent to place: leading-edge production would thus benefit from the 'arts of gracious living' (p. 206), high tech from 'high touch' in an 'urban cocktail' (p. 207). For Lefebvre in the 1970s the Mediterranean was a fantasy space for northern tourists, promoted and experienced as quality not quantity, desire not need, as the consumption of space not the space of consumption (*The Production of Space*, 352–3). For Castells in the 1990s such place-specific qualities (desires, consumable spaces) are added value in the global competition for high tech investment, grist to the invisible mill of techno-dreams (*Technopoles*, 193). The ideal location for the technopole (be it northern California or southern Spain or Australia) is thus at once particular and generalizable, picturesquely different and familiarly the same. The stylized *mise en scène* of the technopole serves to reintegrate, on a fantastic level at least, sociality and technology, festivity and everyday life, work and product.

More intractably the technopole also introduces a term apparently excluded from the real-time global economy: duration. For as Castells frequently reminds us, the time scale required to verify the value of investment in the informational city far exceeds both the short-term business cycle and the political election cycle (p. 247), one reason, perhaps, why Japan provides his only example of the most developed form of technopole in the world. It is thus worth turning to Castells's earlier essay on 'The Reconstruction of Social Meaning in the Space of Flows'[42] in order better to understand the implications of the fate of La Cartuja for Spanish cities and the rise of the new technologies for urbanism in general.

In a more abstract, diagnostic manner (a theoretical 'world view'), Castells gives an almost apocalyptic analysis of the triumph of the space of flows over the space of places: 'asymmetrical networks . . . which do not depend on any specific locale [form] a variable geography [which] denies the specific productive meaning of any place outside its position in a network whose shape changes relentlessly' (p. 494). This 'supersession of place by a network of information flows' eludes controls which 'depend upon territorially based institutions' (p. 495). The resulting 'social disintegration' is all the more disturbing because it reveals 'no tangible oppression, no identifiable enemy, no centre of power'. Self-perpetuating ('the flows of power generate the power of flows'), flows and places come to constitute 'two disjointed spheres of human experience . . . People live in places, power rules through flows.' The death of sociality leads to the birth of 'tribalism', the 'fundamentalist' assertion of localized identities which are inaccessible to fellow citizens: 'Between ahistorical flows and irreducible identities . . . cities and regions disappear as socially meaningful places' (p. 496). Such a process can lead only to catastrophe: 'Societies will fracture into non-communicative segments whose reciprocal alienation will lead to destructive violence and to a process of historical decline' (p. 498).

This diagnosis of the urban experience (of globalization and fragmentation, of irreducible difference and inexplicable violence) is strikingly similar to Goytisolo's dystopian metropolis of the 1980s. Indeed, even in the 1970s Lefebvre had written on the incompatibility of human rhythms and economic flows (*The Production of Space*, 206); and warned that computer science's 'abolition' of distance would 'shatter' or 'pulverize' space

---

[42] This essay is taken from *The Informational City* of 1989; I cite via LeGates and Stout, *The City Reader* (pp. 494–8).

(p. 334). But unlike Goytisolo, who nihilistically embraces the catastrophe of tribalism, Lefebvre offers a remedy for the loss of social meaning in the informational city, writing that the 'only possible alternative' to the terror of the centralized state is the 'challenge from "local powers"', powers which might 'replace the state's machinery by data processing machines fed and managed from below' (p. 382). Castells repeats this double strategy, claiming that only local governments have the flexibility and adaptability to take on global corporations and to 'reconstruct an alternative space of flows on the basis of the space of places [and] the new informational technologies' ('Reconstruction', 497). Reversing asymmetrical information flows, this 'utopian vision' also reverses 'the logic of domination . . . reintegrat[ing] knowledge and meaning into a new Informational City' (p. 498). Such a network would be a new kind of popular monument, lighter even than Calatrava's harps and javelins, but one which shared with those visionary structures the promise of technological utopia.

The final failure of La Cartuja 93 (which remained in 1995 a desolate cityscape suitable neither for technology nor festivity) is an ironic rejoinder to Castells's vindication of strong local governments, compared at one point to the city states of the Renaissance, which also emerged in tandem with a new global economy (p. 497). But Castells himself stresses the unpredictable effects of the social and spatial reorganizations produced by both technological and regional development. And if Spain's experience of IT has proved less radical than its experiment with the devolution of central power to the regions[43] then still the attempt (in Castells's words) to 'reconstruct the meaning of the locality' (p. 497) is well served by that unrepeatable urban *œuvre* (that unique space of festivity) which goes by the name of Seville.

4. From Flow to Rhythm

In a recent 'fiction' based on his experiences in besieged Bosnia,[44] Goytisolo gives an ultimate vision of the death of the city, which rewrites motifs familiar from *Paisajes*. A nameless observer looks down from his ruined hotel room at a 'naked panorama of ruins': 'skeleton buildings, charred trams, melted kiosks' (p. 15). But this privileged and voyeuristic viewpoint offers access not to the rhythmic 'ballet' of Greenwich Village or Le Sentier, but to the sidewalk crawl of a lone woman, dragging herself on her knees through Sniper Alley (p. 17). A sudden explosion kills not her

[43] For the limited take up of IT in Spain see Alonso Zaldívar and Castells's *España, fin de siglo* (pp. 181–203).

[44] *El sitio de los sitios* (Madrid: Alfaguara, 1995). As 'sitio' means both 'place' and 'siege', Sarajevo is presented as the urban space par excellence.

but him; and the subsequent fragmentary narrative stages the search for his mysteriously missing body.

The text thus reworks, in a new, more urgent mode, topoi we have seen elsewhere: the death of sociality and deconstruction of the monument (an equestrian statue persists unnoticed throughout the carnage); the loss of the body in tribalist or terrorist violence; the persistence of nature and history even *in extremis*: a soft snow settles over a city whose traces bear witness to ancient and diverse residents. But where once Goytisolo celebrated the incommensurate cultural differences of the metropolis, here his mood is less sanguine: the unintelligible graffiti of Paris are now 'prolegomena' to ethnic wars, 'symptoms' of a siege to come (p. 32); now the narrator asks whether heterogeneity is the cause or the effect of social indifference and his 'ideal' vision of the '*cives*' as 'crucible' of cultures gives way to the 'tribal' violence which erupts between 'ghettos' (p. 36). Goytisolo thus restates the problem posed by Castells: how to heal urban wounds without appealing to irreducible, non-communicable identities.

Taking a walk through central Madrid in 1995, novelist Antonio Muñoz Molina[45] offers a more hopeful vision, eerily similar to Goytisolo's evocation of Paris in 1982. From the intimate and 'provincial' squares of Chueca and Tirso de Molina, via the tawdry grandeur of the Gran Vía and the Telefónica, Muñoz encounters an urban 'heart' which is irreducible to the stereotypes of both Left and Right administrations (neither the Socialists' utopia of 'modern' nightclubs nor the Partido Popular's inferno of drugs and crime). It is a dense and crowded public space, a continuing rebuke to López's monumental vacuums, to the nostalgic conservationism attacked by Calatrava's commentators, and to Castells's sterile technopole with its 'campus-like atmosphere'. With its junkies and transsexuals, Hindus and Muslims, African vendors and Quechua-speaking maids, this Madrid shows the persistence of the metropolis as a milieu of innovation, at once conceived and lived: of novelty within repetition, density within difference, texture within traffic.

Most significantly that dimension of history that has been evacuated by the restless and instantaneous motion of the 'flow' returns here in the intersection of spatial and temporal patterns as rhythm. In Lefebvre's words: 'as on the surface of a body of water, or within the mass of a liquid, rhythms are forever crossing and recrossing, superimposing themselves on each other' (*The Production of Space*, 205). Lefebvre's 'general rhythmology of the living body and its internal and external relationships' (expressed, he says, par excellence in music and dance) might look something like the rich and brave lives of the retiring, surviving inhabitants of traffic- and crime-plagued Chueca, who produce their own representa-

---

[45] 'Viaje al centro de Madrid', *El País Semanal* (19 Feb. 1995).

tions of space in an area long abandoned by those arch conceptualists, the police and the planners.[46] The persistent and inexplicable survival of urbanism in Spain shows that the pun in Lefebvre's most famous slogan 'le droit à la ville'[47] (as in 'le droit à la vie') is not casual. Rather urban dynamism is stimulated, as Castells recommends, by competition between rival city states (Madrid and Barcelona)[48] led by strong and flexible local governments. If *El País*'s dream house is a chalet in the sierra, then at least one post-Franco film has the perfect housewife burn down her ideal country home as the family return, relieved, to the city.[49]

The four figures I have discussed here (Goytisolo, López, Calatrava, and Castells) testify to the restless space of flows in which a cultural or intellectual 'home' is inseparable from abroad: the circulation of bodies and works, the globalization of both arts (literature and painting) and sciences (engineering and sociology). But perhaps what links them all (even the López whose city is evacuated and citizen isolated) is the notion of rhythm. Lefebvre writes, anticipating and contradicting Castells, that:

the notion of *flows* (of energy, matter etc.) is self-sufficient only in political economy. It is in any case always subordinate to the notion of space. What we *live* are rhythms—rhythms experienced subjectively. . . . Here at least 'lived' and 'conceived' are close. (*The Production of Space*, 206)

The rhythm of Goytisolo's sidewalk ballet, the rhythm of Calatrava's structures (form unfolded into movement), the rhythm of Castells's milieux of innovation (marrying technological change and quality of life), each testifies to the continuing coincidence of the work and the product (the lived and the conceived) in the Spanish and the global city. Even López's architectonic fruit and vegetables point perhaps to the temporality and humanity that have been so brutally expelled from his urban 'world views'. Lefebvre suggests in a final axiom that it is in 'the artistic sphere' that a space which 'contains the potentialities of works and of reappropriation' is first to be found, 'inaugurat[ing] the project of a different space' (p. 349). The recovery of place and time (the celebration of the centre and of sociality, of density and festivity) seen in the works of these Spanish citizens can be read as a gesture towards or an exploration of this different urban space, a space which is as utopian as it is necessary.

[46] Chueca has in recent years experienced regeneration at the hands of lesbian and gay homeowners, now resident in a neighbourhood they previously visited for entertainment.

[47] *Le Droit à la ville* (Paris: Anthropos, 1968); translated in Kofman and Lebas's *Writings on Cities* (pp. 63–181).

[48] For a graphic recreation of the rivalry between the two cities see the special issue of *El País Semanal* (28 Apr. 1996) in which aspects of each city are confronted with one another on facing pages.

[49] *Las verdes praderas* ('Fresh Fields') (José Luis Garci, 1979).

PART III

Subjectivity

7 | Back to Front: Alberto Cardín's Queer Habitus

Why is there no queer theory in Spain? The answer might be historical, institutional, or theoretical. Historically, the long Francoist separation of economic modernization from cultural modernity prevented the emergence of intellectual disciplines such as occurred in other countries. If, as Graham and Labanyi have recently argued, there is no indigenously Spanish cultural theory (analogous to those of Germany and Italy),[1] then we could hardly expect a theorization of the smaller and more marginal field of homosexuality. Institutionally, the persistence of positivism in Spanish universities has meant that trends such as psychoanalysis and deconstruction have had comparatively little influence in the humanities.[2] Unwilling to abandon objectivist scientific thought, Spanish humanists are unlikely to embrace feminism or queer studies, tainted as they are with subjectivism. Theoretically, Spanish scepticism towards gay or lesbian identity has led to a failure to construct a coherent public space for a homosexuality which remains for many a bundle of private pleasures and practices which require no social symbolization.[3] If the Spanish state is unable to support a gay press, it is unlikely to evolve the complex mechanisms of distribution and authorization necessary for the academic discipline of queer theory.

Let us imagine, then, a fantasy figure: an openly gay Spanish writer who was historically active from the leftist gay liberation of the 1970s to the small but courageous AIDS movement of the 1980s; who was institutionally based, with a teaching position at a major university and some

[1] Helen Graham and Jo Labanyi, *Spanish Cultural Studies: An Introduction* (Oxford: Oxford University Press, 1995), 3–4.

[2] For the 'few lasting effects' in Spain of the explosion of critical theory in the 1970s see Silvia L. López, Jenaro Talens, and Darío Villanueva, 'Introduction', in *Critical Practices in Post-Franco Spain* (Minneapolis: University of Minnesota Press, 1994), pp. ix–xxv (p. xi).

[3] For the lack of existence of a gay community or identity in Spain see my account of early liberationist texts in *Laws of Desire: Questions of Homosexuality in Spanish Writing and Film 1960–90* (Oxford: Oxford University Press, 1992), 7–8.

twenty books, academic and non-academic, to his credit; and who was theoretically sophisticated, as well read in anthropology as he was in Marxism and psychoanalysis. Such a figure would surely be a dream date for an Anglo-American Hispanist seeking congenial company. It is surprising, then, that Alberto Cardín did indeed exist; and that his works remain almost unknown both in Spain and abroad. Cardín, who was born in Asturias in 1948 and taught cultural anthropology in the fine arts department of the University of Barcelona, is to my knowledge unique, not only because he publicly declared his HIV positive status in 1985 and lived openly with AIDS until his death in 1991, but because he created and embodied an anomalous and unprecedented figure in the Spanish critical field: the homosexual intellectual.

In this chapter I read a selection of Cardín's works in the light of the habitus, a concept I take from Pierre Bourdieu.[4] The habitus is the self-regulating discursive consensus which at once precedes and reconfirms the words and actions of empirical subjects: in Bourdieu's words it is the 'transformation of past effect into an expected objective . . . immediately prescribed in the present—things to do or not to do, things to say or not to say—in relation to a probable, upcoming future' (p. 53). A self-perpetuating prophecy (the projection of a past whose history is forgotten into a future whose development is perceived as inevitable), the habitus correlates 'objective probabilities and subjective aspirations [in such a way that] the more improbable practices are . . . excluded as unthinkable in a kind of immediate submission to order' (p. 54).

What I shall argue, briefly to anticipate, is that Cardín's life and work constituted an anomaly in the habitus of post-Franco cultural life, an unexpected turn or improbable practice which was immediately and unthinkingly excluded from serious consideration, from things that could be done and things that could be said. As we shall see, the habitus (as a 'scheme of perception, thought, and action which tends to guarantee the "correctness" of practices and their constancy'; p. 54) served more subtly and thus more reliably than 'formal rules or explicit norms' to silence Cardín's voice. As the intersection of the subject, discipline, and institution, the habitus is thus particularly appropriate for the study of Cardín's concerns: 'race', psychoanalysis, and AIDS. Indeed its primary meaning, unused by Bourdieu, is that of 'bodily constitution': 'the general appearance of the body, symptom of a state of health or sickness.'[5]

[4] Where no source is given, the text I cite is 'Structures, Habitus, Practices', in *The Logic of Practice* (Cambridge: Polity, 1992), 52–65. I have also referred to *In Other Words: Essays towards a Reflexive Sociology* (Cambridge: Polity, 1994).

[5] Paul Robert, *Dictionnaire alphabétique et analogique de la langue française* (Paris: SNL, 1976), s.v. 'habitus'.

The history of intellectuals in post-Franco Spain has yet to be written. When that project is attempted it would do well to address both Bourdieu's critique of the self-authorizing intellectual, never more implicated in power relations than when proclaiming his or her disinterestedness, and Cardín's vituperative attacks on the institutionalization of knowledge in the Transition, when a discursive consensus was being forged in and by Cardín's *bête noire*, *El País*, the new newspaper of the democracy. Cardín's vicious polemics against such contributors to *El País* as Juan Goytisolo, Fernando Savater, and Francisco Umbral might seem ephemeral, marked as they are by the intemperate spirit of the time and place in which they were written. But posterity has proved him right. For, just as the habitus projects a principle of consistency and probability into the future, even as that future throws up hitherto inexplicable events, so the chronicle of the constitution of a discursive consensus in the progressive press is also the prehistory of the unprecedented AIDS epidemic which followed it. The establishment of a common-sense order in which homosexuality could not be spoken in the first person and same-sex practice was incompatible with cultural capital was thus a precondition for the impossibility of addressing, indeed the impossibility of seeing, the AIDS crisis in the decade which followed.

What is the nature, then, of Cardín's anomaly, the factor which rendered him invisible and silent? I would suggest that Cardín's characteristic quality is to provoke embarrassment. Thus in the only work on Cardín of which I am aware (a brief survey of his texts on AIDS), José Miguel García Cortés apologizes to his reader for writing about Cardín at all: why dedicate so much space to such a figure?[6] Or again, Cardín's name tends to turn up in unexpected places. He looms large in the memoirs of Federico Jiménez Losantos, the now ultra-right commentator of *ABC*. In the nostalgic introduction to the polemically titled *Lo que queda de España* (first published in 1979; reprinted in 1995), Jiménez Losantos paints a vivid picture of the libertarian Barcelona of the late 1970s, in which queens such as Cardín or the drag diva Ocaña took the Ramblas by storm.[7] Jiménez Losantos's affectionate narrative of a joint sexual and political education (he and Cardín co-edited the short-lived psychoanalytic journal *Diwan*) reveals, nonetheless, Cardín's unerring tendency towards subjective aspirations which (in Bourdieu's terms) did not correlate to the objective probabilities of the

[6] 'A Alberto Cardín in memoriam', in Juan Vicente Aliaga and José Miguel G. Cortés (eds.), *De amor y rabia: acerca del arte y el SIDA* (Valencia: Universidad Politécnica, 1993), 167–75 (p. 171).

[7] *Lo que queda de España: con un prólogo sentimental y un epílogo balcánico* (Madrid: Temas de Hoy, 1995).

Transition and would therefore be overruled or undermined by the habitus.

Thus Cardín was a Castilian speaker who clung to his language even as Catalunya proclaimed its linguistic autonomy, signing in 1981 the 'Manifesto of the 2,300 Intellectuals' against the 'normalization' of Catalan; he was also an ex-Marxist militant seduced by a Lacanian psychoanalysis which was soon to be dismissed in *El País* as a passing intellectual fad; and he was a gay man whose insistence on genital homosexuality was incompatible with the decorous assimilationism offered by the new regulators of cultural capital to those they patronized as *marginados*. For even as Cardín railed against the familialism of the newly legalized PCE, so homosexuality (like communism) was normalized as a mere staging post on the road to modern democracy, no sooner accepted than abandoned. For Jiménez Losantos, a surprisingly sympathetic observer, the flagrant homosexuality of the 1970s is as passé in the 1990s as another equally vulgar phenomenon contemporary with it: the *destape* or 'disrobing' of Spanish actresses (p. 34). If the title of one of Cardín's collections of stories is 'Back to Front' (*Detrás por delante*),[8] then Cardín paid the price for such insistent inversion, disrupting the continuity and regularity of the habitus and dismissed as improbable and extravagant as a result.

Let us examine three characteristically embarrassing moments in Cardín's career. The first is Jiménez Losantos's description of Cardín at a clandestine oppositional meeting in the German Institute in Barcelona, which served in the mid-1970s as a cover for the PCE. Cardín was dressed, we are told, in a brilliant red fur coat, golden eyeshadow, and a single earring. While, Jiménez Losantos says, it was perfectly normal to see all kinds of gays in the Ramblas, what was unheard of was to hear someone with such an appearance spouting an impeccably Marxist and revolutionary discourse: against the family, against convention, against everything and anything ('antiloquefuera'; p. 29). The second moment is an episode from a story in the collection *Lo mejor es lo peor*, called simply 'Sauna'.[9] Here the first person narrator's attempted advances to shadowy queens in the bathhouse cots are greeted not by the expected embraces but by vigorous kicks (p. 149). Balancing on the shoulders of another anonymous companion, he fears he will fall at a very intimate moment. And indeed, once the sexual transaction has been completed, the narrator's careless partner leaves him literally hanging, swinging like a pendulum from the metal bar to which he clings (p. 150). The third moment is darker in tone. In the unpublished 'Afghan chronicles' of 1988, the pseudonymous Cardín describes a meeting with the embryonic govern-

---

[8] (Barcelona: Laertes, 1986).
[9] (Barcelona: Laertes, 1981), 138–51.

ment of the Mujahedin.[10] Fearing for the explosion of AIDS amongst com-
batants, and more particularly for the youths whom Cardín claims are
used for their sexual services by the troops, Cardín and his colleagues ask
permission to carry out a public health campaign to promote the use of
condoms amongst the Afghan guerrillas. The chiefs' hoots of laughter at
this, Cardín writes, could be heard as far away as the Khyber Pass (p. 26).

The revolutionary cell, the sauna, the battlefield: each is a contested
space; and for all their diversity, in each Cardín is characteristically out of
time and out of place. In the German Institute, his appearance is incompatible with his speech; in the bathhouse, his sexual exploits are undercut
by his humiliating predicament; and in the battleground, his concern for
public health is irreconcilable with the very different priorities of Islamic
jihad. While such incongruities may register as humour, they also serve as
an index of a breach in the habitus, with Cardín's subjective aspirations
brutally deflated by objective probabilities. Note also the radical embodiment of Cardín, even as he voices the impeccably abstract discourses of
revolutionary Marxism or occidental health care. It is symptomatic that
the sauna, for Cardín, is not a space for erotic reverie on the problem of
Spain as it is in Goytisolo's *Reivindicación del conde don Julián* (1970); still
less is it seen from the sovereign viewpoint of a positivist sociologist such
as Oscar Guasch in his *La sociedad rosa*.[11] Yet the disputed genre of each of
these texts (tendentious memoir, comic narrative, pseudonymous report
from the battlefield) suggests that we cannot take such embarrassing
moments straight as confessional truths. Rather, Cardín's stress on the
necessary embodiment of discourse is a blow against positivism (insisting
that objects of knowledge are constructed not recorded); and an argument
for psychoanalysis (insisting that the subject, however excluded, denigrated, or abused, has no other existence than the fragments of his own
discourse). While Bourdieu seeks in his practice as a sociologist to 'escape
from objectivism . . . without falling back into subjectivism' ('Structures',
52), Cardín, even in his professional role as an anthropologist, steps down
from the sovereign viewpoint of objectivism only to take up a subjectivism
which, I would argue, is brandished, insistently and embarrassingly, as a
strategy that is not so much personalist as psychoanalytically heuristic.

Indeed in his major anthropological work *Guerreros, chamanes, y
travestís*[12] (based partly on fieldwork carried out with the Plains' Indians in
Canada), Cardín is scathing about the narcissistic subjectivism which
passes off the observer's relation to the object as the object itself. North

---

[10] Fragments appear as 'Crónicas afganas', in the special gay literature issue of Barcelona
cultural magazine *Literal*, 2.12 (Dec. 1995), 26–7.

[11] (Barcelona: Anagrama, 1991).

[12] (Barcelona: Tusquets, 1984).

American activists who, on the slenderest of evidence, claim the most diverse tribal peoples as members of a global gay community are attacked for their 'ghetto-centric' world view and recuperative and justificatory quest for a 'canon' of exotic homosexualities (p. 18). Deriding, but not denying, the relation between sexual tourism and ethnology, Cardín also inveighs against the 'ego psychology' of certain US anthropologists (p. 43), hinting even here at his most drily academic at the possibility of a deconstructive or Lacanian ethnology. Typically the conclusion to the study lists not only thanks but also 'curses' ('imprecaciones'; p. 228), principally directed against the Anthropological Library of the Consejo Superior de Estudios Científicos, which (Cardín claims) refused him entry.

But Cardín's understanding of homosexuality as a certain relation to the other led him to explore 'race' also in his erotic fiction. It is thus appropriate that *Lo mejor es lo peor* (1981) should sport on its cover an illustration by another luminary of the Barcelona Transition, comic artist Nazario. In the drawing a white queen, complete with wig, gloves, and earrings, toasts her naked black beau in the dumpster they are sharing on a derelict street. The image wittily suggests how the pleasures of the cross-cultural encounter can arise amongst the varied detritus of the dustbin of history. And a repeated figure in the stories is the high culture queen from Europe succumbing with vertiginous inevitability to the attractions of North African youths. Thus 'Un nuevo Charles de Foucauld' (a story which is continued as 'Aschenbach en Berbería' in *Detrás por delante*) stages the ritual humiliation of an impeccably Marxist and married theoretician at the hands of rough trade in Tangiers. Parodying homophile aestheticism and sublimation, Cardín (or his mouthpiece) insists that a 'pure' relationship between a European and an Arab is impossible (*Detrás*, 95). Or again, Cardín's bitterest attack on Goytisolo, 'El expreso de mediodía', shows the celebrated contributor to *El País* 'Álvaro Sologaitas' rewriting a piece for public consumption under the baleful eye of his Arab houseboy. Omitting such embarrassing episodes as the beating he received in a hammam, his arrest on a public morals charge, or the time he was robbed by ephebes in the entrance to a mosque, the great author pens a protest on Western ethnocentrism, which is so ignorant of the lived experience of Muslim cultures (*Lo mejor es lo peor*, 71, 78). But if Cardín attacks Goytisolo here (as elsewhere) for reticence, for excising the messy materiality of homosexual practice in the Sotadic zone and for displacing his testimony from the first to the second person in novels such as *Reivindicación*, it is not because Cardín is advocating a confessional tone in the US style. Rather it is because he sees Goytisolo's strategy as an attempt to drape his erotic preferences in the more decorous garb of anti-racism. While Goytisolo 'goes swimming and keeps his clothes' (publishing in the most respected of new Spanish newspapers even as he claims that the new democracy is identical to the old dictatorship), Cardín remains shamelessly naked, self-consciously stripped of erotic and discursive props.

If for Cardín anthropology is fiction (with objectivists passing off their relation to the ethnographic object as the object itself), then fiction is anthropology (with the subjectivist viewpoints of narrative giving way to empirical observations on the encounter with the other culture). But, as Jiménez Losantos notes, the reason for Cardín's theoretical shift from Marxism to psychoanalysis in the 1970s is that the latter contains a theory of the subject lacking in objectivist political economy (*Lo que queda*, 51). And in his non-fiction works Cardín attempts to elaborate an ethics of psychoanalysis which precedes and underwrites his experience of AIDS. An unclassifiable book such as *Como si nada*,[13] written between 24 February and 3 March 1980, self-consciously presents the act of writing as a short session: a frenzy or spasm irreducible to conscious control. Yet the broadly Lacanian account of subjectivity (as dejection, shame, and baroque extravagance; p. III) and of the self as 'nullity', worth no more that the sum of the discourses which it emits (p. 8), is curiously juxtaposed with the minutely historical detail of literary polemic, such as the rejection by *El País* of Cardín's avowedly partial review of an edition of Freud's correspondence (p. XVI). In the final section of *Como si nada*, an essay whose text is constantly qualified by side notes, Cardín theorizes this historicity by defining writing as a temporal 'monument' in which the 'truth of the perverse' takes pleasure in concealing itself (p. 84). Claiming, in deconstructive style, that truth is no longer the adequation of word to thing (p. 72), Cardín recommends what I have called elsewhere the 'fatal strategy' of making good a loss one has already suffered with a loss one brings on oneself.[14] Cardín thus attempts to gain strength from weakness ('sacar fuerza de flaqueza') and render himself invulnerable through the shameless exhibition of psychic wounds (*Como si nada*, 13).

Bourdieu identifies the unconscious with the habitus: 'embodied history, internalized as second nature and thus forgotten as history' ('Structures', 56). Cardín's promiscuous blend of time-bound invective and timeless subjectivity is also a form of embodied history in which the strident denunciation of institutional injustice is combined with a subtle

---

[13] (Valencia: Pre-Textos, 1981).

[14] See my 'Fatal Strategies: The Representation of AIDS in the Spanish State', in *Vision Machines: Cinema, Literature, and Sexuality in Spain and Cuba, 1983–93* (London: Verso, 1996), 101–26 (p. 123). The phrase is Adrian Searle's description of the work of sculptor Pepe Espaliú.

reflection on the nature of the self. However, if Marxism offered solidarity without subjectivity (and was thus intolerable to the narcissistic Cardín), psychoanalysis offered subjectivity without solidarity (and would thus prove incapable of transcending solitude): Cardín's works on AIDS are testimony to this theoretical double bind in which the encounter with the other cannot be combined with the, equally urgent, exploration of the self. Thus in the pathetic postscript to the second edition of *Detrás por delante* (1986), Cardín laments that the complete absence of readers and reviews of his work has provoked him to self-absorption ('ensimismamiento'; p. 134). Ominously, however, the process by which he seeks external aid in order to 'prop himself up' ('sustentar[se]') as a professional writer is strikingly similar to the way he will later describe gay identity in Spain: as a fragile, even fictitious, construct, requiring the constant help of external supports in order to survive.[15]

Bourdieu describes intellectuals as a 'dominated fraction of a dominant group' which experiences the successive revolutions of the critical field as 'questions of life and death' even when such revolutions involve nothing more than the redeployment of intellectual capital (*In Other Words*, 144–5). What, then, of the intellectual with AIDS, who belongs to a dominated group *tout court* and for whom matters of life and death are no longer played out on a symbolic level? If we examine Cardín's brief but important texts on AIDS we see not only a stress on self-effacement and solitude which is foreshadowed by his theoretical training, but also a courageous redeployment of the intellectual capital he had earlier invested in the analysis of 'race' and psychoanalysis: the use of technical terminology, the exploitation of linguistic competence (mainly in English and French), and the appeal to erudite reference. The arsenal of literary polemic, once lived as a matter of life and death, is thus retrained on the medical arena.

For example Cardín's brief introduction to the collection he edited with Armand de Fluviá praises his co-editor's thankless and invisible scholarly work as Barcelona's only gay archivist.[16] And the texts themselves, overwhelmingly drawn from North America, reveal Cardín's academic skills as an editor and translator at an early period when the Spanish epidemic was met, Cardín claims, with equal indifference by gays, doctors, and the press (p. I). Cardín proposes, with typical intransigence, a choice of options each of which implies a new attitude by gay men to their bodies: thus they can continue to see their body instrumentally as a replaceable tool; or they can attempt to preserve it as an 'investment' for new purposes which have suddenly become incompatible with sexual pleasure (p. IV).

[15] See *Lo próximo y lo ajeno* (Barcelona: Icaria, 1990), 56.
[16] *SIDA: ¿maldición bíblica o enfermedad letal?* (Barcelona: Laertes, 1985), unnumbered.

This somewhat chilling objectivism is characteristically combined, however, with a narrative in the first person: Cardín's account of his 'calvary' from one medical institute of the Generalitat to another in a search for advice on and treatment for a swollen gland in the neck (p. II). At a time when his condition could not be confirmed, Cardín argues (bizarrely perhaps) that hypochondriacs deserve urgent medical support: the needs of the *malade imaginaire* are not to be neglected (p. III).

Six years later the dynamic is reversed. The introduction to another volume[17] translated and edited by Cardín begins pragmatically with a less sanguine view of gay men's options: the previous conception of the body as a pure instrument of pleasure must now be replaced by that of an ailing body ('un cuerpo doliente') whose limited strengths require careful marshalling. Moreover the Enlightenment ideal of freedom of choice (the basis of the citizen's freedom) can only be exercised if people with AIDS are provided with accurate information (p. 10). But Cardín soon wanders from this pragmatic path. On the one hand, he claims, Western science's objectivist view of the body as a 'machine' is wholly inadequate (p. 11); but on the other hand, the Oriental treatments which Cardín thanks for preserving his own life are also problematic: while Cardín had planned his book as an informative proposal of the real possibilities of alternative therapies, it has now become the 'literary' proposal of 'imaginary' possibilities, difficult to realize in practice. The 'utopianism' of such therapies is, however, vindicated subjectively by their validity for those who can 'identify' with them and strategically as a means for the patient to become an agent, and thus free himself from the ineffectual but intrusive hands of Western 'experts' (p. 13). Just as Cardín saw in 'race' the interpenetration of anthropology and fiction and in psychoanalysis the mutuality of the institution and the subject, so his hard-won familiarity with AIDS reveals to him the coexistence of efficacy and identification, of the concrete and the imaginary, in the experience of mortal illness. Stepping down from the sovereign viewpoint of Western medicine, Cardín is reconciled to the abjection of the body, an abjection to which his theoretical training had already accustomed him with its stress on the Lacanian subject as weakness and wound, nullity and dereliction.

For Bourdieu one empirical example of the habitus ('the immanent law inscribed in bodies'; 'Structures', 59) is that 'people tend to talk about politics with those who have the same opinions' (p. 61). Never one to accept tacit agreement, Cardín was a man for whom (in Jiménez Losantos's words) fighting ('pelear') was the normal relation to other people (*Lo que queda*, 29). The verb is significant. Abandoning early on the privileged positions of Marxist objectivism, Cardín divested himself of the

[17] *SIDA: enfoques alternativos* (Barcelona: Laertes, 1991).

dignity of revolutionary struggle ('lucha' as opposed to 'pelea'). And in his abortive career in the intellectual field, Cardín was not the fortunate recipient of cultural capital from more established agents, but could only reap the meagre benefits of recognition from maverick right-wingers such as Jiménez Losantos or indeed from his own preposterous female pseudonyms (an admiring blurb for *Lo mejor es lo peor* is attributed to 'Veneranda Cuahutemoc'). Excessively explicit where sex was concerned, Cardín proved as keen an embarrassment in academia as he had been in the revolutionary cell, the sauna, and on the Afghan battlefield. Yet if his texts, fiction and non-fiction, are indeed ephemeral, 'date-tied' in the journalistic jargon, then like Bourdieu's conception of the 'cultural field'[18] they reveal nonetheless the particularity of the general (with Cardín bringing into focus the specific discursive configurations of the Transition) and the generality of the particular (with those broader implications uniquely expressed in Cardín's versions of writing, 'race', and AIDS). If, then, we must avoid what Bourdieu calls 'the illusion created by hindsight in which all the traces of a life . . . appear as the realization of an essence that seems to preexist them' ('Structures', 55), then still we can acknowledge that Cardín's pre-AIDS texts provide an intellectual preparation for his unique engagement with the epidemic. Just as the unspoken consensus of the Transition (the agreements on things to do or not to do, things to say or not say) foreshadowed the apparently inexplicable indifference of a progressive society to the epidemic which was to engulf it, so Cardín's anthropology and fiction, experienced and dismissed as anomalous or extravagant, laid the foundations for his sometimes puzzling, but always fiercely intelligent, understanding of AIDS. It was Cardín's achievement to challenge the repeated refrain that homosexuality (homophobia, racism) was 'not a problem' in post-Franco Spain;[19] and to insist with embarrassing frequency on genital same-sex practice at a time when homosexuality was everywhere tolerated as an open secret and nowhere acknowledged as a public position.

For Bourdieu 'the presence of the past in the false anticipation of the future performed by the habitus [is] most clearly seen . . . when dispositions are ill-adjusted to objective changes because of a hysteresis effect' (p. 62). Bourdieu's example here is taken from Marx: it is Don Quijote. Defiantly untimely, unwilling or unable to adjust his quixotic dispositions to objective changes (and thus to go quietly to his death like his fellow writers Jaime Gil de Biedma and Eduardo Haro Ibars before him), Cardín created the category of 'Spanish gay intellectual', proving Bourdieu's

[18] *In Other Words*, 141.

[19] The absence of homophobia in Spain has been most recently contested by Juan Vicente Aliaga in his and G. Cortés's *De amor y rabia*, 153.

point that while intellectuals may often be accomplices to power, they may also exploit the 'considerable power' of 'naming the unnameable' (*In Other Words*, 149). If, to return to my opening question, there is no queer theory in Spain, then Cardín's queer habitus, his challenge to a discursive consensus which he turned back to front, is an exception that deserves to be honoured and remembered even as the epidemic continues its silent and invisible ravages.[20]

[20] A version of this chapter was first read as a paper in the panel 'Infected Bodies: The Cultural Politics of AIDS and Racism in Spain' on 28 Dec. 1996 at the 112th Convention of the Modern Language Association of America, held in Washington. I would like to thank Teresa M. Vilarós, the panel organizer.

8 | Between Heaven and Earth: Grounding Julio Medem

1. Postnational Subjects

Julio Medem is the cineaste of subjectivity. In his first feature, *Vacas* (1992) the history of 100 years of the Basque Country is replayed as a domestic conflict between two families in a lush valley; in his second, *La ardilla roja* ('The Red Squirrel', 1993), the contemporary comedy of relations between men and women is explored through the lyrical and imaginative means of memory and fantasy; and, finally, in *Tierra* (1996) a cosmic fable of metaphysics and mundanity is performed in an unearthly landscape, as internal as it is external, a landscape which is, in Medem's own words, 'warm, intimate, and subjectivizable'.[1]

This sense of subjectivity is not, however, confined to the plots of Medem's features; it also underwrites their form. Thus Medem is famous for his playful use of cinematic point of view, of 'subjective shots' from the perspective of animals or objects. This is a tendency which I have called elsewhere, after Paul Virilio, 'the vision machine' and which can be defined, briefly, as the cohabitation of self and other, man and machine, in the cinematic apparatus.[2] One point I make in this chapter, however, is that *Tierra* also exploits a rarer and trickier technique, subjective sound. Reviews in sources as diverse as US trade journal *Variety* and French auteurist periodical *Positif* have attacked the 'murky metaphysics'[3] and tiresome 'explication de texte'[4] supposedly embodied in *Tierra*'s voice-over. Read as subjective sound, however, this voice-over tends rather to relativize metaphysics and problematize explanation, to accentuate that

---

[1] Unpublished transcript of interview with author, 8 Nov. 1996; partially published as 'Angels to Earth', *Sight and Sound*, 7.8 (Aug. 1997), 12–14.

[2] See 'Julio Medem's *La ardilla roja* (The Red Squirrel): A Transparent Society?', in my *Vision Machines: Cinema, Literature, and Sexuality in Spain and Cuba, 1983–93* (London: Verso, 1996), 128–45.

[3] Derek Elley, review of *Tierra, Variety* (27 May–2 June 1996), 66–7 (p. 67).

[4] Philippe Rouyer, review of *Tierra, Positif*, 425–6 (July–Aug. 1996), 131.

sense of 'suspension' praised by critics more sensitive to *Tierra*'s oblique irony and crazy comedy.[5]

My own aim is to 'ground' *Tierra*, to read it in the multiple and shifting contexts of Basque postnationalism, of film form, of tributary text (the published script and supplementary narrative authored by Medem), and, finally, of production and distribution history. The *OED* defines 'grounded' in the transferred sense as 'having one's actions or activities curtailed, especially as a punishment'.[6] To ground Medem, however, is not to curtail his work by reducing it to its national or industrial context, but rather to rescue his films from metaphysical readings which invoke such clichés as 'blood and passion', 'mystical continuity', or 'the soul and its relation to the land'.[7] Sceptical of ethnic identity and community (denying point blank the relation between land and nationality),[8] still Medem gestures towards the possibility of a cohabitation or shared residence on earth which will rescue the subject from his or her isolation, whether existential or sexual.

In interviews and in texts reprinted in press notes and accompanying the published version of the script, Medem has repeatedly described *Tierra* as a 'coming to earth' ('aterrizaje'). His short essay 'Ángel's Complex'[9] describes the film's protagonist (played by Medem regular Carmelo Gómez) as a solipsist existing 'within himself' who must 'land' ('aterrizar') and live on the same scale as the rest of humanity. For Medem the film is 'profoundly subjective, imbued [*teñida*] with the look [*mirada*] of the [main] character'. The metaphysics (of character and film) are thus not absolute, but rather relative (p. 11) and undermined by humour (p. 12). *Tierra* is 'a journey from the abstract of [Ángel's] personal world to the concrete of human life', from the complex to the simple. Over-interpreting everyday events, Ángel experiences the world as 'a succession of enigmas' (p. 13); and obsessed with the 'intermediate space' of the sky (between the infinite emptiness of the cosmos and the microscopic realm of the soil) he must also choose between two women, the domesticated Ángela (Emma Suárez) (Plate 11) and the wild child Mari (Silke) (Plate 12): his 'cosmic conflict', caused by a 'split personality' ('desdoblamiento de personalidad'), is thus fused or confused with a conflict of love (p. 14).

[5] See Jonathan Romney, review of *Tierra*, *Sight and Sound*, 7.8 (Aug. 1997), 56.

[6] *The New Shorter Oxford English Dictionary* (Oxford: Oxford University Press, 1993), s.v. 'grounded'.

[7] These phrases derive from Stephen Holden's review of *Vacas* in *New York Times* (30 Mar. 1993).

[8] Interview with author.

[9] Julio Medem, 'El complejo de Ángel', in *Mari en la tierra/Tierra: guión para largometraje* (Barcelona: Planeta, 1997), 11–15; reprinted in English in the UK press book (London: Metro Tartan, 1997).

Anticipating critics who were to complain of 'cosmic claptrap'[10] and 'overblown aestheticism',[11] Medem writes that his film is hostile to transcendence and mysticism, its aim being rather to 'accept human smallness, to hold tight to the earth'.

Now, it is clear that no director, however literate and articulate, can determine the range of interpretations to which his work is open; indeed, even as he seeks to legitimize a particular reading of his work (claiming that Ángel is 'mistaken' and *Tierra*'s cosmic visions take place only in the character's imagination, pp. 11, 12), Medem also disclaims responsibility for the finished film, claiming that *Tierra* belongs not to him but to its audience and that the creative process is unconscious, beginning as it does not with a clearly articulated idea but rather with an indistinct mood or sensation.[12] Moreover, as we shall see, Medem's career (backed from the beginning by the powerful media consortium PRISA) was founded on the promotion of the auteur as spokesman for his films,[13] whether in the domestic context of a supposed 'new generation' of Basque film-makers[14] or the international context of the festivals at which his films compete for foreign sales with rival art movies. If Ángel is caught between heaven and earth, Medem is trapped also between the autonomy of the creative artist and the dependency of the industrial employee, a dependency reduced but not eliminated in *Tierra*, for which Medem received for the first time financial resources equal to his artistic ambitions.[15]

Set in an unidentified landscape whose Martian redness is enigmatically interspersed with Basque toponymics (such as 'Basterretxe') and at an unspecified time (when the high tech fumigation of woodlice is contemporary with a barbaric boar hunt), *Tierra*'s spatial and temporal interzone is best described in negative terms. Thus if the eponymous 'earth' can be read as soil, territory, or planet, *Tierra* reveals little concern for the cultivation of the land (no one objects to the lice which Ángel has come to exterminate) and none at all for the preservation of the homestead or *caserío* (no sense of land as family property such as is found in a classic Basque film of the silent era also named 'Basterretxe');[16] even Ángel's insis-

[10] The phrase is from Elley, *Variety*.

[11] The phrase is from Rouyer, *Positif*.

[12] Interview with author.

[13] See John Hopewell's location report on *Vacas*, 'Waiting for the Cows to Come Home', *Moving Pictures International* (19 Sept. 1991), 25.

[14] Alberto Luchini, '¿De qué va el nuevo cine español?', *El Gran Musical*, 419 (Sept. 1995), 46–51. In this overview of Spanish cinema of the 1990s Medem is named as the most important of a group of young film-makers almost all of whom are Basque.

[15] Interview with author.

[16] The complete script of Mauro Azkona's *El mayorazgo de Basterretxe* (1928) is reproduced in Alberto López Echevarrieta, *Cine vasco: ¿realidad o ficción?* (Bilbao: Mensajero,

tence on the earth as a planet, a 'tiny island' of life and light in the cosmic desert, is abandoned as he learns to live on a human scale. The earth is not nature or purity (the ecological impact of Ángel's poisonous fumes goes unremarked); but nor is it ground or foundation: rather, the characters claim, it is 'hollow' and 'moves beneath the feet'. Deprived of nostalgia for tradition and of affection for the localism of landscape, *Tierra* also undoes opposition in ways which undermine narrative expectations and dramatic conflict: Mari has come from the (unnamed) city, but there is no sense in the film (as opposed to the 'diary' of her character authored by Medem) that her urban frankness is contrasted with rural modesty; likewise no social conflict is shown between the gypsies and the *payos* who inhabit the same bleak landscape. Etymologically a messenger, Ángel bears no message (his cosmic musings are an internal soliloquy); any symbolic dimension of his character seems related to the interzone of the skies once more: theologically, angels are the lowest order of the celestial hierarchy, the closest to earth.

Tierra's poster is typically abstracted: solid blocks of blue sky and orange earth, with a stylized black tree on the horizon, and the massive logo of the title filling the frame. Only the single credit ('A Film by Julio Medem') grounds the film, branding it as cinematic property or patrimony. This dichotomy, then, of physical and metaphysical, abstract and concrete, will be played out by repeated patterns of splitting and doubling, on the one hand, and fusion and identification, on the other. These patterns manifest themselves at the level of the plot, in film form, in print, and in production; but in spite of the variety of these sources one concern remains central: the reconciliation of the subjective and the intersubjective in an ideal of differentiation without isolation and unity without violence. What remains to be seen is whether *Tierra*'s dualisms are indeed transcended by Ángel's fall to earth; and whether Medem's dazzling and disorientating use of subjective vision and sound opens up a cinematic space for new subjectivities, most particularly for Basques and for women.

Medem has refused to take up the public position of 'Basque filmmaker', bravely resisting those who appeal to violence in support of a dualistic and antagonistic nationalism.[17] And it may be no accident that recent debates around 'postnationalism' in a Basque context repeat both general moves and particular motifs which appear in a more lyrical and oneiric form in *Tierra*. Intellectuals such as Jon Juaristi, Juan Aranzadi,

n.d.), 175–215. The plot revolves around a moneylender's attempt to appropriate the homestead of the title, and the film is notable for its *costumbrista* treatment of rural traditions.

[17] See my 'Angels to Earth'.

and Patxo Unzueta have sought, like Medem, to disentangle nationality from the land (and language) with which it is so frequently fused, viewing the mirage of independence as an 'act of termination'[18] rather than a new beginning for the Basque people. Taking their cue from foreign scholars better known in the UK and the USA than in the Spanish state, such as Hannah Arendt, Eric Hobsbawm, and Benedict Anderson, these Basque internationalists ground metaphysical nationalisms by treating them sceptically and analytically as localized forms of anti-Semitism, as the invention of traditions, or as imagined communities. Thus Juaristi's 'genealogy' traces the peculiarly unstable location of Basque identity: the 'compulsive' search for Basque roots in the sixteenth century is, paradoxically, an expression of 'Hispanic patriotism'.[19] Posing as the pre- or proto-historic Spain (an originary nobility which required no proof of its racial purity), the Basque nation reinforced unitary Spanish conservativism, even as it sought to separate itself from it (*Vestigios*, 5–6). Appropriating and confusing Jewish traditions (claiming their descent from the twin Tuvals of the Bible whom they mistakenly fused into one, p. 24; displacing conversos from the scribal positions they themselves coveted, p. 12), Basques founded their sense of self on a myth of originary language (divine, angelical, animal; p. 75), usurped from Hebrew. The 'spirit of the nation' was thus fused with the 'genius of the language' (p. 80) in a mythical triad: original purity, fall, and redemption (p. 74).

For Juaristi, then, all identity, whether national or individual, is imposed from outside: 'in the depths of every one of us lives the Other and to him belong our dearest fantasies' (p. 104). Hence the inexplicable persistence of anti-Semitism (for Juaristi the very origin of Basque nationalism) long after the expulsion of the Jews had left an 'empty ghetto':[20] attempting to legitimize a new ideology through appeal to literature, nineteenth-century nationalists[21] invented a pseudo-medieval tradition (a 'genealogy of the Basque Imaginary or of the imaginary Basque'; *El linaje*, 18) which would at once differentiate their people from other Spaniards and separate them from the biblical precedents of earlier Basque mythologies (p. 96). Medieval myths rewritten at the time (such as

---

[18] I take this phrase from the collective volume by these three scholars, *Auto de terminación: raza, nación, y violencia en el País Vasco* (Madrid: El País/Aguilar, 1994). The only article I know to have (briefly) cited Juaristi in discussing Medem is Aitor Yraola, 'El discurso de la muerte en *Vacas* de Julio Medem', in George Cabello-Castellet et al. (eds.), *Cine-Lit*, ii: *Essays on Hispanic Film and Fiction* (Portland: Portland and Oregon State Universities and Reed College, 1995), 163–8 (p. 167).

[19] *Vestigios de Babel: para una arqueología de los nacionalismos españoles* (Madrid: Siglo XXI, 1992), 5, 6.

[20] 'El gueto vacío', in *Auto de terminación* (pp. 115–36).

[21] *El linaje de Aitor: la invención de la tradición vasca* (Madrid: Taurus, 1987).

the tale of the 'woman with the feet of a goat'[22]) characteristically combine misogyny and anti-Semitism with classic locations such as the boar hunt. In a further paradox, then, the ultra-Catholicism of early nationalists gave way to a polytheistic Aryanism which took the late Christian conversion of the Basques to be a badge of honour: a dialogue by Pío Baroja of 1922 cites Urtzi, the ancient god of thunder, as the wielder of a hammer which will 'shatter the servile, hypocritical world of Catholicism and implant the free worship of nature' (*El linaje*, 288). Returning from his exile in the 'frozen Northern deserts', Urtzi-Thor will restore the 'original and spontaneous vitalism of the Basque people' (p. 277). While the purpose of such myth-making was to produce through the work of art a 'collective subject' (p. 19) its effect was rather to ensure the 'lethal self-absorption' of the Basque people, mesmerized by a Golden Age or 'past before History' (p. 290). Bringing separatist myth-making down to earth with a bump, Juaristi dates national identity, supposedly immemorial, to 1836 precisely, when a forgotten pamphleteer 'began to dream our nightmare'.

Juan Aranzadi also makes the move (like Medem) from the metaphysical to the physical, from the abstract to the concrete.[23] For him the racism on which Basque nationalism is founded is a 'conceptual break with the logic of the concrete' (which he calls 'earthly feeling'; pp. 36, 37); or again 'traditional rural beliefs' ('the name Mari, the hearth, the souls of the ancestors') enact an 'indissoluble fusion of Earth–House–Family–Race–Nobility' (p. 77) backed by the 'theology' of Euskera as 'angelic speech, language of Paradise' (p. 81). For Juaristi again,[24] nationalism is to be 'weakened' or 'secularized' (pp. 97, 98), and the role of historiography is to 'bring down [*descender*] the nation from the heaven of myths and submerge it in temporality' (p. 111). The loss of nationalism is not, however, an easy affair: like the loss of God, it provokes 'anguish', 'a desire without object', and 'the burden of the consciousness of death' (p. 113). ETA's 'theology' is thus also a 'necrology' or 'necrologic', legitimized through crazy causality: for Patxo Unzueta[25] 'the consequence of terrorist action [state repression] is passed off as the inevitable cause of that action' (p. 144); for Aranzadi[26] nationalist movements call into being the national 'entity' of which they claim to be the natural expression (p. 202). The question of ethnicity and violence is thus also and most importantly the question of the subject: an ethnic group is defined not by objective charac-

---

[22] 'La dama pie de cabra' (1843), reprinted in Jon Juaristi (ed.), *La tradición romántica: leyendas vascas del siglo XIX* (Pamplona: Pamiela, 1986), 47–76.

[23] I cite two articles from *Auto de terminación*: 'Racismo y piedad' (pp. 27–43) and 'La religión abertzale' (pp. 63–95).

[24] 'Postnacionalismo', in *Auto de terminación* (pp. 97–113).

[25] 'Del monte al llano', in *Auto de terminación* (pp. 139–55).

[26] 'Etnicidad y violencia en el País Vasco', in *Auto de terminación* (pp. 201–33).

teristics but by subjective opposition to other groups (p. 202); the purpose of terror is not to achieve an objective end but rather to establish 'subjective reversion', that is to say the fact that the agent is oneself and no other (p. 212); and the efficacy of such actions is 'global, abstract, and not concrete' (p. 216) anchored in 'false, fetish subjects, such as the people . . . in which the individual self is doubled, projected, alienated, and empowered' (pp. 218–19).

It is not to curtail the lyrical and romantic power of *Tierra* to argue that the film can be read within the context of the postnationalist debate with which it is contemporary. Indeed the postnationalists share with Medem not only their impatience with national boundaries and antagonisms but also their engagement with fantasy and irrationality. Juxtaposing film and text we might read *Tierra* as an allegory of a Basque nationalism brought down to earth. Ángel the celestial messenger is perhaps also the imaginary Basque whose riddling speech appears to have special access to both the divine and the animal. Moreover he is an initially 'pure' creature who falls only to be redeemed by human love. But while Medem invokes the genealogy of the Basque Imaginary (the numinous Mari, the boar hunt, even the gypsies as substitute for the empty ghetto of the Jews) and sets his action in a frozen northern desert, he dissolves the fusion of Earth–House–Family, dislocating the links with which abstract nationalism so violently binds them together. Hence the Earth is displaced (the film is shot not in Euskadi, but in Aragón), the House is defiled (the patriarch cheats on his wife), and the Family is dispersed (the father is killed and the mother spurned).

Ángel will thus be led out of his lethal self-absorption through his engagement with the twin love objects, sensual Mari and domestic Ángela; and his divine speech will be secularized, reduced to the scale of human existence. Initially obsessed with the anguish of mortality, he expresses himself with crazy necrologic, responding to human crises (such as the attempted suicide of Ángela's father) with abstract discourses on the cosmic void; but later, rejecting the violence of his antagonist Patricio (lover of Mari, husband of Ángela), he will also abandon that subjective splitting in which he doubles and projects himself: the phantom angel who accompanies him, invisible and inaudible to others, will be left behind when Ángel drives from the village with Mari in the final scene. Ángel's split personality, then, is not merely the legacy of psychiatric disorder or the internalization of external conflict; it is the acknowledgement that identity is imposed from outside and the Other inhabits our most intimate fantasies.

2. Formal Dislocations

Tierra's avowed anti-mysticism bears within it a particular charge: that of those 'heretical' nationalists who opposed Christianity as the usurper of pagan vitalism. While the film clearly resists such Aryan nature worship, it does make a specific reference here: Ángel's fumigation company goes by the name of 'Urtzi', the ancient god of thunder also invoked by Baroja. How then might we reread *Tierra*'s apocalyptic opening in a post-nationalist context? The published script is particularly evocative here: I transcribe the first sequences, omitting the voice-over which is described as the 'Voice of the angel'.

1. NEGRO Y ESPACIO CÓSMICO (NEGRO CÓSMICO). EXTERIOR.

Sobre una pantalla absolutamente negra aparece lentamente, en letras blancas . . .

TIERRA

Funde a negro y oímos una voz cercana, serena.

Comenzamos a sentir 'el sentido de la angustia' al tiempo que aparecen esos diminutos destellos fluctuantes que señalan que nos encontramos, moviéndonos suavemente, en medio del espacio cósmico.

2. NUBES Y VISIÓN AÉREA DE LA COMARCA. EXTERIOR. DÍA.

A. NUBES.

Poco a poco (sobre el fondo cósmico de la sec. anterior) entra una espesa y cada vez más resplandeciente masa de nubes que atravesamos a gran velocidad.

Repentinamente, tras sobrepasar la última nube, toda la imagen se despeja . . .

B. VISIÓN AÉREA DE LA COMARCA.

Vemos la tierra desde el cielo, como una aparición serena en la que se ha desvanecido la sensación de velocidad. Se trata de 'la comarca', un paisaje de viñedos cultivados sobre suaves y confortables colinas de tierra pardorrojiza. Estamos en invierno, así que las cepas se muestran desnudas de hojas.

Encadena a . . .

3. GALERÍA BAJO LA *TIERRA*. INTERIOR. DÍA.

Una cochinilla (popularmente bicho bola) ocupa toda la pantalla mientras camina por el interior de una galería bajo la tierra.

4. IMÁGENES DE LA COMARCA (PARA CRÉDITOS). EXTERIOR. DÍA.

Comienza a llover abundamente con acompañamiento de rayos y truenos, sobre diversas imágenes de la comarca:

— Una gruesa cepa sin hojas, en primer término, sobre un fondo de suaves colinas de tierra rojiza salteada de viñedos.
— Gotas penetrando la tierra.
— Visión interior de un seco maizal que recuerda a un tupido bosque de estrechos troncos amarillos.

Subjectivity

— Huellas de tractor en un camino sobre las que discurre el agua de la lluvia.
— Un rayo cae sobre un árbol solitario, partiendo la mitad de su tronco, que cae sobre la tierra.

En sobreimpresión han ido apareciendo los TÍTULOS DE CRÉDITO.

Funde a negro cósmico. (pp. 19–21)

1. BLACK AND COSMIC SPACE (COSMIC BLACK). EXTERIOR.

On an absolutely black screen there slowly appears, in white lettering . . .

TIERRA

Fade to black and we hear a calm voice, close by.

We start to hear 'the sound of anguish' as tiny twinkling glimmers appear, signalling that we find ourselves smoothly moving though cosmic space.

2. CLOUDS AND AERIAL SHOT OF THE DISTRICT. EXTERIOR. DAY.

A. CLOUDS.

Little by little (over the cosmic background of the previous sequence) there comes into view a thick and increasingly bright mass of clouds through which we pass at great speed.

Suddenly, after passing through the last cloud, the whole picture clears . . .

B. AERIAL SHOT OF THE DISTRICT

We see the earth from the sky, like a serene apparition in which the sensation of speed has faded away. It is 'the district', a landscape of vines growing on gentle, comfortable hills of reddish earth. We are in winter, and the vines have no leaves.

Dissolve to . . .

3. GALLERY UNDER THE EARTH. INTERIOR. DAY.

A woodlouse fills the whole screen as it walks through the inside of a gallery dug under the earth.

4. SHOTS OF THE DISTRICT (FOR THE CREDITS). EXTERIOR. DAY.

It starts to rain heavily, accompanied by thunder and lightning, over varied shots of the district:

— A thick vine stump without leaves, in the foreground, on a background of gentle hills of red earth scattered with vines.
— Drops of rain sinking into the earth.
— Shot from inside a dry maize field which looks like a dense forest of narrow yellow trunks.
— Tractor tracks on a path over which rainwater is running.
— A thunderbolt falls on a solitary tree, splitting half of its trunk, which falls onto the earth.

The CREDITS have been superimposed over these shots.

Fade to cosmic black.

154

The sequence stages the fall to earth of camera, character, and audience. It is an apparently continuous movement (from deep space, to upper atmosphere, to sodden soil) created by a characteristic editing style of fades, dissolves, and masked cuts. But this spatial journey is also temporal, the shift from darkness into light recreating a pagan cosmogony, the creation *ex nihilo* of the earth (and, perhaps, of cinema). The script repeatedly uses the first person plural pronoun; and through helicopters and digital effects (the aerial shot and the animatronic insect), the audience is encouraged to adopt the impossible, omniscient viewpoint of the vision machine, at once human and inhuman, or of the ancestral gods, both celestial and chthonic. This sense of subjectivization is reinforced by the use of sound, which serves to heighten affectivity even here in the realm of cosmic myth-making: the angel's voice remains calm and close whatever the image it plays over; the strings of Alberto Iglesias, Medem's long-time musical collaborator, swell and swoon. Vertiginous changes in point of view and in scale are thus disavowed by the film form which initially promotes fusion and identification.

The brief shots which follow serve economically to establish some of the locations featured in the film and to hint at narrative exposition: the vines are the initial motive for Ángel's arrival in the district; the maize field is the setting for the boar hunt; the tractor belongs to Ángel's antagonist Patricio, who will be struck by lightning. But just as the voice-over tells us that Ángel has come to this place for something other than his overt mission (the extermination of the woodlice), so the intensity of these images exceeds their denotative value within the diegesis. In the Basque cosmology invoked by the name Urtzi (and, indeed, Gernika), the thunderbolt and the tree bring with them mythical connotations of violence and vitalism, of spirituality and continuity. But the earth to which 'we' fall is not substantial but, rather, hollow: shot through (according to the voice-over) with 'holes of mystery', the great 'gallery of the woodlouse' repeating and reversing not just the human habitation but also the cosmic void above it. In a double gesture, then, *Tierra* re-enacts and undermines the founding myths of a planet and a nation, which stand revealed as fragile 'islands' in space and time. Medem thus stages a narrative of subjectivity (of 'thrownness'[27] into the world) which employs a pantheism with no nature principle, a mysticism with no divinity, and an allegory with no fixed literal term. After the tree is shattered we are returned once more to the ever enigmatic and 'anguished' cosmic black.

As *Tierra* proceeds, film form is used in this sceptical and ironical way with the effect of splitting and doubling, rather than fusion and identifi-

[27] For this Heideggerian term see my reading of Medem through Gianni Vattimo in *Vision Machines*, 130.

cation. Thus when Ángel first walks over the land to the gypsies, carrying a teasingly emblematic 'lost sheep' on his shoulders, the cinematography shifts abruptly from smooth tracking and steadicam shots to a jerky hand-held camera. When he engages Ángela and her family in conversation, the slow and ominous performance style (most particularly Emma Suárez's eloquent looks and pregnant pauses) cuts against the grain of the crazy causality of the dialogue. The placid and muted rhythm of such interiors is violently contrasted with the quick cuts and deafening Dolby sound of such action exteriors as the race between the tractor and Mari's motorbike or the boar hunt in the maize field.

Most complex is the dislocation of sound- and image-tracks, frequently effected by the incursion of the angel's voice-over, a subjective sound which (according to the script) only Ángel seems to hear (p. 38), the aural equivalent of the distinctive view through the 'geoscope' which is also accessible only to Ángel and the audience. The most moving sequence rings the changes on on and off screen sound. When Ángel phones Ángela at home we hear her voice as if distorted through a telephone: first, over a travelling exterior shot of the phone cables; next, over an interior of her speaking in her kitchen; and finally, also in the kitchen, but with her lips not moving. Simultaneously we hear Ángel's (non-telephonic) voice: first, when he is out of frame; second, as his mute angelic companion approaches Ángela in the kitchen; and finally, as the angel moves his lips (while Ángela's stay still even as she speaks). Working against the cosmic fusion of the opening sequence, such complex scenes register the pleasures and the problems of terrestrial life in which modern technology both promotes and frustrates the desire for spatial and temporal simultaneity, for a phantasmal cohabitation between subjects and sexes. Medem's play with subjective sound and vision is thus a cinematic equivalent of that splitting and doubling we have seen in both Basque (post)nationalism and the psychodrama of 'Ángel's complex'.

A later sequence also problematizes point of view in a vertiginous and contradictory switching of viewpoints. Ángel, once more in the kitchen, attempts to console Ángela after her father's suicide attempt. Standing behind her, we see from his point of view ('posición subjetiva'; p. 110) a 'slight movement' towards the back of her neck. The next 'frontal shot' of Ángela (a 180-degree shift) reveals Ángel has not in fact moved. The script specifies a change in depth of field achieved by the Hitchcockian technique of inverted tracking and zoom before a cut to the previous point of view from which we see two pairs of arms encompassing Ángela, a 'double embrace' by the character and his angelic companion. Towards the end of the film, depth of field is repeatedly used in a similar way to express the simultaneity and the separation of Ángel from his alter ego: a surprise shot from the corridor of Ángela's house reveals in order of increasing distance from the camera a 'foreshortened' back view of the angel; Ángela's daughter spying on her mother; and Ángel the man addressing Ángela the mother inside the kitchen (p. 138). Or again as Ángel leaves the house (in a frontal tracking shot; p. 140) we see behind him and slightly out of focus the image of his angel beside the two Ángelas.

Unusually precise as to camera movement and actor positioning in such scenes, the script also suggests subjective identifications between characters in addition to those already made explicit by their sharing the same names. Thus the reader (but not the spectator) is told that the invisible angel covers Ángela's face with kisses as tenderly as Mari had kissed Ángel the man (p. 147); or again, when Ángel leaves the bar to follow Mari, we are told that he looks back to see the pale face of the angel wearing an 'identical expression' to that worn by the abandoned Ángela (p. 149). Such elaborate symmetries (which have their counterpart in repeated camera movements which are also specified in the script) establish intersubjective fusions which transgress the fixed frontiers of male and female, real and fantastic.

The fact remains, however, that in the film itself the point of view, whether single or double, is consistently that of the twin Ángels. And while Medem has claimed in interview that gender is indifferent to *Tierra*'s narrative,[28] the only character subjected to sexual objectification is the nymphomaniac Mari. Indeed the script repeatedly defaces her: the unknown figure on a motorcycle is, we are told, Mari 'whose face we do not see' (p. 48); when first spotted in the bar she is 'with her back towards us' (p. 59); and Ángel later 'glimpses a shoulder . . . a hip with two half-open legs' (p. 61). Given this fetishistic fragmentation, perhaps the most surprising of *Tierra*'s cross-gender identifications and subjective shifts is Medem's own authorship of the character's 'diary', bound with the published script, but printed back to front and upside down. 'Mari en la tierra' was, we are told, first the working title of the film and then the basis of a low budget feature which Medem intended to shoot simultaneously with *Tierra* in black and white and from Mari's point of view. Dedicated to novice actress Silke ('more beautiful than in the imagination'), the diary was used in the lengthy rehearsal process to provide Mari (previously the 'slave of the script'; p. 9) with an internal dilemma equal and opposite to Ángel's. The 'other side' of *Tierra*, her look would be as 'subjective' as his (p. 10). Following a supplementary logic, however, this additional text transformed the original it was intended merely to complement, 'infiltrating' itself into the final version of *Tierra* and 'taking out' of Medem 'a character [he] did not know [he] had' within him (p. 11).

[28] Interview with author.

But if Mari 'changes [Medem's] point of view' (p. 13) and if the twin stories are the 'subjective looks of characters in the process of finding one another' (p. 14), then still the spectator of the film is left with only half of that 'intermediate world in which [the couple] can live together' (p. 14); and even the reader of the 'diary' will be left in some doubt as to the 'complementarity' of the exchange that it claims to perform. On the one hand, Mari's perspective does lend a social and political specificity to *Tierra*'s dream landscape: riding her motorbike past the gypsies she worries that she looks like 'the boss's daughter' (p. 41); she denounces Patricio's apparent 'racism' (only implicit in the film; p. 86); and with her 'great experience of the big city' (p. 44) she can dismiss Ángela's best clothes as examples of 'village vulgarity' (p. 124). But if the film's enigmas and triangles are reversed (with male motivation now mysterious and the woman forced to choose between two men), still Mari is deprived of intimacy and history. Thus Medem has her write repeatedly that she will 'speak in the present tense' looking neither forward nor back (pp. 20, 21, 23); and she will discuss neither the 'shadow' which hangs over her nor the phantom city from which she has escaped (p. 20). And if Mari's story fills gaps in the narrative (most particularly by establishing a loving friendship between her and her rival Ángela), still it confines her to a temporal and spatial immediacy born of an obsessional sexuality no less pathological than Ángel's hyperactive imagination.

But this internal play of duplication and identification enacted by film and text narratives is (as Medem's acknowledgement of Silke's contribution to *Tierra* suggests) also acted out in such external questions of the film's production history as casting. Perhaps the most public of these substitutions is Silke's displacement of Emma Suárez as Medem's muse: Suárez, the browbeaten mother of *Tierra*, was the leather-clad girl on a motorcycle in his previous feature, *La ardilla roja*. Likewise, according to the trade press,[29] aquiline Carmelo Gómez as Ángel was a substitute for the previously cast Antonio Banderas, a more likely love object for what *Variety* called 'two striking femmes'. Finally Silke, cast as a 'sex genius' in this her first role, has repeatedly insisted that the character had 'nothing in common with herself'[30] and indeed she was strikingly different in the two films she made with young women directors immediately after *Tierra*, in which her persona is more mundane and less frankly sexual.[31]

---

[29] Anonymous note in *Screen International*, 991 (20 Jan. 1995), 10.

[30] Ricardo Aldarondo, 'Julio Medem propone en *Tierra* un viaje al "mundo desconocido que nos rodea"', *El Diario Vasco* (24 May 1996). The occasion of this piece is the première of *Tierra* in San Sebastián, which was attended by Medem and most of his cast. I would like to thank the staff of the Euskadiko Filmategia/Filmoteca Vasca in Donostia/San Sebastián for providing press clippings on Medem.

[31] Icíar Bollain's picaresque *Hola, ¿estás sola?* and Mónica Laguna's comedy of city folk in

Silke's sudden celebrity as a cover star of Spanish magazines no doubt aided *Tierra*'s unlikely box office success in the domestic market: for several weeks it was the only Spanish film to figure in the top ten grosses.[32] But more important was the continuing support of PRISA, Spain's biggest media corporation which embraces TV, radio, and the most prestigious daily newspaper, *El País*. Medem's first feature *Vacas* had been the first venture into feature production by Sogetel, the film division of PRISA, and its international success, spearheaded by prizes in festivals in Turin and Tokyo, had been essential to the producer's recoupment of costs which could no longer be satisfied by revenue from the home market.[33] *La ardilla roja*, panned by home critics, was extravagantly praised by the French and awarded the prize for best foreign feature in the Directors' Fortnight at Cannes.[34] With this record, Medem's budget for *Tierra* permitted the use of Spain's best-known cinematographer Javier Aguirresarobe (a veteran of Erice and Saura), whose widescreen work *Variety* called 'stunning', and the use of technical effects (also voted 'tops'). Part funded by Canal+, Europe's biggest subscription TV channel, the *Tierra* which presents itself as an unrepentant art film with an uncompromisingly abstract concept is also a mainstream movie in the production context of the national and European industries. In a Spanish cinema which in 1995 set out to court youthful audiences with young directors and actors and in which state funding was now directed according to more commercially motivated criteria,[35] an apparently left-field project such as *Tierra* looked to be a solid investment, even without the stellar presence of Spain's only international star, Antonio Banderas.

But if *Tierra*'s production history is relatively simple, its distribution is more problematic. While Medem claims that the film was given adequate space in Spanish theatres and was not pulled before it had completed an

the country *Tengo una casa* (both 1996). Medem is credited for his collaboration in the former's script, published as *Hola, ¿estás sola?: guión original de la película* (Barcelona: Planeta, 1997).

[32] In its third week of release *Tierra* remained at number five in the national ranking, having taken over $350,000 in thirty-three theatres; source: *Screen International* (28 June 1996), 25. Further proof of *Tierra*'s popular and critical success are the facts that it was voted best film of the year by readers of *El País Semanal* and received two Goya awards.

[33] See Hopewell, *Moving Pictures International*.

[34] Typical of French praise for this film is the interview-feature by Gilles Boulenger and Vincent Lebrun, 'L'Échappée belle,' in *Le Cinéphage*, 16 (Jan. 1994), 7–11 which hails the birth of an 'immense cineaste' (p. 7).

[35] Rocío García, 'El cine español mira al público: inicia su recuperación con 2,5 millones de espectadores más que en 1994', *El País* (24 Dec. 1995). *Tierra* was one of a slate of features announced by PRISA in San Sebastián in collaboration with powerful producer Andrés Vicente Gómez; Rocío García, 'Sogetel amplía alianzas para coproducir 15 filmes españoles en el plazo de tres años', *El País* (23 Sept. 1995).

appropriate run,[36] in English-speaking countries foreign-language films have become endangered species, a tiny, fragile island in a sea of US product. Shown only in festivals in the USA, Medem's films are also threatened in the UK, where they have indeed received theatrical release. Screened at the London Film Festival in October 1996, *Tierra* was not shown commercially until almost a year later;[37] and its reception was mediated by apparently extraneous factors, at once general and specific to it. Amongst the general factors was the collapse in art house audiences, caused in part by the near disappearance of subtitled cinema even on the minority channels of terrestrial TV. Factors specific to *Tierra* are its director's lack of English, which problematizes promotional interviews; the abstraction of the press notes he authored, rendered ridiculous by inadequate translations; and a crisis in the British distributor-exhibitor which acquired *Tierra*, the only house in the country known for Spanish-language films, whose well-regarded owner died suddenly. In such circumstances, although *Tierra* found favour in the pages of a semi-academic film journal such as *Sight and Sound*, it was unlikely to receive sympathetic coverage from the general press. But Medem's films have not always received positive notices even in his local Basque papers, which faithfully report, however, every stage of the production process, from the award of government subsidy, through the first day of shooting, to the inevitable première in Medem's native San Sebastián/Donostia.[38]

Medem denies the existence of a distinctively Basque cinema, whether it is based on artistic or commercial criteria: he claims to have nothing in common with other Basque directors of his 'generation' (such as Juanma Bajo Ulloa or Alex de la Iglesia); and attacks the Basque autonomous government for pulling the plug on film-makers and technicians just as the prospect of a national industry became possible.[39] Excessive attention to the commercial constraints of production and distribution is surely reductive, even punitive, when applied to films as enamoured of mystery

[36] Medem contrasts *Tierra*'s good distribution with the less happy fate of other domestic hits of the same season, such as Mariano Barroso' s *Extasis*; see my 'Angels to Earth'.

[37] At the Metro Cinema in the West End on 8 Aug. 1997.

[38] See, in the case of *La ardilla roja*, the following reports in *El Diario Vasco*: Manuel Mediavilla, 'Julio Medem, uno de los doce subvencionados por el ICAA' (11 June 1992); Ainhoa Ondarzabal, 'Comienza hoy en San Sebastián el rodaje de *La ardilla roja*' (17 Aug. 1992); and Ricardo Aldarondo, 'Emma Suárez: "Julio Medem reta y engrandece a sus actores"; el equipo de *La ardilla roja* presentó en San Sebastián la nueva película' (24 Apr. 1993). *El Diario Vasco* also announced that remake rights had been sold to the USA: EFE, 'La versión americana de *La ardilla roja* costará 1.600 millones' (24 May 1994). Returning from Cannes, where *Tierra* was shown in competition, Medem claimed to Ricardo Aldarondo that his third film had been sold to fifteen countries; 'Arregi acabó con el cine vasco', *El Diario Vasco* (24 May 1996).

[39] See my 'Angels to Earth'.

and fantasy as Medem's. But I hope to have shown that to 'ground' Medem in his national and industrial context is a critical enterprise parallel and sympathetic to his own cinematic journey in *Tierra*. Caught between art and commerce, film and text, Medem is an artistic equivalent of his creation Ángel, 'a brave man with shaky hands';[40] and the space he has carved out for himself is, like the interzone of Urtzi's sky or of the anonymous red landscape, a terrain which is at once difficult to define and uniquely distinctive.

At the end of the film the landscape 'takes leave' of Ángel 'showing [him] its marks which are [his] own footprints', the trace of his journey through time and space. It is a revelation of 'earthly feeling' (Aranzadi's phrase) which is at once intimate and concrete. Transcending the anguished and lethal self-absorption caused by the lost objects of the Catholic God and the nation state, Ángel and the audience are led to view the earth on which they were thrown as both the horizon of freedom and the precondition of interpretation: in Heidegger's words 'the putting into work of truth'.[41] If (as the voice-over puts it) 'the mystery of the woodlouse will not be solved', then it is Medem's achievement not only to hold fast to his narrative enigmas but also to rework and untie those rapturous myths which, most particularly in the case of the Basque Country, bind land so violently to language and to nationality. Reconciling the subjective and the intersubjective (imagination and cohabitation), *Tierra* suggests, in spite of its cosmic ambitions, that we may indeed find solace for our solitude at a personal, national, and existential level, but only if we take our leave of murderous metaphysics and live on a strictly human scale.

[40] Metro Tartan press book, 5.
[41] For this Heideggerian reading of art and earth see my *Vision Machines*, 141–2.

9 | Cross-Cut: Gypsy

1. The Subject of Everyday Life

By the mid-1990s the themes of the gypsy and of flamenco (irreducible to and inseparable from one another) acquired unprecedented prominence in Spanish popular culture. No fewer than four major films released in 1995 featured this motif: Julio Medem's *Tierra* (as we have seen) located a gypsy community in the bleak stasis of a lunar landscape; Almodóvar's *La flor de mi secreto* ('The Flower of my Secret') featured dancer Joaquín Cortés in his first dramatic role; flamenco fusion group Ketama were shown performing both in the multicultural London of Fernando Colomo's *El efecto de mariposa* ('The Butterfly Effect') and in the ethnically diverse Madrid of Chus Gutiérrez's *Alma gitana* ('Gypsy Soul').[1] My hypothesis in this final chapter is that this disproportionate presence of the gypsy in everyday Spanish life is symptomatic of recent social change. More particularly, the gypsy is presented as a new, hybrid subject, both strange and familiar, who is at once a response to and a displacement of Spaniards' confrontation with a more radical otherness: that of global immigration to the Spain that was for so long a nation of net emigration. Indeed two other films, also of 1995, centre on immigration from sub-Saharan Africa and Eastern Europe, respectively.[2] The fantasy of an original miscegenation (of the Spanish heritage and of flamenco as a hybrid derived from Jewish and Arab roots)[3] thus serves as a screen for a more immediate social relation which cannot be projected so safely into the distant past.[4]

[1] For a journalistic survey which testifies to this phenomenon see Joaquín Albaicín, 'Los gitanos en el cine', *El País: Babelia* (Saturday supplement) (30 Mar. 1996), 2–3. My thinking on gypsies, 'race', and popular culture was aided by two papers at the Spanish Cultural Studies conference held at the Institute of Romance Studies in the University of London, 5–6 June 1997: Jo Labanyi, 'Musical Battles: Mediations of the High/Low Cultural Divide in the Early Francoist Folklórica'; and Isabel Santaolalla, 'The Dark Side: Racial Configurations in Contemporary Spanish Culture'.

[2] Imanol Uribe's *Bwana* and Icíar Bollaín's *Hola, ¿estás sola?*.

[3] Typically fantastic is the derivation of *jondo* from Hebrew *yom tod* (*sic*; for *yom tov*) in Joaquín García Lavernia, *El libro del cante flamenco* (Madrid: Rialp, 1991), 26.

[4] By 1991, with the precipitous decline of the Spanish birth rate, the greater part of popu-

As a locus of the intersection of modernity and tradition, home and abroad, same and other (of contradictions in time, space, and subjectivity), the gypsy takes on the role of an alterity that is also a proximity and a supplementarity; all too close to notions of authentic Spanishness (as shown by such ambivalent traditions as the *feria* of Seville), the gypsy comes to substitute for that 'proper' culture and to represent it both at home and abroad. Of course the centrality of such phenomena as the *feria* (in which non-gypsies temporarily adopt gypsy-derived dress) need not demonstrate sympathy for or understanding of gypsy culture; indeed it could be argued that those *payos* most enamoured of flamenco have most reinforced the dependency of gypsy performers and the devaluation of their culture. Thus recent anthropological studies have strongly contested stereotypes of 'soul' and 'passion' that are themselves legitimized by the purist nostalgia of aficionados. Timothy Mitchell has described a 'passional culture' in which intensity of emotion is inseparable from social structures such as a pernicious patronage system and a ruinous reliance on alcohol;[5] William Washabaugh has stressed the socio-political context of performance in an age of mass media, an approach which makes him sympathetic to such controversial hybrids as Cortés;[6] finally, Génesis García Gómez has given a socio-cultural interpretation of the subgenre of miners' flamenco, a song form that has evolved in an industrial, proletarian milieu.[7] García Gómez is particularly scathing about those with 'the loudest voices' who claim that flamenco cannot be studied because it is 'mystery, enigma, obscurity, and *duende*' (p. 7).

It is also salutary to be reminded by García Gómez that there remain academics in Spain who reject flamenco because it is socially stigmatized (p. 7). Yet the social history of gypsies in Spain is complex and contradictory.[8] Unlike elsewhere in Europe, the process of enforced sedentarization began early: in 1499 the Catholic Monarchs ordered gypsies to settle and take up a trade; in 1610 the Cortes legislated dispersal and surveillance; and in 1633 Philip IV proclaimed that gypsies would be known not by origin or nature but by adopted way of life. Laws of Forced Assimilation

---

lation increase was due to immigration; see Carlos de Vega, 'Los flujos de inmigrantes apuntalan la caída de la población autóctona en toda Europa', *El País* (14 July 1997). The statistics cited here are from the Eurostat Agency.

[5] *Flamenco: Deep Song* (New Haven: Yale University Press, 1994). See also his earlier *Passional Culture: Emotion, Religion, and Society in Southern Spain* (Philadelphia: University of Pennsylvania Press, 1990) for a sociological account of Semana Santa.

[6] *Flamenco: Passion, Politics, and Popular Culture* (Oxford: Berg, 1996).

[7] *Cante flamenco, cante minero: una interpretación sociocultural* (Barcelona: Anthropos, 1993).

[8] I take this historical sketch from Bernard Leblon, *Gypsies and Flamenco* (Hatfield: Gypsy Research Centre/University of Hertfordshire Press, 1995).

succeeded one another in the eighteenth century, culminating in the brief but traumatic General Internment of 1749. Charles II's Law of 1783 severely penalized any manifestation of distinctiveness in language, costume, lifestyle, and trade. In the light of this history of violent assimilation, Timothy Mitchell plots a past and predicts a future for flamenco that is 'beyond ethnicity' (*Flamenco*, 216): when differential criteria have strayed from 'race' or 'blood' to profession and even urbanization ('payo' originally designated the non-gypsy as a 'rural dweller'), it proves impossible to draw the line between self and other: a constitutionally hybrid category, 'gypsy' throws into crisis those criteria by which the subject is properly known and recognized.[9]

In this chapter, then, I do not address the question of artists' self-identification; and the four cultural phenomena I treat are typically hybrid. The first is *Carmen* (1983), the dance-cinema collaboration between choreographer-performer Antonio Gades and director Carlos Saura; the second *Alma gitana* (1995), Chus Gutiérrez's narrative feature film with musical interludes, mentioned above; the third the popular flamenco fusion music of Ketama, a group which formed in the early 1980s; and the fourth Joaquín Cortés's touring dance spectacle *Pasión gitana* ('Gypsy Passion'; first performed in 1995). While my stress on dance and song is as inevitable as it is regrettable (only Medem sees fit to cast a flamenco performer solely for his acting ability)[10] I intend to read dance and song not as spontaneous effusions of voice and body, but rather as practices of everyday life: means by and through which subjects make their way in time and space.

The Practice of Everyday Life is the English translation of the work by Michel de Certeau whose French title is *Arts de faire*: skills of making, doing, and making do (of artistic creation, social action, and cultural diversion).[11] For Certeau such practices as 'walking in the city'[12] or 'telling stories' are bodily or verbal 'arts' which deserve and require close attention if they are properly to be understood or adequately described. A pioneer of now familiar emphases of cultural studies, such as the positivity of consumption and subversion through the 'turning' of a pre-existing artefact,

[9] Antonio Gades, a non-gypsy dancer who also claims that ethnicity is irrelevant, compares the fluidity of a flamenco dancer to that of a Calder mobile; see Pierre Lartigue, *Antonio Gades: le flamenco* (Paris: Albin Michel/L'Avant-Scène, 1984), 58, 59.

[10] Musician Juan José Suárez 'Paquete' plays the part of Manuel, the gypsy leader.

[11] (Berkeley and Los Angeles: University of California Press, 1984). All references to Certeau are to this text. Certeau is best known in English for *Heterologies: Discourse on the Other* (Minneapolis: University of Minnesota Press, 1986), a collection with no French original.

[12] As this reference suggests, Certeau's work on the city and everyday life acknowledges the influence of Henri Lefebvre (see *Practice*, 205 n. 5).

Certeau has wider ambitions, attempting as he does to render visible the lost continent of unsymbolized 'ordinary culture'; to contest the 'arts of theory' of Foucault and Bourdieu; and to reinvent such categories as space, language, and belief. These debates clearly have implications for the subject. Thus Certeau's study is dedicated to the 'ordinary man'; but this does not imply 'a return to individuality', but rather the 'individual [as] locus in which an incoherent . . . plurality of determinations interact' (p. xi). 'The fragmentation of the social fabric today', he writes, 'lends a *political* dimension to the problem of the subject' (Certeau's emphasis; p. xxiv). Or again, Certeau claims that Foucault's 'scattered technologies' of the body or Bourdieu's enforced alignment of dispositions with structures through the habitus (pp. 45, 57) deprive subjects of the knowledge which speaks through them: 'they bear witness to it without being able to appropriate it' (p. 71). Finally, spatial technologies (beginning with the railway) 'abstract' travellers from landscapes that are no longer their own and are no longer 'proper places' (p. 112), just as reproductive technologies 'cut' or mediate the voice, transforming 'the sound of the body' into 'the copy of its own artifact' (p. 132). With the 'devaluation of belief', writes Certeau, 'one is a socialist because one used to be one' (p. 177); or again: 'It is as if belief could no longer be expressed in direct convictions, but only through the detour of what others are thought to believe' (p. 188). I will argue in a moment that gypsies may be identified precisely with these 'subjects supposed to believe'.[13]

Perhaps the most influential of Certeau's distinctions, however, has been that between 'tactics' and 'strategies'. Tactics are 'indeterminate trajectories' or 'lignes d'erre' (p. 34). They 'drift over imposed terrain', enacting a 'temporal movement through space' (p. 35). In the 'absence of a proper locus' there is in the tactic 'no delimitation of exteriority or autonomy' (p. 37) and hence no stable or definitive sense of self. Inversely strategies are functional, rational, and formal (p. 34). They reduce the trajectory to the figure or line (p. 35) and posit a 'place that can be delimited as [one's] own and serve as the base from which relations with an exteriority . . . can be managed' (p. 36). Establishing and speaking from 'the proper', strategies embody 'the triumph of space over time' (p. 36). The notion of tactic thus enables a reworking of nomadism (of the 'ligne d'erre') not as identity but as a cultural practice, a reworking that is particularly appropriate perhaps for Spanish gypsies who have been sedentary yet culturally distinct for so long. Moreover it also allows a revaluation of the hybrid: for the tactic 'boldly juxtaposes diverse elements' (p. 38), privileging 'the rapidity of movement . . . relations among

[13] I take this formulation from Slavoj Zizek, 'The Supposed Subjects of Ideology', *Critical Quarterly*, 39.2 (Summer 1997), 39–59.

successive moments in an action, . . . intersections of durations and heterogeneous rhythms' (p. 39). There could be no clearer theoretical account of the contemporary practice of flamenco dance and music, heterogeneous and rhythmic phenomena that must repeatedly establish their claim to legitimacy in a field (that of mass media) that is never wholly their own. Certeau writes, pertinently, that the tactic is the 'art of the weak' (p. 37).

Certeau's own trajectory is somewhat wayward and erratic: tactical rather than strategic in method. And commentators have questioned the validity of the division between tactics and strategies: surely the powerful have exploited the tactical properties of confusion and seduction as successfully as the powerless?[14] Yet Certeau's military metaphors encourage us to view flamenco as the product of discipline (rather than the supposed licence and spontaneity of the *juerga* and *jaleo*); and to explore the implications for gypsy subjectivity of the distinction between proper and improper time and space. My argument, broadly, will be that *Carmen* and *Alma gitana* refuse modernity, nomadism, and hybridism and thus align themselves with the strategy's 'establishment of a proper place'; and that Ketama and Cortés attempt to incorporate those same contemporary characteristics, appealing to the tactic as the utilization of time in a shifting space that is not one's own. The fantasy of origin (of a strategic delimitation of the self and tradition) thus gives way to the confrontation with actuality (a tactical alliance with the other), a practice that is seen most spectacularly perhaps in Ketama's collaboration with West African kora virtuoso Toumani Diabate. If, however, flamenco is stereotypically tainted with a nostalgia for another, simpler time and place, then it has also served as another point of view, a subjective perspective on personal and national histories. Such a viewpoint is found, as we shall see, in both the fetishizing abstraction of *Carmen* and the infantile back story of *Alma gitana*. In both films gypsies will be positioned as 'subjects supposed to believe': dogged defenders of traditional notions of gender and nationality, of festivity and fatality.

2. Preserving the Proper: Carlos Saura's *Carmen* and Chus Gutiérrez's *Alma gitana*

The opening titles of the dance film *Carmen* tell us both that the project is inspired by Mérimée and Bizet and that director Carlos Saura and dancer Antonio Gades share the credit for script and choreography. Critics have not failed to pick up on the hybridity of the film and the way it poses

[14] Jeremy Ahearne, *Michel de Certeau: Interpretation and its Other* (Oxford: Polity, 1995), 162. Ahearne is opposed to the common 'heterological' reading of Certeau.

subjectivity as crisis. For Marvin D'Lugo, author of the standard monograph on Saura,[15] the identity of the Gades character (known also as 'Antonio') is 'contradictory': he is at once performer, choreographer, and spectator (p. 205); or again, for Robin Fiddian and Peter Evans[16] the film attempts to 'pick up the pieces of a lost identity' (p. 7) which is at once individual and national: the 'Europeanization of Carmen' they describe charts both the dereliction and the allure (p. 85) of traditional notions of masculinity and nationality. Most recently Evlyn Gould[17] has described the challenge to authority inherent in the 'oscillation' between two auteurs (Saura and Gades), a challenge she locates both in the formal duplicity of the film, so reminiscent of Mérimée's ironically self-reflexive novella, and its ambiguous role in 'shaping or shifting boundaries of Europeanness' (pp. 153–4) at a time when Spain was about to enter the then EEC.

At first sight *Carmen* does indeed seem to confront both formally and thematically practices of everyday life in the heterogeneous forms of modernity, nomadism, and hybridism. Shot almost entirely in the sterile box of a rehearsal room (Plate 13) (one of the walls is a window giving access only to a wintry treescape; another is a mirror in which the dancers discipline their own bodies), *Carmen* allows brief cutaways to equally modern and everyday settings: the prison in which Carmen visits her incarcerated husband; the street in which she drives herself to a nocturnal assignation with Antonio. Costume is also studiously subdued: in rehearsal dancers wear leg warmers or jeans; when Carmen pays her late night visit she comes in beige and cream, hair severely up. Between punishing bouts of rehearsal, the camera tracks over the prone bodies of the dancers, apparently caught off guard and no longer subject to the discipline of professional display. Although there are no concrete references to contemporary events in the film, the constant switching between on- and off-stage action suggests a certain engagement with actuality, a refusal to surrender to that abstraction of time typical of both the *españolada* and flamenco.

If modernity is implied by a certain austerity of *mise en scène*, then nomadism and hybridism are implicit in other cinematic techniques. Thus, as we have seen, this self-consciously Spanish film is based unashamedly on French precedents; and on the image- and soundtrack

[15] *The Films of Carlos Saura: The Practice of Seeing* (Princeton: Princeton University Press, 1991).

[16] *Challenges to Authority: Fiction and Film in Contemporary Spain* (London: Tamesis, 1988).

[17] *The Fate of Carmen* (Baltimore: Johns Hopkins University Press, 1996). Two important critics read the film as an attempt to create a specifically Spanish form of movie musical: John Hopewell, *Out of the Past: Spanish Cinema after Franco* (London: BFI, 1986), pp. 151–7; Vicente Molina Foix, *El cine estilográfico* (Barcelona: Anagrama, 1993), 214–16.

the foreign and the domestic are seamlessly woven together. In the first sequence after the credits (nineteenth-century *costumbrista* engravings) the camera slowly tracks and pans in a single virtuoso movement from the dancers rehearsing in front of the mirror, to the musicians essaying a *bulería*, to Antonio threading a tape of Bizet's opera into a player. Just as the multiple action takes place in a single location, so the various sound sources merge to form a single aural landscape. Saura then cross-cuts between the tape and the musicians as the latter attempt to improvise a flamenco version of the operatic aria which has interrupted their folk song. We are thus presented with a concrete and apparently spontaneous example of that active consumption (that 'turning' of the pre-existing object) that is for Certeau characteristic of the continuous and anonymous practice of everyday life. The fluidity and mobility of the camerawork thus speaks as eloquently as the collage-like soundtrack (flamenco and opera, Spanish and French) of the heterogeneity of contemporary space and language. This 'Europeanization of Carmen' reveals that the most familiar of Spanish stereotypes is, like the figure of the gypsy it is made to represent, curiously strange, inhabited from its inception by an alterity that is also a proximity, an otherness borrowed from and redirected to the neighbouring nation.

Antonio gives his Carmen (Laura del Sol) a copy of Mérimée's novella to read. And reciting in voice-over from it (miming the foreigner's words), he equates the gypsy woman with animality and deceit. Yet if Carmen is generic (the 'eternal feminine'), she is not individual but plural, a locus of intersecting discourses. Arriving late for rehearsal she teams a (modern, casual) denim jacket with the red flounced skirt of the traditional femme fatale; or again, she alternately reassures Antonio in traditional style of the authenticity of her love and defiantly announces in modern tones that she reserves the right to personal and sexual autonomy. Appearing first in his fantasy as a parodic vision of femininity (complete with mantilla and red rose), she later adopts the same costume for herself in the real-life festive scene when the company stage an improvised entertainment for the birthday of one of the musicians. Finally, she at first submits to Antonio's direction (even his request that she become 'more feminine' by imitating his movements), only to demand subsequently that he dance the *farruca* for her before she sleeps with him. If Carmen is unable to appropriate the knowledge which she puts into play (unable to reconcile the heterogeneous roles she is made to perform) still she uses dance as a practice of making do: of procuring pleasure and profit for herself within a pre-existing cultural field (from Mérimée and Bizet to Saura and Gades) over which she has no control.

The subject is thus abstracted even as he or she rehearses the discipline of dance, the art of making do. Antonio is never shown outside the studio (except for a brief visit to the dance academy where he discovers Carmen). The studio may be his 'proper place' (he repeatedly sweeps it with his all-seeing gaze), but it remains suspended outside everyday life. Similarly the flamenco voice, so often praised for its authenticity, is here mediated and 'cut'. While singers and musicians are frequently present within the frame (and indeed take on active roles within the dramatic action) at key moments the soundtrack is 'unjustified' with no source specified in shot. And always in the background is the operatic tape, played on Antonio's oversize machine. The constant shift between diegetic and extradiegetic sound thus reinforces that intermittence of costume and characterization noted above. Each of these cinematic resources can be read as a pointer to nomadic personal (and national) subjectivity.

It should be clear that so far I have argued for a 'tactical' reading of *Carmen*, in Certeau's sense of the term. Indeed dance would seem to epitomize that drifting trajectory and that temporal and temporary move-ment through space that Certeau praises and prizes in everyday life. However while the diversity, rapidity, and rhythm of the tactic are recreated in Gades's dance and Saura's mobile camera, the twin auteurs' *mise en scène* also serves to emphasize one technique more characteristic of the strategy: the delimitation of exteriority. Rarely straying from the hermetic space of the rehearsal room, still the action heightens the tension between inside and outside: from her car Carmen glimpses Antonio's shadow, magnified on the blind; on his release her husband presses him-self against the window behind which she rehearses; or again while Antonio discusses Carmen's performance with her jealous, older rival Cristina (Cristina Hoyos), we see her appear between and behind them through a two-way mirror. Obsessive and neurotic, Antonio is thus shown as constantly delimiting a space that is his own, shaping and shifting boundaries. Asserting in the studio his panoptic power (a fundamental characteristic of Certeau's 'strategy'), his look in and through the mirror and the window establishes a proper place (however provisional and vulnerable) in which he proclaims his autonomy and from which he bases his relations with a stubbornly unknowable exteriority: the gypsy woman.

It is perhaps no accident that the story boards for *Carmen* resemble military maps, with sweeping arrows plotting the deployment of dancers.[18] For in his choreography Gades also enforces discipline, reducing the

---

[18] See Carlos Saura and Antonio Gades, *Carmen: el sueño del amor absoluto* (Barcelona: Círculo de Lectores, 1984). As well as the script, photos, and graphic material related to the film, this volume also includes an essay by Diego Galán and interviews with Saura and Gades. For pseudo-military story boards see, for example, the dance diagram for the Tabacalera sequence (p. 95).

errant trajectory to the fixed figure or line. Thus in the pre-credit sequence the massed ranks of dancers advance towards him (towards 'Antonio'), performing strictly under his gaze; and Gades has spoken in interviews of the 'austerity' of male flamenco performance, in which arm and hand movements must be rigorously controlled.[19] It thus follows that while many critics believe that the ironic or self-reflexive framing of the narrative in *Carmen* serves to problematize traditional notions of gender and nationality (demonstrating their 'dereliction' as well as their 'allure'), the grammar of the dance itself, strictly delimited and gendered, clearly fails to do so. If for Fiddian and Evans the studio is a 'room of eternal rehearsals' (*Challenges*, 88) in which there can never be a fixed or final performance, then it might also be seen as a site of forced sedentarization in which women and gypsies are confined, abstracted, fetishized.

In the final sequence of *Carmen* Antonio, enraged by his leading lady's infidelities, knifes her, just off screen. Her body falls to the ground and the camera pans left to reveal the rest of the company relaxing, oblivious to what has happened. The extradiegetic score (Bizet once more) suggests we take the sequence as Antonio's lurid fantasy, undercut by the continuing anonymous practice of everyday life. However the published script claims that Carmen is indeed dead (p. 164). Beyond, then, the dereliction of masculinity and traditionalism, Saura and Gades ultimately reconfirm that fatality through which the strategy delimits its space and imposes its power on the subtle, but fragile, tactics of the weak.

The opening sequence of *Alma gitana*, a flashback to a child's point of view, economically establishes dance as a tactic: at once a movement in space and a trajectory in time. In grainy black and white with appliquéd details of red we see a woman's curling hand and swirling shawl. It is the protagonist Antonio's mother, partnered by her gypsy lover Darío (Peret). When both parents are killed in a car crash in Seville director Chus Gutiérrez cuts from a close-up of the child shielding his eyes from the carnage to the now adult Antonio (Pedro Alonso) making the same gesture with his hand as he dances in a tourist *tablao* in Madrid. This graphic match or visual hook thus not only suggests that bodily gesture is a fragile but material source of subjective continuity; it also initiates an Oedipal rivalry with the father and love for the mother which will be inextricable from gypsy–*payo* relations.

Antonio works by day in a bar and performs by night in the club; he is shown from the start to be wayward and irresponsible, even as a student of the flamenco so deeply and obscurely linked to his sense of self. His future love interest Lucía (intelligently played by novice Amara Carmona) is

[19] See *Carmen: el sueño del amor absoluto*, 51–2.

established quite differently. First shown studying late at night for an exam the next day, she refuses to warm up her brother's dinner. Responsible and reliable, Lucía contests both the rapacious sexual stereotypes of *Carmen* and the repressive conventions still enforced by tradition: accepting chastity and monogamy, still she demands freedom of choice in the fields of education, work, and marriage. Lucía thus makes do, a tactical move made also by actress Amara Carmona in press interviews. For while director Gutiérrez claims that the anti-racist aim of the film is simply to 'reverse stereotypes' and contribute to the (widely ignored) International Year of Tolerance,[20] Carmona claims simultaneously and contradictorily that gypsies must 'struggle' to make themselves known as they truly are; that the film succeeds in making the 'differences' between gypsies and *payos* 'disappear'; and that those traditions which differentiate between the two groups (such as chastity before marriage) can only be appreciated from inside the minority culture.[21] Focusing on the dangers of intimacy between cultures, press coverage of the rather chaste kiss between the two protagonists (there are no sex scenes in the film) claimed both that Carmona was the only gypsy girl willing to kiss a non-gypsy on camera and that her father would beat her if she were to repeat that action in real life.[22]

If the gypsy woman, whether character or actress, can 'turn' tradition only while remaining within it, the alterity of that tradition is also marked by its intimate proximity with the dominant, secular culture. Lucía's brother Jesús plays in the band which accompanies Antonio; the two lovers coincide at the same nightclub for a performance by Ketama (real-life relations of Carmona), although Lucía is safely chaperoned by male members of her family. There are, however, schematic oppositions between the two cultures at the level of *mise en scène*: Antonio's neurotic and truncated family (his warring aunt and uncle) take their tense meals in a sombre flat; Lucía's family home is richly coloured and cluttered (compared by the script to an 'auction house'),[23] dense with bodies, voices, and movement. The impoverishment of *payo* sociality is implicitly contrasted with the cultural wealth of gypsy communality: the church at

---

[20] Cristina Estrada, 'La vida está tan cargada de tópicos que es maravilloso darles la vuelta' (interview with Chus Gutiérrez and location report), *Ya* (4 Feb. 1995); Gema Delgado, 'Amores difíciles' (location report), *Cambio 16* (13 Mar. 1995).

[21] Cristina Gil, 'Los gitanos tenemos que luchar para que se nos conozca de verdad', *Ya* (30 Jan. 1996); Beatriz Cortázar, '*Alma gitana*: un estreno con "duende"', *ABC* (30 Jan. 1996); Nuria G. Noceda, 'El alma gitana de Chus Gutiérrez', *Diario 16* (30 Jan. 1996). Noceda reports that the 'new star' Amara Carmona has been nominated for a Goya award.

[22] Nuria Barrios, 'Amara Carmona', *El País de las Tentaciones* (12 May 1995).

[23] '*Alma gitana*: guión de Joaquín Jordá, Chus Gutiérrez, Antonia Conesa y Juan Vicente Córdoba. Adaptado de una obra original de Timo Lozano' (unpublished typescript; n.p., n.d.), fo. 19.

which Darío serves as a lay preacher is packed with an effortlessly musical congregation; a later set piece of a gypsy wedding displays a lost continent of traditional culture (of ritual, costume, music, and dance) inconceivable and inaccessible to the fractured *payo* family.

Substituting for the lost 'proper' culture, gypsy music becomes a resource for new forms of urban sociality, new practices of everyday life. Thus it is no accident that the lovers should meet at a concert by Ketama, for, as we shall see, their flamenco fusion music is a locus for the intersection of multiple cultures. In *Alma gitana* they perform a Latin-tinged rumba entitled 'Loko', a prime example of the song forms that make a 'return' or 'round trip' journey between Europe and the Americas. The openly gypsy-identified Ketama, prominently featured in the film, thus exemplify that nomadism and hybridism held to be characteristic of the modern metropolis. And *Alma gitana* holds out the possibility of new, tactical alliances between ancient and modern minorities: the next performance attended by the lovers is by mixed race group Congo Bongo; and when one of the latter's musicians (an illegal African immigrant) is confined in prison, Lucía pretends to be his girlfriend in order to gain access to him on behalf of his friends. 'Some couple,' murmurs the racist prison guard, bracketing together representatives of diverse groups which had not hitherto considered the possibility of communality or, indeed, criminality: the dialogue establishes that neither has set foot in a prison before.

However while the diversity, rapidity, and rhythm of 'world music' is offered as a primary (indeed solitary) practice of cultural creation and social action, elsewhere in *Alma gitana* heterogeneity is repeatedly associated with culpable confusion, even chaos. Antonio's promiscuous relations (his ex-girlfriends include a Japanese, a North American, and a Spaniard) are unfavourably contrasted with Lucía's chastity, as is her sober Coca Cola with his Tequila and cocaine. The noisy exterior of the Rastro, where Antonio's multiethnic friends man a market stall, gives way to the still and silent interior of the upmarket antique shop owned by Lucía's father. The shop, like the gypsy home, church, and *sala de fiestas*, is a proper place in both senses of the word: the bastion of a restrictive moral code that asserts autonomy only by enforcing exteriority. It is Antonio who is the nomadic outsider, roaming the metropolis on his motorbike (Plate 14). The gypsies, and not just the women, lead lives of discipline, even bourgeois propriety: Lucía's father is as concerned by the future of his business as by the good name of his daughter. *Payo* promiscuity thus provokes and reinforces gypsy monogamy and endogamy. And, relatively reticent in showing evidence of racism, the film does not present such traditions as an 'art of the weak' in Certeau style. Indeed its director

Gutiérrez, who praises the vital heterogeneity of the city, also extols the 'strength' of the gypsies in refusing assimilation.[24]

Reinvestigating gender and nationality for the 1990s, then, Chus Gutiérrez suggests, against the fatal stereotypes of Saura in the 1980s, that passion can be modulated by discipline and ethnic identity by social circumstance; while Carmen is the story of an 'absolute love', *Alma gitana* is the tale of a 'difficult affair',[25] less abstracted and more pragmatic. It remains the case, however, that dance serves in *Alma gitana* as a fetishistic and ritualized romance that transcends and transgresses any social consciousness. For in the converging professional and personal *Bildungsroman* (in Antonio's joint education as consummate dancer and unconsummated lover) flamenco serves as the freezing of time, the fusion of space, and the fixing of identity. One motif straddles the introductory flashback and the main narrative: it is a richly embroidered shawl, given first by Darío to Antonio's mother and then by Antonio to Lucía. The gift of the shawl not only links Seville 1975 with Madrid 1995 (Darío dances with Lucía as once he had danced with Antonio's mother); it also identifies Antonio himself with his phantom father Darío, his mother's gypsy dancing partner and lover. The question of miscegenation is left open: we are not told if Darío is Antonio's biological parent. But this is because the film suggests, even as it praises the strength and endogamy of the gypsies, that a 'gypsy soul' is beyond ethnicity: Antonio claims that in dancing he becomes 'a little' gypsy. By following quite literally in the steps of his artistic or fantastic father Antonio incorporates or assimilates Darío as the subject supposed to believe: the martyr who sacrifices his life to his love and his art. The climactic conversation in which the older man confesses his love for the younger man's mother is filmed in a sustained two shot, stressing the continuity between and the contiguity of the male couple. It can be compared to one of the spatial tactics that Certeau identifies with childhood: that identification and differentiation of self that means at once 'to be the other and to move toward the other' (*Practice*, 110).

Chus Gutiérrez has compared *Alma gitana* to Stephen Frears's films of multicultural lovers; Spanish critics asked when the gypsy Spike Lee would appear to direct similar narratives of 'racial pride'.[26] Unlike Frears's

---

[24] In conversation after a screening of *Alma gitana* at the London Film Festival (17 Nov. 1996).

[25] See the title of Gema Delgado's feature, cited above: 'Amores difíciles'.

[26] In Diego Muñoz, 'El cine español se pone flamenco con *Alma gitana* de Chus Gutiérrez', *La Vanguardia* (5 Feb. 1995), Gutiérrez cites Frears's *Sammy and Rosie Get Laid* as an inspiration; Joaquín Albaicín looks for the gypsy Spike Lee in 'Los gitanos en el cine'; Lee is also invoked by Fernando Herrero, who compares 'gypsy racial pride' to 'negritude'; '*Alma gitana*' (review), *El Norte de Castilla* (Valladolid) (11 Mar. 1996). One of the few

London or Lee's New York, however, the Madrid of Gutiérrez's musical romance is as lacking in racial conflict as it is in mordant irony or humour. The last sequence of *Alma gitana* has Antonio pursue on his motorbike the bus in which Lucía has chosen to travel to Seville, away from both her restrictive family and her wayward lover. The camera tilts down to the white line in the centre of the road, the image of a trajectory that is incomplete, defiantly open. It is an inconclusive conclusion that gestures toward the more critical and mobile subjects implied by the music of Ketama and the dance of Joaquín Cortés.

3. Changing their Times: Ketama and Joaquín Cortés

Ketama, formed in the early 1980s and still prominent fifteen years later, are the major proponents of new flamenco. An article in an *El País* dossier devoted to the state of the art headlines its feature on Ketama 'The American Dream' and describes them with the English term 'crossover'.[27] Citing perhaps their best-known couplet ('No estamos lokos, I sabemos lo ke keremos' ('We're not crazy I we know what we want')), the author infers that Ketama did indeed know what they wanted: resounding commercial success. Now they can fill sports stadiums in Spain and reach the top of the pop charts. It is not incidental to this success that they have recorded since 1990 with the multinational Polygram.

Like Joaquín Cortés, then, Ketama have been attacked (and not just by the sentimental purists known as 'flamencólicos') for blurring artistic boundaries and straying from their proper place.[28] Yet the history and lyrics of the group suggest a strong, even 'strategic', sense of the limits or delimitations of the autonomous self. Thus Ketama are proud of and praised for their inheritance: sons of the most prestigious flamenco masters (known as 'patriarchs') Habichuela and Sordera, the Carmona cousins (Antonio, Juan, and José Miguel) and one-time collaborator José Soto claim that flamenco cannot be learned from books, but is instilled by birth and by intimate acquaintance from infancy (*Historia*, 98). Resident in Madrid still they bear proper names charged with autochthonous authority, from Granada and Jaén respectively. Even Juan's nickname ('el Camborio') evokes Lorca's gypsy ballads. Patriarchal tradition is re-

hostile reviews is from Gutiérrez's native Granada, a city she praises for its supposed mestizo tradition; Felipe Santos, '*Alma gitana*' (review), *Ideal de Granada* (3 Apr. 1996).

[27] José Manuel Gamboa, 'Ketama: el sueño americano', *El País Semanal* (7 July 1996), 60–1. Earlier proponents of 'neo-flamenco', such as Veneno and Pata Negra, no longer exist.

[28] I take the history of Ketama from Pedro Calvo and José Manuel Gamboa's excellent *Historia-guía del nuevo flamenco: el duende de ahora* (Madrid: Guía de Música, 1994), 97–118. Calvo and Gamboa also give a full discography (p. 118) and reproduce selected lyrics (pp. 210–11, 213).

affirmed by flexible performance conditions: Soto sings a plangent *soleá* with his companions' respected father; the massed 'young Habichuelas' assemble for a one-off gig of some twenty performers in 1993 (*Historia*, 118). Ketama's hit rumba 'Vente pa' Madrid' celebrates the centrality of the capital to neo-flamenco; on the release of their sixth album *Pa' gente con alma* (For People with Soul) they are invited to represent Spain in New York at celebrations for the Quincentennial (*Historia*, 110). Surely 'gypsy soul' has never been so culturally central and so socially accepted.

This domestic assimilation is echoed in Ketama's career abroad: they have opened for the world tour of the Artist Formerly Known as Prince and played five nights at London's Town and Country, at that time the most fashionable medium-size venue in the city. And if we consider the lyrics to Ketama's crossover album, *Y es ke me han kambiado los tiempos* ('So My Times Have Been Changed/So Times Have Changed Me') of 1990, we find beneath the self-evident *mestizaje* or hybridism an uncompromising sense of self. Thus the opening rumba 'Loko' (which featured in *Alma gitana*) is a romantic and seductive address to a gypsy girl, who is described in conventionally sensual terms: 'cuando ella me mira con sus negros ojos | esa gitanita me rompe el coco | cuando beso yo sus labios rojos | siento yo morirme poco a poco' ('when she looks at me with her dark eyes | that gypsy girl drives me crazy | when I kiss her red lips | I feel like I'm dying oh so slowly'). 'Pirata' is a *bulería* of lost love and fatal destiny: 'quiero una cosa que es imposible | mi destino es así | quiero verte una vez más | en mi noche solitaria no dejo de pensar en ti' ('I want an impossible thing | that is my fate | I want to see you just one more time | I can't stop thinking about you'). The *sevillanas* of 'Puchero light' undermine the transatlantic nomadism of the first stanzas (with their musical and lyrical references to Havana, Rio, and Harlem) with the repeated refrain: 'Ketama somos gitanos | aunque hagamos música universal' ('Ketama are gypsies | but we make universal music'). The facility of the move between the particular and the general reinforces on a subjective level that apparent fixity of place implied by Ketama's emphatic appeal to their ethnic and cultural roots. Whether the mood is light (as in the praise of the *juerga* in the hybrid *bulesalsa* 'Shivarita') or austere (as in the lament for solitude and fate in the *soleá* 'Y es ke me han kambiado . . .') the themes are equally traditional, equally grounded in popular practice.

A closer look at both the history of the band and their compositions reveals a different and more complex story. For if Ketama claim flamenco is an originary knowledge born in the home, they also state that that their aim is to 'take [the genre] out of itself [*hacia afuera*]' (*Historia*, 98); and if they are now signed to Polygram, they spent years of apprenticeship with the specialized labels Nuevos Medios in Madrid and Hannibal in London.

Current crowd-pleasers in Spain, until recently they complained that they were more appreciated in Britain and France. And their ground-breaking album with Malian Diabate was passed over at home, while winning 'World Music' awards abroad.

The songs of *Y es ke . . .* are also more ambiguous and fluid than an initial reading of the lyrics would suggest. A love song to a stereotypically sensual gitana, 'Loko' is also and more importantly a lyrical evocation of the fading of the male subject as he contemplates the female object: 'cuando yo miro sus ojos | pierdo el sentío poquito a poco [When I look into her eyes | I slowly lose my senses]'. The melancholic 'Pirata' works against the generic conventions of its song form (the *bulería* whose origins lie in festivity); and an unexpected burst of electric guitar cuts through the plangent lute. The proudly asserted identity of 'Puchero light' is not individual but communal, even plural, with the singer claiming that his song is the product of 'the culture of a people' and the experiences 'we' have had with guitars in our hands. Gypsy identity is thus 'vivencia': a 'quest for life' and an education in the 'laws' 'taught' by 'gypsies of old cadences'. This is a communal memory which cannot be allowed to die: 'que no se pierda lo nuestro | nuestra cadencia flamenca' ('Let's not lose what he have | our flamenco cadence'). If 'Shivarita' celebrates the traditional male freedom to take pleasure as he wishes (the singer awakes with a hangover only to look forward to the coming night's *movida*), still it is preceded by a vigorously voiced wake-up call from Antonio's mother. Celebrating, like all popular music, the submerged continent of everyday life, *Y es ke . . .* also strives to memorialize the present and to incorporate it into an unwritten cultural history that is always on the point of disappearing and has no proper place in which it can be preserved: the solitary voice of the title *soleá* not only laments that his times have changed (or that times have changed him); he also proclaims his intention of incorporating a past that is as fluid and evanescent as music itself: 'hoy quiero beber la [*sic*] agua del pasado | la llevaré en el recuerdo para la vida' ('Today I want to drink the water of the past | I'll keep it in my memory as long as I live').

The intergenerational collaboration on this piece (which is dedicated to the band's fathers) could thus be read in Certeau's terms not as a strategy (an enforcement of patriarchal privilege) but as a tactic (a movement through a territory that belongs to another). As Certeau writes, such a process requires 'a tight rope walker's talent and sense of tactics' if it is to achieve its end: 'the implantation of memory' in a place that is already occupied by the enemy (*Practice*, 37). But it is in the densely and delicately textured soundscapes of *Songhai* (1988), the collaborative work that was so ill received in Spain, that Ketama most clearly make that move to a third, provisional artistic practice that stands between modernity and tradition, home and abroad, same and other. Thus the heterogeneous elements (West African lute, Spanish guitars and percussion, jazz bass by Briton Danny Thompson) drift or stray over and under one another, without priority or authority. The instrumental 'Jarabi' has the shimmering treble of the kora bear the melody while the flamenco and bass hold back; but in 'A Toumani' José Soto's traditional vocal line (in which he calls on the forces of nature to help him in his love song) is taken up only subsequently by Diabate's strings. Or again, as the titles might suggest, 'A mi tía Marina' is guitar led; 'Ne Ne Kiotaa' kora led. Even the hit rumba 'Vente pa' Madrid' (a love letter to the metropolis composed for a cousin exiled in Alicante), with its domestic theme and salsa call-and-response structure, ends at the fade out with a brief murmured vocal from Diabate in an African language. As a 'puchero light' (a stew in which the elements remain distinct) this is no facile melting pot but rather a mobile and temporary combination (an 'African paella'), characterized by the diversity, rapidity, and rhythm of Certeau's tactic. According to the sleeve notes the initial collaboration between Ketama and Diabate was improvised in a single day before being performed in the London which served as a third place between the twin homes of Madrid and Mali.

Diabate claims that the ease and fluidity of the fusion of West African and gypsy musics is because neither is written down (sleeve notes). Yet illiteracy, of course, does not imply lack of sophistication; and, coming like the Ketama cousins from a celebrated line of musical masters, Diabate claims that griots like himself have served to preserve Malian history as an auditory 'library'. In spite of their commercial success, then, earned after a full decade of neglect, Ketama might also be seen as occupying a similar, problematic position: the repository of cultural memory in a society in which literacy has not always been highly prized. And in their constant references to Arab culture (their name is taken from a village famous for its kif) Ketama suggest not so much the quest for fantastic miscegenation (for a return to the multicultural utopia of Al-Andalus) but an engagement with everyday social (and, indeed, narcotic) practice in the Spanish metropolis. Moreover Ketama embody the problematic modernity of popular culture which, Certeau wrote 'cannot be confined to the past, the countryside, or primitive peoples' (Practice, 25). Indeed they have always been at the centre of sophisticated, urban contemporaneity, from the first album with its cover by Ceesepe, a graphic designer best known for his work with Pedro Almodóvar. Gypsies of the movida, Ketama may have lost with their urban contemporaries a sense of their proper place (and hence the respect of purist flamencólicos), but still they testify to that qualified but necessary autonomy which derives from the perilous but pleasurable confrontation with modernity.

There is no doubt that Joaquín Cortés is the best known of contemporary flamenco fusion dancers. A principal at the Ballet Nacional de España until 1990, he left to found his own company and experienced unprecedented success in Spain and abroad with his second show, *Pasión gitana*, which premièred in Madrid in March 1995 and is still touring at the time of writing. Dancer, choreographer, musical arranger, and company director, Cortés is truly a hybrid or plural subject; and as a self-styled 'gypsy ambassador' his 'feral'[29] figure (long black hair and dark eyes) evokes Certeau's description of popular traces or traditions, which 'move, like dancers, passing lightly through the field of the other' (*Practice*, 131).

Yet, like fellow fusion artists Ketama, Cortés has always stressed in interview the fixity of his roots.[30] Born outside Córdoba into an assimilated gypsy family who (Cortés claims) never experienced racism at the hand of their *payo* neighbours, Cortés's vocation was encouraged by his family: he was inducted into the fierce discipline of flamenco dance by his uncle Cristóbal Reyes, later to be a featured artist in his nephew's show. Promoted as an Andalusian (in spite of his lengthy residence in Madrid, where he attended the national ballet school), Cortés presents his career as a series of challenges in which he struggled to excel in successive spheres. Certainly he has targeted those places most central to the various cultural worlds through which he has migrated. Thus, after great success as a performer in both flamenco and Spanish classical dance, Cortés leapt as a director from small theatres such as the Nuevo Apolo in Madrid to the largest and most prestigious venues in foreign metropolises: the Royal Albert Hall in London and Radio City in New York, the first time a Spanish dancer had headlined that venue. The newly revised version of *Pasión* (autumn 1997) toured bull rings in sixty Spanish cities, a unique use of the largest arenas in the country.[31] When Cortés made his debut in cinema, it was with Almodóvar and Saura, respectively the most commercially successful and the most intellectually revered directors in Spain. When he required new costumes for the world tour of *Pasión*, it was to Giorgio Armani that he turned. The supposed embodiment of Spanish gypsy tradition, Cortés also poses as an icon of cosmopolitanism and modernity.

[29] The adjective is used by Tina Jackson in her interview 'Joaquín Cortés', the cover story in the *Big Issue*, the London magazine devoted to the homeless (10–16 Feb. 1997), 12–13. This piece stresses Cortés's 'explosive combination' of 'art and politics', a rare emphasis in Cortés's extensive press coverage.

[30] I take the history of Cortés from press cuttings and the documentary *The Making of Joaquín Cortés* (BBC 2, 1996).

[31] Julio Bravo, 'Joaquín Cortés: el amor brujo', *Blanco y Negro* (9 Mar. 1997). Bravo notes in passing the public funding that has supported Cortés's commercial success: his studio is the former headquarters of the Compañía Nacional de Danza, provided for him by the Ministry of Culture.

With the naming of a town square after him, Cortés would seem (like Almodóvar who has received the same honour) to have achieved the untouchable status of a cultural monument and acquired a 'proper place' in the most literal sense.

Pasión itself appears initially at least (as the title might suggest) to reconfirm gypsy stereotypes of fatality and festivity: the first half of the plotless show is devoted to typically tragic themes; the second culminates in a 'great fiesta'. And from the start there is a nostalgia for the fantastic origin of mystical miscegenation. In the first number 'Leyenda' Cortés makes his way through the audience, bare chested and wrapped in a skirt, to a stage wreathed in smoke and lit by giant menorahs.[32] Freezing into his trademark 'eagle' posture (head and legs bent, arms stretched horizontally and hands raised vertically), Cortés makes a virtue of immobility, a fetishistic fixing of the figure. And while Cortés's first hand movements are defiantly feminine (breaching that choreographic code of male austerity that Gades has defended so long), he is joined on stage for the second number ('Ambigüedad') by the female corps de ballet, dressed in tight-fitting men's suits. 'Romance amargo' continues the wilful confusion of genders and genres as a male duet danced in Spain (but not on the world tour) to the recitation of Lorca's homoerotic poem and featuring Cortés's collaborator Marco Berriel (formerly of Maurice Béjart's company). The choreography (credited to both dancers) is clearly disparate, with Berriel's classical footwork and ports de bras contrasting with Cortés's more sober *farruca*. After the interval disparate music and dance idioms are again juxtaposed without being resolved. In 'Perdidos' the musicians mix traditional *minero* flamenco with a number by contemporary icon Camarón de la Isla; and Cristóbal Reyes's no frills traditionalism is followed by Marco Berriel's most audacious and classical experiment: a solo with and in the train of a flamenco frock, which he alternately embraces and trails behind him. Berriel's *élévation* here (his exploitation of the verticality of classical jumps) could hardly be further from Reyes's earth-bound *taconeo*. Stage space dynamics are also heightened by extreme contrast between numbers: 'Sentires' is a jazzy threesome with Cortés fingering a double bass with two female dancers in swinging bias cut frocks in fashionable brown; 'Irradian' a fast-moving ensemble number in which the female corps de ballet

[32] My sources for this account of *Pasión gitana* are performances at the Nuevo Apolo, Madrid (Mar. 1995), and the Royal Albert Hall, London (Oct. 1996); and the video *Joaquín Cortés: In Celebration of Gypsy Passion* (1997), shot at Barcelona's Teatro Tívoli in 1995. The show has been frequently revised. When classical ballerina Aída Gómez left the Ballet Nacional de España to join Cortés's company in 1996 she lamented the poor state of dance in Spain, both artistically and financially; Miguel Mora, 'Trinidad Sevillano y Aída Gómez muestran su desolación por el estado del baile español', *El País* (4 Sept. 1996).

criss-crosses the stage in black velvet gowns with white petticoats. Finally, Cortés's solo 'Oscura luz' (bare chested once more) is contrasted with the Latin-tinged finale 'Naciente' in which he sports an unaccustomed homburg.

The extreme diversity of set, costume, and lighting design (aspects of performance for which Cortés has shown particular interest) thus effects a certain abstraction of time and space: for example the 'legendary' opening number cites both Jewish and Galician culture (Cortés claims in the programme notes to be dancing the *curandero* of popular medical tradition); but 'Leyenda' also exhibits angular postures and gestures clearly reminiscent of Martha Graham.[33] *Mise en scène* and dance idiom thus interact in unexpected ways. This cultural and choreographic nomadism, which suggests that there is, in Certeau's terms, no frontier (no boundary between 'legitimate space and alien exteriority'; *Practice*, 127), is, however, contradicted by Cortés's semi-nudity, the image most consistently reproduced in press photos. For if his musculature is highly contemporary (suggesting as it does the gym-honed dancers' torsos of recent times, so different from Gades's pigeon chest), then this self-conscious disrobing also implies a return to a tabula rasa or original authenticity that is pure physicality, pure passion. Cortés's much quoted distaste for the frilly shirts of his predecessors is thus not merely an aesthetic distinction; it also suggests a subjective shift similar to his insistence on live music in his show: only the naked body and the natural voice can speak from and of gypsy passion.

This rhetoric of the proper place is, however, undermined by Cortés's equal and opposite stress, so typical of the contemporary performer, on the discipline on which his art is dependent and the market forces within which he moves. Thus for all the abstraction of his 'legendary' art design, Cortés's modernity lies in his embrace of the logistics of the tour. His Italian manager and producer, Pino Sagliocco, is credited with bringing for the first time a rock and roll infrastructure to a dance troupe. Travelling with their own sets, lights, and sound equipment Sagliocco and Cortés ensure the same experience is recreated whatever the differences between venues. More particularly, the use of giant video screens enables the reappropriation of pre-existing spaces (such as sports stadiums) intended for other purposes and never before used for dance. The extended tour (in which numbers and performers are supplemented and substituted) thus serves as a trajectory in Certeau's sense: in spite of the military manœuvres required to coordinate over one hundred people, Cortés's mobile spectacle is no abstract 'map' of the territory, but rather an

---

[33] Cortés's choreography for Almodóvar's *La flor de mi secreto* is also clearly reminiscent of Graham.

'itinerary' traced over the terrain, the image of the tactic which (Certeau says) 'dances through the city' (*Practice*, 120).

The appeal to the logistics of rock is a tactical alliance echoed in the juxtaposition of dance idioms in Cortés's choreography. Thus if Cortés collaborates with his uncle Cristóbal Reyes, the epitome of familialism and traditionalism, and if he is most frequently photographed in his climactic solos, still he collaborated for many years with Marco Berriel, principal in Brussels and choreographer in Turin. And Cortés's duet with Berriel was proclaimed by *El País* 'an uncompromising story of fierce love between men'.[34] Where conventional flamenco dance practice enforces a frontier between gendered movements and relationships, Cortés has embraced dance (in Certeau's terms once more) as a 'bridge' in which the limits between the legitimate and the alien (the same and the other) are dissolved, temporally and temporarily, in movement through space. He thus poses the problem of intersubjectivity. As Certeau asks: 'Of two bodies in contact, which one possesses the frontier that distinguishes them? Neither. Does that amount to saying: no one?' (*Practice*, 127)

Flamenco fusion may thus lead to a more radical blurring of bodily and subjective boundaries than has hitherto been acknowledged; and Cortés's engagement with film and fashion can also be reread in similar style. For if Cortés has performed for the most authoritative of Spanish cineastes he has also contested their limited take on the gypsy: stereotyped as a thief and seducer in Almodóvar's *La flor de mi secreto* Cortés's character is also (in the dancer's own contribution to the script) a sophisticated choreographer exploring the Oedipus complex in dance; and in Saura's abstracted *Flamenco* (an austere performance movie shot in an abandoned Seville railway station) Cortés preserves his autonomy and modernity even though, like all of the artists who appear, he receives no on-screen credit. Likewise, Cortés has used the apparently frivolous arena of fashion to contest stereotypes and suggest new cultural connections, typically modelling for the most cerebral foreign designers (such as Romeo Gigli and Dolce e Gabbana) or with the most unexpected partners (black Briton Naomi Campbell).[35] Refusing to be bound by the temporal or spatial limits of ethnicity, this paradoxical 'gypsy ambassador' (the representative of a people with no fixed territory to call their own)

[34] Roger Salas, 'Joaquín Cortés deslumbra con *Pasión gitana*', *El País* (9 Sept. 1995). This very positive review stresses the originality of Cortés's dance idiom in strictly choreographic terms, a rare emphasis in press coverage. Hostile British reviewers tended to deny Cortés both stylistic originality and the ethnic authenticity they expect of flamenco; see Jenny Gilbert, 'Full of Far Eastern Promise', *Independent on Sunday* (13 Oct. 1997).

[35] Cortés models Dolce e Gabbana for *El País Semanal* (19 Febr. 1995); see also the cover story for British *Elle* (Apr. 1997) ('Fashion Meets Passion: Naomi and Joaquín Get Physical'), a photographic shoot at which the couple first met.

attempts a repeated and risky engagement with other times and places, a gamble which can never be guaranteed to pay off. As the most temporary and contemporary cultural phenomenon, fashion is a battlefield that can never be definitively conquered: Armani's brown is the colour of winter 1996, but may not look so fresh the following season; the bull rings and foreign amphitheatres will always return to their 'proper' uses when the gypsy tour has passed on.

It is in this context that Cortés's cinematic choreography (and his recent use of live video screens) should be seen. For as in pop video (a clear inspiration for Cortés's youthful niche marketing) discontinuity of time and dislocation of space serve to suggest that the body is always mediated in its movement and the voice (however 'live') always 'cut' by technology. Cortés's relentless exploitation of his own image, therefore, reconfirms Certeau's intuition that the subject of popular culture is always 'the copy of its own artifact'. Accepting and exploiting this problematic practice, Cortés exemplifies that art of the weak in which tactical rapidity and virtuosity outwit the less fleet-footed strategies of power.

4. From Strategy to Tactic

The 1997 documentary called, significantly, *The Making of Joaquín Cortés* ends with the dancer wandering through the streets of his long-time home, Lavapiés, the same central working-class area of Madrid which served as the location for *Alma gitana*. As Certeau suggested, 'walking through the city' and 'telling a story' can be tactics or practices of everyday life: in this case Cortés's immersion in the multicultural urban barrio and his narrative of his own life (the result of mutual exploitation by star and press) show both his easy engagement with a hybrid modern space and his more conflictive relationship with mediatized times: Cortés's brief and ill-fated affair with Naomi Campbell was exhaustively documented by *Hola* magazine and its British spin-off *Hello*.[36] The otherness of the everyday life of global celebrities was thus temporarily and intrusively brought close to its public in paparazzi shots of the couple in metropolitan airports and restaurants, shops and streets.

Such trivia are ruthlessly excluded from Saura's feature *Flamenco* (1995), in which both Cortés and Ketama appear. Isolated and aestheti-cized, dancers and musicians perform without an audience and amidst a production and lighting design that privileges geometry and abstraction: anonymous bodies shot against red spots, black silhouettes on white back-grounds. Even as the austerity of its *mise en scène*, so reminiscent of

[36] See cover story of *Hello* (18 Jan. 1987). The couple's romance was widely held to be a publicity stunt.

Carmen over a decade earlier, pays homage to the gravity of flamenco, the film's claustrophobia (its refusal to transgress the limits of an empty space suspended outside time) tends to deny flamenco performers that broader social arena which they have so recently conquered within Spanish popular culture. For if the *tablao* and the *juerga* corresponded to strictly delimited criteria of time, space, and subjectivity (in which the traditional performer was positioned as the patron's dependent) then the new cultural forms I have discussed in this chapter transcend those limits, appropriating and diverting central spaces: the big screen of Gutiérrez's feature film, the international distribution of Ketama's major record label, the bull rings and amphitheatres of Cortés's dance tour. No longer are self-identified gypsies restricted to the fatal stereotypes that Saura and Gades attempted, with only intermittent success, to modernize. Rather, working within those stereotypes ('making do') gifted artists in film, music, and dance have both contested ancient wrongs and asserted modern civil and social rights.

Cortés and Ketama also coincided at another ambivalent event, the memorial concert held at Madrid's Las Ventas bull ring in September 1997 in honour of Miguel Ángel Blanco, the young Basque politician kidnapped and brutally murdered by ETA. The assembled cast made strange bedfellows indeed, with the gypsy modernists sharing a stage with such unashamed supporters of the new Partido Popular administration as the histrionic Raphael and *folklórica* Rocío Jurado, vocal revenants of previous eras.[37] Presented, in patronizing fashion, as the epitome of gypsy 'raza', Ketama surprised with a dignified Caribbean-style *bulería* called 'Pillar of Salt'. In it Antonio Carmona sang that he would not be turned into a pillar of salt, even though he would look back behind him. In an evening which featured such festive levities as Los del Río's 'Macarena' (an invitation to dance too readily taken up by Las Ventas's audience), Ketama's was one of the very few contributions equal and appropriate to the seriousness of the event the concert was intended to commemorate. Insisting that proper remembrance of the past must not paralyse engagement with the present and hope for the future, Ketama revealed once more the unique potential of flamenco to comment acutely on national trauma and to trace the trajectory of modern Spain.

Shifting, then, from margin to centre (from tradition to modernity, from foreign to domestic, from other to same) the challenge for flamenco fusion is to resist homogenization or assimilation, however benevolent it may be when compared to the terrible violence of the past. The good

---

[37] Members of the cast took a photo call with Prime Minister Aznar at Moncloa; Antonio Burgos, 'El fin y los medios' (media roundup), *El Mundo* (14 Sept. 1997). Cortés went on to play Las Ventas with *Pasión gitana* three days later.

intentions of, say, Chus Gutiérrez, whose 'positive images' of a gypsy family merely reconfirm traditionalist bourgeois and patriarchal values, are exemplary of this liberal double bind. Until progressive *payos* in Spain acknowledge the difficult practice of everyday life in a multicultural society (most particularly the paradox that respect for other cultures involves the recognition that those cultures may reject the progressive values on which multiculturalism is based), they will produce works as initially pleasurable, and as ultimately superficial, as *Alma gitana*. As the film reveals in spite of itself, there can be no easy synthesis (no fusion) of the free floating hedonism so typical of contemporary, *payo* Spain and the gypsy moralism centred on those very proper places, the workplace, the chapel, and the home.

After *Carmen* Gades did not perform in Madrid for thirteen years. And returning in 1997 he spoke ambivalently at best of innovatory dancers such as Cortés; moreover he clung to an idealized socialism (which idolized Fidel Castro) which had fallen far out of fashion.[38] Hybrid subjects par excellence, the talented and versatile artists of a new generation essayed new tactical alliances: Amara Carmona starred in a second feature with Cuban Jorge Perugorría; her Ketama cousins also collaborated with Cuban exile salsa star Celia Cruz. However, as I argued in the introduction to this chapter, the popularity of gypsy culture need not prove that it is accepted by the majority who consume it; and, in spite of the sexual and international innovations of, say, *Pasión gitana*, gypsies still serve at home and abroad as 'subjects supposed to believe': a British journalist writing of a rival dancer to Cortés (the title of whose show shamelessly echoes its predecessor) could say that the former embodied 'all the virility and machismo that mark out the good flamenco male'.[39] The preservation of such stereotypes thus seems to become all the more necessary as they diverge from the lived experience of everyday life in a European Union in which (in Spain as in Britain) the workforce is increasingly female and multicultural. Spaniards are thus as vulnerable as other Europeans to ethnic nostalgia; and while some are proud to point to the origin of their national identity in the *convivencia* of the Middle Ages (the supposed peaceful coexistence of Jew, Muslim, and Christian), they are less likely to be able to locate a kosher or halal butcher in the modern metropolis.[40] Still less will they question the all pervasiveness of the

---

[38] Ritama Muñoz-Rojas, 'Antonio Gades baila en Madrid después de 13 años de ausencia', *El País* (10 Sept. 1997); Pepa Roma, 'Antonio Gades, bailarín: "Yo no lo veré, pero el comunismo tiene futuro" ', *El País* (14 Sept. 1997).

[39] The quotation is from Nicholas Dromgoole writing in the conservative *Daily Telegraph*; cited in publicity material for Paco Peña's *Arte y pasión*, playing at the Sadler's Wells Peacock Theatre in Nov. 1997.

[40] For a collection of articles on the difficulty of cohabitation see the dossier 'España

Catholic calendar which, with its frequent festivities, continues to punctuate their secularized social relations. The heterodox 'subject supposed to believe' is thus difficult indeed to incorporate into the familiar routines of everyday life.

For Certeau, the creative activity of the consumer is comparable to Freud's version of wit: 'cross-cuts, fragments, cracks, and lucky hits in the framework of a system' (*Practice*, 38). Rapid and rhythmic hybrid subjects, the artists I have treated here have exploited such heterogeneous formal techniques as the cross-cut to produce cultural products that are at once artistically innovatory and commercially successful, enthusiastically welcomed by domestic and foreign consumers scanning the global market place of world music and dance. Self-identified Spanish gypsies, as well as *payo* performers of flamenco, are thus well placed to negotiate future circumstances even as they look back to confront a problematic past, positioned as they are between dominant and emergent cultures, between fatality and festivity, between strategic manœuvres and tactical alliances.

mestiza: la difícil convivencia en tres zonas del país con alta concentración de inmigrantes', *El País* (25 Aug. 1996).

Conclusion: Chronicles of Seduction

In June 1997 the European outpost of the Guggenheim Museum was completed in Bilbao. Along with a bridge by Santiago Calatrava[1] and the long postponed metro by Norman Foster, Frank Gehry's titanium structure was acclaimed for its role in the 'renaissance of a city'.[2] An apparently exemplary instance of the regeneration of urban space through culture, still the Guggenheim received mixed notices from Basque scholars. Joseba Zulaika (professor of the Basque Studies Programme in the University of Nevada) traces the 'chronicle of a seduction'.[3] Charting the negotiations, month by month, between Thomas Krens, controversial director of the Guggenheim Foundation, and the embattled Basque nationalist politicians, Zulaika intersperses his chronology with quotations from Baudrillard, Beckett, and popular songs in Euskera. He also cross-cuts between differing locations: from Krens's opulent office on Fifth Avenue to the desolate and derelict banks of the Nervión. Finally he insists (against Gehry himself who tells Zulaika that the latter is simply hostile to American imperialism; p. 15) that the 'seduction' of US cultural capital is not 'deception' and transcends any simple idea of truth and lie (p. 17). Rather, Zulaika argues, the 'incongruity' of the project points to a postmodern perspective in which the Guggenheim represents the supreme example of the 'evaporation of the aura' in the avant-garde work of art (p. 303).

Jon Juaristi (the postnationalist theorist whom I cited in relation to

---

[1] Calatrava was named by daily *El Mundo* one of the 100 'Spaniards of the Year' in 1996; other nominees examined in this book are La Cubana (acclaimed for their 'great success' *Cegada de amor*), Cristina García Rodero (who won the National Photography Prize), Ketama ('fusion stars of 1996'), Julio Medem (for *Tierra*); Rafael Moneo (who won the Pritzker Prize); actresses Emma Suárez and Silke (for *Tierra* and other films); and Francisco Umbral (winner of the Príncipe de Asturias Prize for Literature); see www.el-mundo.es/larevista/num63/textos/espac.

[2] Special issue of *El País Semanal* (1 June 1997).

[3] *Crónica de una seducción* (Madrid: Nerea, 1997).

Medem) gives an equally ironic but more sober account of the museum.[4] Juaristi traces the halting and faltering history of Basque cultural policy until the present, a history strewn with unbuilt projects. And he locates the Guggenheim within a Bilbao whose situation is problematic when sited in the geography of a ruralist Basque nationalism suspicious of the hybrid metropolis. Finally he suggests that for all its reference to local typological models (the metallic skin cites Bilbao's lost steel foundries, the soaring projections the sails of its once prosperous fleet), the showy spectacle in which locals now take such pride is profoundly alien to their aesthetic and subjective traditions: a typically 'British' austerity and modesty.

While both critics are sceptical of the Guggenheim (Zulaika sees it as an outpost of Wall Street, Juaristi as a ship of fools slipping into the *ría*), their theoretical approaches are very different. Zulaika combines pastiche and fragmentation in a postmodern style familiar in the US academy, lamenting and celebrating a society of the spectacle in which the impossible promises of seduction have replaced the material rewards of production. Juaristi also believes that for the Basque nationalists modernization has become the 'accumulation of signs' (p. 36); but, with a stylistic sobriety appropriate to his subject matter (and consistent with his earlier archeology of Basque myths), he grounds the lofty ambitions of architectural practice and postmodern theory in the temporal, spatial, and subjective conditions of national, regional, and civic history.

My own practice in this book has been closer to Juaristi's than to Zulaika's. The problem with applying postmodern theory to contemporary Spanish culture is that it becomes tautologous: performance, play, and particularity (the all too familiar signs of postmodernity) simply map onto a Spanish cultural scene which, since the *movida*, is commonly thought by both academic and popular commentators to embody those same elements. The sociologically inspired theory with which I have engaged in this study, less spectacular and more sober perhaps than, say, the seductions of Baudrillard, attempts to reconcile the abstract and the empirical in a logic of practice which permits the cultural commentator a certain critical distance from his or her object. Thus we have seen that even Lyotard and Vattimo do not abandon the possibility of historicity in their analyses of postmodern time; that Lefebvre does not neglect the specificity of individual cities (or 'works') even as he gives a general account of the production of urban space (or 'products'); and finally that Certeau pays minute attention to the subjective practices of everyday life while attempting to integrate those same practices into an objective account of cultural consumption. Such theorizing is not incompatible with that of the scholars of the Spanish state who have rehistoricized central and

[4] 'Bilbao: la metamorfosis de una ciudad', *El País Semanal* (1 June 1997), 26–9, 36.

peripheral nationalisms and whose work I addressed in my chapters on cinema. Certainly it reinforces Bourdieu's discursive analyses of the intellectual field, the judgement of taste, and the rules of art.

Calatrava's Bach de Roda bridge in Barcelona (Plate 10), intended to be a 'place maker' in an anonymous peripheral site, is now scarred by graffiti, its elegant arches too tempting a challenge to adventurous urban youth. The pedestrian staircases that descend either side from 'hanging plazas' lead not to a pleasant park but to what is still a desolate wasteland, pockmarked by the mattresses and bonfires of the destitute. The interaction of design and environment (the inscription of time into space) thus remains unpredictable. And Spanish culture since the defeat of the Socialists in 1996 is ambiguous in its nature and effects. The practitioners of *ensayo* have not generally proved to be more explicitly political, focusing, still, on stylistics.[5] While commercial indicators for cinema seem positive (with the market share of domestic features increasing at home), the artistic quality of the most successful titles is questionable.[6] The three cross-cut topics remain equally ambiguous. The year 1998 saw a spectacular replaying of cultural history in the massive centenary celebrations for Lorca's birth, celebrations which in general edited out all reference to the poet's political commitments and sexuality.[7] The Spanish urban landscape continued to boast new 'Pharaonic' monuments beyond the Guggenheim, notably the neoclassical folly of the Teatre Nacional in Barcelona and the ruinously expensive rehabilitation of the Opera in Madrid.[8] The gypsy fashion also continued unabated, with Joaquín Cortés fêted at home once more when the 'Passion' tour finally reached Manhattan.[9] Hence if Spanish (Basque, Catalan, Andalusian) culture remains 'tactical' or, in

[5] For Jordi Gracia the 'consecrated style' of Spanish *ensayo* after the eclipse of oppositional politics is still defined by irony, scepticism, and literary artifice (*El ensayo español, v: Los contemporáneos* (Barcelona: Crítica, 1996), 56).

[6] See *Variety*'s special pull-out on Madrid (20–6 Apr. 1998) which cites a boom in all three areas of production, distribution, and exhibition. The biggest recent domestic hits, however, were genre pictures: Juanma Bajo Ulloa's *Airbag* ('party-on road movie'), Alex de la Iglesia's *Perdita Durango* ('Tex-Mex actioner'), and the highest grossing film of all time, Santiago Segura's *Torrente, el brazo tonto de la ley* ('Torrente, the Wrong Arm of the Law', described as 'spoof cop flick'). See John Hopewell, 'B[ox] O[ffice] Reflects Big Changes', 31, 34. The increased box office share taken by local production was seen in other European countries, but, as in Spain, was dependent on a small number of titles. See the survey for which Hopewell was Spanish contributor 'Euro Pix Revel in Plextasy: As Overall Aud[ience]s Grow, Local Fare Upstages Hollywood', *Variety* (27 Apr.-3 May 1998), 1, 70–2.

[7] For the implications of the Lorca centenary see my *The Theatre of García Lorca: Text, Performance, Psychoanalysis* (Cambridge: Cambridge University Press, 1998), 1, 12.

[8] See Andrés Fernández Rubio, 'Los arquitectos del Teatro Real se declaran la guerra en los últimos toques de la reforma', *El País* (31 Jan. 1997).

[9] Roger Salas, 'El bailarín Joaquín Cortés consagra su singularidad en Nueva York', *El País* (4 June 1998).

Certeau's words, an 'art of the weak', it still seems well placed to make its mark in the global market place, its hybrid and deterritorialized products freely recombining in new forms and loosing themselves from old locations in time and space. What remains unanswered, however, is Castells's question as to whether economic modernization can 'leapfrog' social belatedness and, most particularly, if Spain can jump directly to the informational utopia of the technopole when much of the population has not fully experienced the culture of literacy.[10]

Perhaps the answer is provided to some extent by Pedro Almodóvar, Spain's most sophisticated exploiter of the rules of art. For his twelfth feature *Carne trémula* ('Live Flesh', 1997) realizes all the promises of the *movida*, so celebrated and denigrated almost twenty years earlier. Artistically equal to any in the European Union, the film was produced not with Spanish state subsidy, but through a private coproduction deal with France. Spanning twenty years of Spanish history (from dictatorship to democracy), it testifies to the personal and collective cost of historical process. And in its glossy surface and mobile camera, it suggests the sensual seductions of 'the moderns' even as it contests frivolity and chronicles the irrevocable nature of political change. Spain, the voice-over tells us over a final shot of crowded and festive city streets, is no longer afraid. If Spain has not moved 'beyond postmodernity'[11] (and theory teaches us that such definitive changes must always be interrogated), then its contemporary culture reveals the pleasures and the problems of breaking with a past that will always insist, nonetheless, on being replayed.

[10] Carlos Alonso Zaldívar and Manuel Castells, *España, fin de siglo* (Madrid: Alianza, 1992), 60.

[11] I take the phrase from Gonzalo Navajas's *Más allá de la postmodernidad: estética de la nueva novela y cine españoles* (Barcelona: EUB, 1996). In spite of its title, this study makes no detailed reference to cinema. Navajas's analyses of the 'retrieval of the past' and 'new subjectivity' in narrative are, however, parallel to my own in other media.

Filmography

El espíritu de la colmena ('The Spirit of the Beehive', 1973), director Víctor Erice
(Chapter 2)

Production company/
Executive Producer   Elías Querejeta
Screenplay   Ángel Fernández Santos and Víctor Erice
Director of Photography   Luis Cuadrado
Music   Luis de Pablo
98 mins

Cast:
Fernando Fernán Gómez   Fernando
Teresa Gimpera   Teresa
Ana Torrent   Ana
Isabel Tellería   Isabel

1940. Two children, Ana and Isabel, attend a travelling film show of James Whale's *Frankenstein* in the Spanish village of Hoyuelos. Meanwhile their father Fernando tends to his hives and their mother Teresa cycles to the train station to post a letter. Fascinated by the film, the girls discuss it that night in bed; Ana asks why the little girl and the monster were killed; Isabel replies that they aren't really dead, cinema is a trick—the monster is a living spirit, you only have to announce yourself and he will come. Fernando listens to his crystal set and writes out a quotation from Maeterlinck's *Life of the Bee* at his desk where he falls asleep, coming to bed at dawn; Teresa, also awake, feigns sleep. At school the children have an anatomy lesson. Isabel tells Ana that the spirit lives in a barn at the top of a field; Ana finds a footprint. Later, Isabel attempts half-heartedly to strangle the cat, smearing her lips with the blood she draws from a scratch and then playing dead as a practical joke on Ana. Ana finds and befriends a fugitive soldier who hides in the barn, giving him Fernando's coat containing his musical watch. There is shooting at the barn, and later Fernando goes to the village hall where the soldier's corpse is laid out under the cinema screen, and collects his watch. At breakfast Ana notices Fernando has his watch back and goes to the barn to find it empty but blood-stained; she flees from Fernando, who has followed her there. The village sends out search parties. Sitting by the river, Ana sees the monster approaching her. At dawn she is found in a ruin. Isabel sits next to Ana's bed and calls to her. That night, Fernando falls asleep over the same Maeterlinck passage, and Teresa covers his shoulders with a jacket. As the moon rises Ana comes out of her coma, gets a drink of water, and goes to the open French windows calling softly, 'It is Ana. It is Ana.' (Verina Glaessner)[1]

La teta i la lluna ('The Tit and the Moon', 1994), director Bigas Luna (Chapter 5)

Production companies	Lolafilms, in association with Cartel and Hugo Films (Paris)
Producer	Andrés Vicente Gómez
Screenplay	Cuca Canals, Bigas Luna
Director of Photography	José Luis Alcaine
Music	Nicola Piovani
88 mins	

Cast:

Biel Durán	Tete
Mathilda May	Estrellita
Miguel Poveda	Miquel
Gérard Darmon	Maurice

Tete is a 9-year-old child growing up on the Catalan coast. We first see him struggling to climb up a human tower or *castell*, a traditional activity at local festivals. He is the *anxaneta* whose role is to stand on top of all the other participants. Urged on by his nationalistic and machista father, still Tete 'does not have the balls' to reach the crowning position. One older participant in the tower is Miquel, a Catalan-speaking adolescent whose parents come from the south of Spain. Jealously watching his mother breastfeed his baby brother, Tete vows that with the help of the moon he will find a breast for himself; and overhearing his parents making noisy love, he longs for the 'milk' which men fill women with. A suitably seductive women is not long in making an appearance: she is the French Estrellita ('little star'), a ballet dancer at a cheap cabaret, married to her colleague Maurice, the *pétomane* or professional farter. Although Maurice is impotent, Estrellita remains devoted to him, willingly lending herself to perverse sex games: devouring baguettes between his legs or amorously preserving his tears in a flask. Both Tete and Miquel fall for the seductive Estrellita, who initially rebuffs their advances. Tete offers her his pet frog; Miquel courts her with hoarse-throated flamenco. In his rich fantasy life Tete imagines Estrellita filling his mouth with milk from her breast. Prompted by his father's obsession with the supposed classical origins of Catalunya, Tete also imagines himself marching with the ancient armies through Roman ruins. When Miquel's best friend, the muscle man Stallone, is killed in a motorcycle accident Estrellita is finally seduced by Miquel's grief. Savouring his tears, she embarks on a torrid affair with the young man which the older Maurice initially tolerates. Finally he locks her in the caravan where they live and confronts Miquel. After Estrellita and Miquel have made love for the last time (puncturing Maurice's water bed in the process), the French couple leave the town in the night without a word. In our last sight of Tete, the child returns once more to the human tower. This time, as he approaches the top, he glimpses Estrellita on the balcony. Baring her breast to him, she gives him the courage to

[1] *Monthly Film Bulletin* (Nov. 1974).

reach his goal. As he is fêted for his new-found 'balls' by his male collaborators, Tete sees himself in fantasy suckled by Estrellita and his mother in turn. A final, perhaps equally fantastic sequence reveals that Miquel has joined Estrellita and Maurice's cabaret act. In a harmonious *ménage à trois*, he sings along with them to the song by Piaf ('Les Mots d'amour') which was previously the French couple's love theme. (Paul Julian Smith)[2]

Tierra (1995), director Julio Medem (Chapter 8)

Production companies	Sogetel and Lola Films, in collaboration with Sogepaq and Canal+
Executive Producer	Fernando Garcillán
Screenplay	Julio Medem
Director of Photography	Javier Aguirresarobe
Music	Alberto Iglesias
118 mins	

Cast:

Carmelo Gómez	Ángel
Emma Suárez	Ángela
Silke	Mari
Karra Elejalde	Patricio

Ángel, a mysterious young man of possibly unearthly origin, comes to an agricultural region of Spain to fumigate the woodlice infesting the vines. Arriving in a thunderstorm, he visits an old farmer, Tomás, who lives with his daughter and granddaughter, both called Ángela, Ángela's husband Patricio, and bar-owner Alberto, brother of local siren Mari, Patricio's mistress. At the mayor's office, Ángel meets a soldier who used to work at the mental hospital where Ángel was once treated for a 'hyperactive imagination'. Ángel assembles a work crew headed by gypsy Manuel. Mari recruits Ángel for a boar hunt, during which Patricio is shot. Blaming Ángel, Patricio warns him to stay away from Mari. Ángel alienates the gypsies after their wages have gone missing. He helps Ángela save Tomás after a suicide attempt. He grows closer to Ángela, but is also propositioned by Mari. After Patricio's death by lightning, Ángel tells Angela that he did shoot him in the hunt, although it was his other self—his 'angel'—that performed the deed. He sleeps chastely with Mari, but next morning makes love with Ángela who had spent the night with Alberto. Ángela finds the missing wages; Ángel goes to pay the gypsies, but is knocked unconscious by Manuel's son. He awakes in hospital, to be greeted by his till-now absent uncle and Mari. He drives away with her, while his other self is reunited with Ángela. (Jonathan Romney)[3]

[2] *Sight and Sound* (July 1996).
[3] *Sight and South* (Aug. 1997).

Bibliography

A.F., review of *El espíritu de la colmena*, *Cineinforme*, 186 (Nov. 1973), 23–4.

AHEARNE, JEREMY, *Michel de Certeau: Interpretation and its Other* (Oxford: Polity, 1995).

ALBAICÍN, JOAQUÍN, 'Los gitanos en el cine', *El País: Babelia* (Saturday supplement) (30 March 1996), 2–3.

ALDARONDO, RICARDO, 'Emma Suárez: "Julio Medem reta y engrandece a sus actores"; el equipo de *La ardilla roja* presentó en San Sebastián la nueva película', *El Diario Vasco* (24 Apr. 1993).

—— 'Julio Medem propone en *Tierra* un viaje al "mundo desconocido que nos rodea"', *El Diario Vasco* (24 May 1996).

ALIAGA, JUAN VICENTE, and CORTÉS, JOSÉ MIGUEL G. (eds.), *De amor y rabia: acerca del arte y el SIDA* (Valencia: Universidad Politécnica, 1993).

ALONSO ZALDÍVAR, CARLOS, and CASTELLS, MANUEL, *España, fin de siglo* (Madrid: Alianza, 1992).

Anon., review of *El espíritu de la colmena*, *El Pueblo* (17 Oct. 1973).

—— 'El espíritu de la colmena' (synopsis), unpub. typescript in the Filmoteca Nacional, Madrid (n.d.).

Asociación Española de Críticos de Arte, *Ocio, arte, y postmodernidad* (Madrid: Fundación Actilibre, 1986).

AUBACH, MARÍA TERESA (ed.), *Utopía y postmodernidad* (Salamanca: Universidad Pontificia, 1986).

BALCELLS, ALBERT, *La història de Catalunya a debat: els textos d'una polèmica* (Barcelona: Curial, 1994).

—— *Catalan Nationalism: Past and Present* (London: Macmillan, 1996).

BALLESTEROS, JESÚS, *Postmodernidad: decadencia o resistencia* (Madrid: Tecnos, 1994).

BARRIOS, NURIA, 'Amara Carmona', *El País de las Tentaciones* (12 May 1995).

BATLLE I JORDÀ, CARLES, 'Apuntes para una valoración de la dramaturgia catalana actual: realismo y perplejidad', *Anales de la Literatura Española Contemporánea*, 21.3 (1996), 253–70.

BAUDRILLARD, JEAN, *Simulacra and Simulation* (Ann Arbor: University of Michigan Press, 1994).

BHABHA, HOMI, *The Location of Culture* (London: Routledge, 1994).

BIGAS LUNA, and CANALS, CUCA, *Iberian Portraits* (Barcelona: Lunwerg, 1994).

'Bilbao: renacimiento de una ciudad', special issue of *El País Semanal* (1 June 1997).

Bibliography

BOLLAIN, ICÍAR, *Hola, ¿estás sola?: guión original de la película* (Barcelona: Planeta, 1997).

BOOKER, CHRISTOPHER, *Neophiliacs: The Revolution in English Life in the Fifties and Sixties* (London: Pimlico, 1992).

BOU, NÚRIA, 'A la recerca del pit perdut', *Avui* (9 Oct. 1994).

BOULENGER, GILLES, and LEBRUN, VINCENT, 'L'Échappée belle' (interview with Julio Medem), *Le Cinéphage*, 16 (Jan. 1994), 7–11.

BOURDIEU, PIERRE, *Homo Academicus* (Cambridge: Polity, 1988).

—— *The Logic of Practice* (Cambridge: Polity, 1992).

—— *In Other Words: Essays towards a Reflexive Sociology* (Cambridge: Polity, 1994).

—— *Distinction: A Social Critique of the Judgment of Taste* (London: Routledge, 1996).

—— and PASSERON, JEAN-CLAUDE, *The Inheritors: French Students and their Relation to Culture* (Chicago: University of Chicago Press, 1979).

BRAVO, JULIO, 'Joaquín Cortés: el amor brujo', *Blanco y Negro* (9 Mar. 1997).

CALVO, PEDRO, and GAMBOA, JOSÉ MANUEL, *Historia-guía del nuevo flamenco: el duende de ahora* (Madrid: Guía de Música, 1994).

CANALS, CUCA, and BIGAS LUNA, 'La teta y la luna (On parle français)/Guión cinematográfico' (Barcelona: Lolafilms, 1994).

CAPITEL, ANTÓN, introduction to *Oteiza-Moneo: Pabellón de Navarra, Esposición Universal de Sevilla* (Pamplona: Caja de Ahorros Municipal, 1992).

—— and SOLÀ-MORALES, IGNACIO, *Contemporary Spanish Architecture: An Eclectic Panorama* (New York: Rizzoli, 1986).

CARDÍN, ALBERTO, *Como si nada* (Valencia: Pre-Textos, 1981).

—— *Lo mejor es lo peor* (Barcelona: Laertes, 1981).

—— *Guerreros, chamanes, y travestís* (Barcelona: Tusquets, 1984).

—— *Detrás por delante* (Barcelona: Laertes, 1986).

—— *Lo próximo y lo ajeno* (Barcelona: Icaria, 1990).

—— *SIDA: enfoques alternativos* (Barcelona: Laertes, 1991).

—— 'Crónicas afganas', *Literal*, 2.12 (Dec. 1995), 26–7.

—— and FLUVIÁ, ARMAND DE, *SIDA: ¿maldición bíblica o enfermedad letal?* (Barcelona: Laertes, 1985).

CASTELLS, MANUEL, 'The Informational City' (1989), in Richard T. LeGates and Frederic Stout, *The City Reader* (London: Routledge, 1996), 494–8.

—— and HALL, PETER, *Technopoles of the World: The Making of Twenty-First-Century Industrial Complexes* (London: Routledge, 1994).

CASTRORTEGA, PEDRO, et al., *Encuentros sobre modernidad y postmodernidad* (Madrid: Fundación de Investigaciones Marxistas, 1989).

CEBOLLADA, PASCUAL, review of *El espíritu de la colmena*, *Ya* (10 Oct. 1974).

CEBRIÁN, JUAN LUIS, *El tamaño del elefante* (Madrid: Alianza, 1987).

CEREZO, FRANCISCO, 'La Cubana', *Primer Acto*, 256 (Nov.–Dec. 1994), 86–7.

CERTEAU, MICHEL DE, *The Practice of Everyday Life* (Berkeley and Los Angeles: University of California Press, 1984).

—— *Heterologies: Discourse on the Other* (Minneapolis: University of Minnesota Press, 1986).

CHÁVARRI, RAÚL, *La pintura española actual* (Madrid: Ibérico Europeo, 1973).

COMAS, JUAN, 'Víctor Erice nos dice; entrevista', *Imagen y Sonido* (Jan. 1974), 35–6.

CONTE, RAFAEL (ed.), *Una cultura portátil: cultura y sociedad en la España de hoy* (Madrid: Temas de Hoy, 1990).

CORTÁZAR, BEATRIZ, '*Alma gitana*: un estreno con "duende"', *ABC* (30 Jan. 1996)

CRESPO, PEDRO, ' "El espíritu de la colmena" de Víctor Erice', *Arriba* (10 Oct. 1973).

La Cubana, programme for *Cegada de amor* (Madrid: Teatro Lope de Vega, 1996).

DATTNER, RICHARD, *Civil Architecture* (New York: McGraw Hill, 1995).

DAVIS, MIKE, *City of Quartz: Excavating the Future in Los Angeles* (London: Verso, 1990).

DELGADO, GEMA, 'Amores difíciles' (location report on *Alma gitana*), *Cambio 16* (13 Mar. 1995).

DELGADO, MARIA (ed.), *Spanish Theatre 1920–95*, special issue of *Contemporary Theatre Review*, 7.4 (1998).

DE VEGA, CARLOS, 'Los flujos de inmigrantes apuntalan la caída de la población autóctona en toda Europa', *El País* (14 July 1997).

D'LUGO, MARVIN, 'Catalan Cinema: Historical Experience and Cinematic Practice', *Quarterly Review of Film and Video*, 13 (1991), 131–47.

—— *The Films of Carlos Saura: The Practice of Seeing* (Princeton: Princeton University Press, 1991).

—— '*La teta i la lluna*: The Form of Transnational Cinema in Spain', in Marsha Kinder (ed.), *Refiguring Spain: Cinema/Media/Representation* (Durham, NC: Duke University Press, 1997), 196–214.

ELLEY, DEREK, review of *Tierra*, *Variety* (27 May–2 June 1996), 66–7.

EPPS, BRAD, *Significant Violence: Oppression and Resistance in the Narratives of Juan Goytisolo* (Oxford: Oxford University Press, 1996).

ERICE, VÍCTOR, and FERNÁNDEZ SANTOS, ÁNGEL, *El espíritu de la colmena* (Madrid: Elías Querejeta, 1976).

—— and OLIVER, Jos, *Nicholas Ray y su tiempo* (Madrid: Filmoteca Española, 1986).

ESPADA, ARCADI, *Contra Catalunya* (Barcelona: Flor del Viento, 1997).

ESPARZA, JOSÉ JAVIER, *Ejercicios de vértigo: ensayos sobre la posmodernidad y el fin del milenio* (Valencia: Barbarroja, 1994).

ESPELT, RAMÓN (ed.), *Mirada al món de Bigas Luna* (Barcelona: Laertes, 1989).

ESTRADA, CRISTINA, 'La vida está tan cargada de tópicos que es maravilloso darles la vuelta' (interview with Chus Gutiérrez and location report on *Alma gitana*), *Ya* (4 Feb. 1995).

EYRES, H., 'Modern Spain Finds a Voice' (review of *Paisajes después de la batalla*), *The Times* (London) (14 Oct. 1989).

FEITO, ALVARO, review of *El espíritu de la colmena*, *Cinestudio*, 127 (Dec. 1973), 47–8.

FERNÁNDEZ, MANUEL, 'Diez años de "El espíritu de la colmena"', *Ya* (23 Nov. 1983).

FERNÁNDEZ ALBA, ANTONIO, *La metrópoli vacía* (Barcelona: Anthropos, 1990).

Bibliography

Fernández Alba, Antonio, and Gavira, Carmen, *Crónica del espacio perdido: la destrucción de la ciudad en España* (Madrid: Ministerio de Obras Públicas y Urbanismo, 1986).

Fernández Rubio, Andrés, 'Los arquitectos del Teatro Real se declaran la guerra en los últimos toques de la reforma', *El País* (31 Jan. 1997).

Fernández Santos, Ángel, 'Una hermosa elegía inacabada', *El País* (25 May 1985).

—— '"El sol del membrillo", de Víctor Erice y Antonio López, provoca una fuerte división de opiniones', *El País* (12 May 1992).

—— and Erice, Víctor, 'El espíritu de la colmena' (script), unpub. typescript in the Filmoteca Nacional, Madrid (1973).

Fernández Santos, Elsa, 'Los buscadores de luz', *El País* (3 May 1992).

Fiddian, Robin, and Evans, Peter, *Challenges to Authority: Fiction and Film in Contemporary Spain* (London: Tamesis, 1988).

Fondevila, Santiago, 'Bigas Luna apunta con su cámara a Cataluña', *La Vanguardia* (7 Mar. 1994).

Frechilla Camoiras, Javier (ed.), *III Bienal de Arquitectura Española 1993–4* (Madrid: Ministerio de Obras Públicas et al., 1995).

Gallero, José Luis, *Sólo se vive una vez: esplendor y ruina de la movida madrileña* (Madrid: Ardora, 1991).

Gamboa, José Manuel, 'Ketama: el sueño americano', *El País Semanal* (7 July 1996), 60–1.

García, Ángeles, 'Víctor Erice dice que "El sol del membrillo" es para minorías que "están en todas partes"', *El País* (20 Jan. 1993).

García, Rocío, 'El cine español mira al público: inicia su recuperación con 2,5 millones de espectadores más que en 1994', *El País* (24 Dec. 1995).

—— 'Sogetel amplía alianzas para coproducir 15 filmes españoles en el plazo de tres años', *El País* (23 Sept. 1995).

García Gómez, Génesis, *Cante flamenco, cante minero: una interpretación socio-cultural* (Barcelona: Anthropos, 1993).

García Lavernia, Joaquín, *El libro del cante flamenco* (Madrid: Rialp, 1991).

García Rayo, Antonio, 'Ana María Torrent: con nueve años, dos películas', *Ya* (23 Nov. 1975).

García Rodero, Cristina, *España oculta* (Barcelona: Lunwerg, 1989).

—— *España: fiestas y ritos* (Barcelona: Lunwerg, 1992).

Gaya Nuño, Juan Antonio, *La pintura española del siglo XX* (Madrid: Ibérico Europeo, 1972).

Genover, Jaume, review of *El espíritu de la colmena*, *Dirigido Por* (Jan. 1974), 25.

George, David, and London, John (eds.), *Contemporary Catalan Theatre: An Introduction* (Sheffield: Anglo-Catalan Society, 1996).

Gil, Cristina, 'Los gitanos tenemos que luchar para que se nos conozca de verdad' (interview with Amara Carmona), *Ya* (30 Jan. 1996).

Gómez, Lourdes, 'La Cubana la monta', *El País* (14 Aug. 1997).

González Herrán, José Manuel, 'Álvaro Pombo, o la conciencia narrativa', *Anales de la Literatura Española Contemporánea*, 10.1–3 (1985), 99–109.

González Requena, Jesús, 'La conciencia del color en la fotografía cinematográfica española', in Francisco Llinás, *Directores de fotografía del cine español* (Madrid: Filmoteca Española, 1989), 118–65.

GONZÁLEZ SEARA, LUIS, '¿Posmodernidad o espíritu servil?', *ABC* (19 Sept. 1995).

GOULD, EVLYN, *The Fate of Carmen* (Baltimore: Johns Hopkins University Press, 1996).

GOYTISOLO, JUAN, *Paisajes después de la batalla* (Madrid: Espasa-Calpe, 1990).

—— 'París, ¿capital del siglo XXI?', in *El bosque de las letras* (Madrid: Alfaguara, 1995), 177–90.

—— *El sitio de los sitios* (Madrid: Alfaguara, 1995).

GRACIA, JORDI, *El ensayo español, v: Los contemporáneos* (Barcelona: Crítica, 1996).

GRAHAM, HELEN, and LABANYI, JO, *Spanish Cultural Studies: An Introduction. The Struggle for Modernity* (Oxford: Oxford University Press, 1995).

GUASCH, OSCAR, *La sociedad rosa* (Barcelona: Anagrama, 1991).

GÜELL, MARÍA, 'Aunque *La teta y la luna* es un filme muy catalán puede emocionar a un chulo de Chamberí', *ABC* (6 Oct. 1994).

GÜELL, XAVIER (ed.), *Spanish Contemporary Architecture: The Eighties* (Barcelona: Gustavo Gili, 1990).

HARO TECGLEN, EDUARDO, 'Umbral: defensa de la escritura', *Cuadernos Hispanoamericanos*, 450 (Dec. 1987), 39–47.

HEREDERO, CARLOS F., *Las huellas del tiempo: cine español 1951–61* (Madrid: Filmoteca, 1993).

HERRERO, FERNANDO, '*Alma gitana*' (review) *El Norte de Castilla* (Valladolid) (11 Mar. 1996).

HOLDEN, STEPHEN, review of *Vacas, New York Times* (30 Mar. 1993).

HOOPER, JOHN, *The Spaniards* (Harmondsworth: Penguin, 1987).

—— *The New Spaniards* (Harmondsworth: Penguin, 1995).

HOPEWELL, JOHN, *Out of the Past: Spanish Cinema after Franco* (London: BFI, 1986).

—— *El cine español después de Franco* (Madrid: El Arquero, 1989).

—— 'Waiting for the Cows to Come Home' (location report on *Vacas*), *Moving Pictures International* (19 Sept. 1991), 25.

—— 'B[ox] O[ffice] Reflects Big Changes', *Variety* (20–6 Apr. 1998), 31, 34.

—— et al., 'Euro Pix Revel in Plextasy: As Overall Aud[ience]s Grow, Local Fare Upstages Hollywood', *Variety* (27 Apr.–3 May 1998), 1, 70–2.

INGENSCHAY, DIETER, 'Álvaro Pombo: *El héroe de las mansardas de Mansard*: sobre el problemático hallazgo de la propia identidad y la grácil disolución de la realidad', in Dieter Ingenschay and Hans-Jörg Neuschäfer (eds.), *Abriendo caminos: la literatura española desde 1975* (Barcelona: Lumen, 1994), 65–74.

JACKSON, TINA, 'Joaquín Cortés' (interview), *Big Issue* (London) (10–16 Feb. 1997), 12–13.

JACOBS, JANE, *The Death and Life of Great American Cities* (London: Cape, 1962).

JIMÉNEZ LOSANTOS, FEDERICO, *Lo que queda de España: con un prólogo sentimental y un epílogo balcánico* (Madrid: Temas de Hoy, 1995).

JORDÁ, JOAQUÍN, GUTIÉRREZ, CHUS, CONESA, ANTONIA, and CÓRDOBA, JUAN, VICENTE, 'Alma gitana: guión' (unpublished typescript; n.p., n.d.).

Bibliography

JUARISTI, JON (ed.), *La tradición romántica: leyendas vascas del siglo XIX* (Pamplona: Pamiela, 1986).

—— *El linaje de Aitor: la invención de la tradición vasca* (Madrid: Taurus, 1987).

—— *Vestigios de Babel: para una arqueología de los nacionalismos españoles* (Madrid: Siglo XXI, 1992).

—— 'Bilbao: la metamorfosis de una ciudad', *El País Semanal* (1 June 1997), 26–9, 36.

—— ARANZADI, JUAN, and UNZUETA, PATXO, *Auto de terminación: raza, nación, y violencia en el País Vasco* (Madrid: El País/Aguilar, 1994).

KINDER, MARSHA, 'Pleasure and the New Spanish Morality: A Conversation with Pedro Almodóvar', *Film Quarterly* (Fall 1987), 33–4.

—— *Blood Cinema: The Reconstruction of National Identity in Spain* (Berkeley and Los Angeles: University of California Press, 1993).

—— *Refiguring Spain: Cinema/Media/Representation* (Durham, NC: Duke University Press, 1997).

LARTIGUE, PIERRE, *Antonio Gades: le flamenco* (Paris: Albin Michel/L'Avant-Scène, 1984).

LEBLON, BERNARD, *Gypsies and Flamenco* (Hatfield: Gypsy Research Centre/University of Hertfordshire Press, 1995).

LEFEBVRE, HENRI, *The Production of Space* (Oxford: Blackwell, 1991).

—— *Writings on Cities*, ed. Eleonore Kofman and Elizabeth Lebas (Oxford: Blackwell, 1996).

LEGATES, RICHARD T., and STOUT, FREDERIC, *The City Reader* (London: Routledge, 1996).

LLINÁS, FRANCISCO, *Directores de fotografía del cine español* (Madrid: Filmoteca Española, 1989).

LÓPEZ, SILVIA L., TALENS, JENARO, and VILLANUEVA DARÍO (eds.), *Critical Practices in Post-Franco Spain* (Minneapolis: University of Minnesota Press, 1994).

LÓPEZ ECHEVARRIETA, ALBERTO, *Cine vasco: ¿realidad o ficción?* (Bilbao: Mensajero, n.d.).

LUCHINI, ALBERTO, '¿De qué va el nuevo cine español?', *El Gran Musical*, 419 (Sept. 1995), 46–51.

LYOTARD, JEAN FRANÇOIS, *The Postmodern Condition: A Report on Knowledge* (Manchester: Manchester University Press, 1984).

MACTAS, MARIO, *Las perversiones de Francisco Umbral* (Madrid: Anjana, 1984).

'Madrid', special pull out in *Variety* (20–6 Apr. 1998).

MARTIALAY, FÉLIX, review of *El espíritu de la colmena*, *El Alcázar* (12 Oct. 1973).

MEDEM, JULIO, *Mari en la tierra/Tierra: guión para largometraje* (Barcelona: Planeta, 1997).

MEDIAVILLA, MANUEL, 'Julio Medem, uno de los doce subvencionados por el ICAA', *El Diario Vasco* (11 June 1992).

Ministerio de Cultura, *Cuatro direcciones: fotografía contemporánea española* (Madrid: Ministerio, 1991).

MITCHELL, TIMOTHY, *Passional Culture: Emotion, Religion, and Society in Southern Spain* (Philadelphia: University of Pennsylvania Press, 1990).

—— *Flamenco: Deep Song* (New Haven: Yale University Press, 1994).

Moix, Terenci, *Suspiros de España: la copla y el cine de nuestro recuerdo* (Barcelona: Plaza y Janés, 1993).

Molina Foix, Vicente, 'El año en que triunfamos peligrosamente', *El País* (23 June 1983).

—— 'La guerra detrás de la ventana', *Revista de Occidente* (Oct. 1985), 112–18.

—— *El cine estilográfico* (Barcelona: Anagrama, 1993).

Moneo, Rafael, *Sobre el concepto de tipo en arquitectura* (Madrid: Escuela de Arquitectura, 1982).

Montero, Rosa, 'La vida caótica', *El País Semanal* (17 Nov. 1996), 12.

Mora, Miguel, 'Trinidad Sevillano y Aída Gómez muestran su desolación por el estado del baile español', *El País* (4 Sept. 1996).

Muñoz, Diego, '*La teta y la luna* es mi homenaje a Cataluña por encima de los nacionalismos', *La Vanguardia* (6 Oct. 1994).

—— 'El cine español se pone flamenco con *Alma gitana* de Chus Gutiérrez', *La Vanguardia* (5 Feb. 1995).

Muñoz Molina, Antonio, 'Viaje al centro de Madrid', *El País Semanal* (19 Feb. 1995).

Muñoz-Rojas, Ritama, 'Antonio Gades baila en Madrid después de 13 años de ausencia', *El País* (10 Sept. 1997).

Navajas, Gonzalo, *Más allá de la postmodernidad: estética de la nueva novela y cine españoles* (Barcelona: EUB, 1996).

Nieva, Francisco, 'Introduction', *Antonio López García: Paintings, Sculptures, and Drawings, 1965–86* (London: Marlborough Fine Art, 9–31 May 1986), 4–5.

Noceda, Nuria G., 'El alma gitana de Chus Gutiérrez', *Diario 16* (30 Jan. 1996).

Olsen, Donald J., *Town Planning in London* (New Haven: Yale University Press, 1982).

Ondarzabal, Ainhoa, 'Comienza hoy en San Sebastián el rodaje de *La ardilla roja*', *El Diario Vasco* (17 Aug. 1992).

Overesch-Maister, Lynne E., 'Echoes of Alienation in the Novels of Álvaro Pombo', *Anales de la Literatura Española Contemporánea*, 13.1–2 (1988), 55–70.

Palá, José María, 'Conversación con Víctor Erice y Julia Peña', *Film Ideal* (1969), 217–22.

Palou, Josep, 'Bigas Luna: "Sólo el adolescente es capaz de matarse por amor"', *El País* (26 Mar. 1994).

Pando, Juan, 'Ana Torrent: el poder de la mirada', *Dunia*, 18 (1989), 136–7.

Pasajes: Spanish Art Today (Seville: World's Fair, 20 Apr.–12 Oct. 1992).

Pelayo, Antonio, 'El cine español presenta hoy su único filme a concurso en Venecia', *Ya* (8 Sept. 1994).

Pombo, Álvaro, *El héroe de las mansardas de Mansard* (Barcelona: Anagrama, 1983).

Pope, Randolph D., *Understanding Juan Goytisolo* (Columbia: University of South Carolina Press, 1995).

Porter i Moix, Miquel, *Història del cinema a Catalunya* (Barcelona: Generalitat, 1992).

Pujol, Jordi, *Cataluña España* (Madrid: Espasa Calpe, 1996).

Bibliography

RAGUE, MARÍA JOSÉ, 'La Cubana, el gran éxito del teatro catalán en 1989', *Estreno*, 17.1 (Spring 1991), 26–30.

RIAMBAU, ESTEVE, 'La teta de Tete y la luna de Bigas', *Dirigido Por*, 228 (Oct. 1994), 38.

ROCAMORA, PEDRO, 'Francisco Umbral o la "invención" de Madrid', *Arbor*, 118.462 (1984), 53–7.

ROMA, PEPA, 'Antonio Gades, bailarín: "Yo no lo veré, pero el comunismo tiene futuro"', *El País* (14 Sept. 1997).

ROMNEY, JONATHAN, review of *Tierra*, *Sight and Sound*, 7.8 (Aug. 1997), 56.

ROUYER, PHILIPPE, review of *Tierra*, *Positif*, 425–6 (July–Aug. 1996), 131.

ROWE, WILLIAM, and SCHELLING, VIVIAN, *Memory and Modernity: Popular Culture in Latin America* (London: Verso, 1991).

RUBIO, MIGUEL, 'El espíritu de la colmena', *Nuevo Diario* (14 Oct. 1973).

RUBIO CARRACEDO, JOSÉ, *Educación moral, postmodernidad y democracia: más allá del liberalismo y del comunitarismo* (Madrid: Trotta, 1996).

RUEDA, ANA, 'Entre la fascinación y el descrédito: el superhéroe del cómic en la narrativa actual', *Revista Monográfica*, 7 (1991), 350–63.

SALAS, ROGER, 'Joaquín Cortés deslumbra con *Pasión gitana*', *El País* (9 Sept. 1995).

—— 'El bailarín Joaquín Cortés consagra su singularidad en Nueva York', *El País* (4 June 1998).

SALIGA, PAULINE, and THORNE, MARTHA (eds.), *Building in a New Spain: Contemporary Spanish Architecture* (Barcelona and Chicago: Gustavo Gili and Art Institute of Chicago, 1992).

SÁNCHEZ VIDAL, AGUSTÍN, *Sol y sombra* (Barcelona: Planeta, 1990).

SANTOS, FELIPE, '*Alma gitana*' (review), *Ideal de Granada* (3 Apr. 1996).

SANZ, VICTORIA, press release for La Cubana (Barcelona, 18 Dec. 1995).

SAURA, CARLOS, and GADES, ANTONIO, *Carmen: el sueño del amor absoluto* (Barcelona: Círculo de Lectores, 1984).

SAVATER, FERNANDO, *Panfleto contra el todo* (Barcelona: DOPESA, 1978).

—— *Contra las patrias* (Barcelona: Tusquets, 1984).

—— *Las razones del antimilitarismo y otras razones* (Barcelona: Anagrama, 1984).

—— *Ética como amor propio* (Barcelona: Grijalbo-Mondadori, 1988).

—— and BARNATÁN, MARCOS-RICARDO, *Contra el todo* (Madrid: Enjana, 1984).

—— and SÁDABA, JAVIER, *Euskadi: pensar en el conflicto* (Madrid: Libertarias, 1987).

SHARP, DENNIS, *Santiago Calatrava*, 2nd edn. (London: E. and F. N. Spon, 1994).

SMITH, PAUL JULIAN, *Laws of Desire: Questions of Homosexuality in Spanish Writing and Film 1960–90* (Oxford: Oxford University Press, 1992).

—— *Desire Unlimited: The Cinema of Pedro Almodóvar* (London: Verso, 1994).

—— *Vision Machines: Cinema, Literature, and Sexuality in Spain and Cuba, 1983–93* (London: Verso, 1996).

—— 'Angels to Earth' (interview with Julio Medem), *Sight and Sound*, 7.8 (Aug. 1997), 12–14.

—— *The Theatre of García Lorca: Text, Performance, Psychoanalysis* (Cambridge: Cambridge University Press, 1998).

Subirats, Eduardo, *La cultura como espectáculo* (Mexico: Fondo de Cultura Económica, 1988).

—— *Después de la lluvia: sobre la ambigua modernidad española* (Madrid: Temas de Hoy, 1993).

—— 'Postmoderna modernidad: la España de los felices ochenta', *Quimera*, 145 (Mar. 1996), 11–18.

Sullivan, Edward J., 'Deserted Streets and Silent Rooms: Contemporary Spanish Realists', in *Contemporary Spanish Realists* (London: Marlborough Fine Art, June–Aug. 1996), 2–8.

Torreiro, M., 'Dulce Cataluña', *El País* (9 Oct. 1994).

Torres, Augusto M., *Diccionario del cine español* (Madrid: Espasa Calpe, 1994).

Trías, Eugenio, 'La resaca del pensamiento débil', in Rafael Conte (ed.), *Una cultura portátil* (Madrid: Temas de Hoy, 1990), 201–26.

Umbral, Francisco, *El giocondo* (Barcelona: Planeta, 1970).

—— 'Spleen de Madrid: Ana Torrent', *El País* (5 Sept. 1980).

—— *Spleen de Madrid 2* (Barcelona: Destino, 1982).

—— *Un carnívoro cuchillo* (Barcelona: Planeta, 1988).

—— *La escritura perpetua* (n.p.: Mapfre-Vida, 1989).

—— *Y Tierno Galván ascendió a los cielos: memorias noveladas de la transición* (Barcelona: Seix Barral, 1990).

—— *La década roja* (Barcelona: Planeta, 1993).

—— *Los cuerpos gloriosos: memorias y semblanzas* (Barcelona: Planeta, 1996).

—— and González, Alfredo, *Teoría de Madrid* (Madrid: Espasa-Calpe, 1981).

'Una casa para soñar', special issue, *El País Semanal* (30 June 1996).

Vattimo, Gianni, *The End of Modernity: Nihilism and Hermeneutics in Postmodern Culture* (Oxford: Polity, 1988).

—— *La sociedad transparente* (Barcelona: Paidós, 1990).

Vilarós, Teresa, *El mono del desencanto: una crítica cultural de la transición española (1973–1993)* (Madrid: Siglo XXI, 1998).

Washabaugh, William, *Flamenco: Passion, Politics, and Popular Culture* (Oxford: Berg, 1996).

Weinrichter, Antonio, *La línea del vientre: el cine de Bigas Luna* (Gijón: Festival de Cine, 1992).

Williams, Linda, *Hard Core: Power, Pleasure, and the Frenzy of the Visible* (London: Macmillan, 1991).

Yraola, Aitor, 'El discurso de la muerte en *Vacas* de Julio Medem', in George Cabello-Castellet et al. (eds.), *Cine-Lit, ii: Essays on Hispanic Film and Fiction* (Portland: Portland and Oregon State Universities and Reed College, 1995), 163–8.

Zizek, Slavoj, *Looking Awry: An Introduction to Jacques Lacan through Popular Culture* (Cambridge, Mass.: MIT, 1992).

—— 'The Supposed Subjects of Ideology', *Critical Quarterly*, 39.2 (Summer 1997), 39–59.

Zulaika, Joseba, *Crónica de una seducción* (Madrid: Nerea, 1997).

Zunzunegui, Santos, 'Entre la historia y el sueño: eficacia simbólica y estructura mítica en *El espíritu de la colmena*', in *Paisajes de la forma: ejercicios de análisis de la imagen* (Madrid: Cátedra, 1994), 42–70.

ZUNZUNEGUI, SANTOS, *La mirada cercana: microanálisis fílmico* (Barcelona: Paidós, 1996).

—— *El extraño viaje: el celuloide atrapado por la cola, o la crítica norteamericana ante el cine español* (Valencia: Episteme, 1999).

Index

Index

Index